NARCONOMICS

NARCO-NOMICS

How to Run a Drug Cartel

Tom Wainwright

EBURY
PRESS

1 3 5 7 9 10 8 6 4 2

Ebury Press, an imprint of Ebury Publishing
20 Vauxhall Bridge Road
London SW1V 2SA

Ebury Press is part of the Penguin Random House group of companies
whose addresses can be found at global.penguinrandomhouse.com

Penguin
Random House
UK

First published in the United States by PublicAffairs,
a member of the Perseus Books Group, in 2016.
First published in the United Kingdom by Ebury Press in 2016.

www.eburypublishing.co.uk

A CIP catalogue record for this book is available from the British Library

HB ISBN 9781785030406
TPB ISBN 9781785030413

Printed and bound in Great Britain by Clays Ltd, St Ives PLC

MIX
Paper from
responsible sources
FSC
www.fsc.org   FSC® C018179

Penguin Random House is committed to a sustainable
future for our business, our readers and our planet.
This book is made from Forest Stewardship Council®
certified paper.

Crooks already know these tricks. Honest men must learn them in self-defense.

—"How to Lie with Statistics," Darrell Huff

Contents

Photographs appear following p. 124.

Introduction

CARTEL INCORPORATED

"Ladies and gentlemen, welcome to Ciudad Juárez, where the local time is 8:00 a.m." On a chilly November morning on a runway in the Mexican desert, one passenger onboard Interjet Flight 2283 is fiddling nervously with a small package hidden in his sock, wondering if he has made a terrible mistake. Juárez, a brash border city of scorching days and freezing nights, is the main cocaine gateway to the United States. Shoved up against the metal fences of the Texas border, exactly halfway between the Pacific and the Gulf coasts, it has long been a smugglers' hangout: a place where illicit fortunes are made and blown on fast cars, gaudy mansions, and usually before very long, spectacular mausoleums. But the nervous passenger, now blinking in the morning sun as he walks to the terminal, noting the camouflaged, balaclava-wearing marines guarding the exit, is not a drug mule. The passenger is me.

Inside the terminal I find the nearest bathroom, lock myself in a cubicle, and pull out the package, a small, black, electronic gadget, about the size of a cigarette lighter, with a single button and an LED light. A few days earlier, in Mexico City, it had been presented to me by a local security consultant who feared that the naïve young *británico* before him might get into hot water on his trip to Juárez. Now, at the time of my first visit, the place has recently earned the title of "world's most murderous city," thanks to the deadly game of hide-and-seek being played by rival cartel hit men across its colonial downtown and

1

cinderblock slums. Roadside executions, mass graves, and inventive new forms of dismemberment fill the local newspapers and television reports. Inquisitive journalists, in particular, have a habit of disappearing into car trunks, mummified in masking tape. Juárez is not a place to take any chances. So what I should do, the consultant had explained, handing me the device, is press the button when I arrive, wait for the LED to come on, and keep the gadget hidden in my sock. As long as the light is blinking, he will be able to track my whereabouts—or at least those of my right leg—should I fail to check in.

In the cubicle, I quietly take out the tracking device, turn it over in my hands, and press the button. I wait. The light remains dead. Puzzled, I press it again. Nothing. Jabbing, hammering, holding the button down: whatever I do to try to coax the device to life over the next few minutes, the light refuses to blink. Eventually I stick the useless thing back in my sock, gather up my things, and make my way warily out onto the streets of Ciudad Juárez. The gadget is dead, and I am on my own.

•   •   •

This is the story of what happened when a not very brave business journalist was sent to cover the most exotic and brutal industry on earth. I arrived in Mexico in 2010, just as the country was starting to ramp up its war on the narco-cowboys, who, with their gold-plated Kalashnikovs, had reduced some parts of the country to a state of near anarchy. The number of people murdered in Mexico in 2010 would reach more than twenty thousand, or about five times the figure recorded across all of Western Europe.[1] The following year was to be more violent still. News bulletins featured little else: every week brought new stories of corrupted cops, assassinated officials, and massacre after bloody massacre of narcotraficantes, by the army or each other. This was the war on drugs, and it was clear that drugs were winning.

I had sometimes written about drugs from the point of view of the consumer, in Europe and the United States. Now, in Latin America, I was confronted with the narcotics industry's awesome supply side. And the more I wrote about *el narcotráfico*, the more I came to realize what it most closely resembled: a global, highly organized business. Its products are designed, manufactured, transported, marketed, and sold to a quarter of a billion consumers around the world. Its annual revenues are about $300 billion; if it were a country, it would rank among the world's forty largest economies.[2] The people who run the industry may have a sinister glamour about them, with their monstrous nicknames (one in Mexico was known as El Comeniños, or "The Childeater"). But whenever I met them in person, their boasts and complaints tended to remind me of nothing so much as those of corporate managers. The head of a bloodthirsty gang in El Salvador, who boasted to me in his baking prison cell about the amount of territory controlled by his *compañeros*, spouted platitudes about a new gang-truce that could have come directly from the mouth of a CEO announcing a merger. A burly Bolivian farmer of coca, the raw ingredient of cocaine, enthused about his healthy young narco-crops with the pride and expertise of a commercial horticulturalist. Time and again, the most ruthless outlaws described to me the same mundane problems that blight the lives of other entrepreneurs: managing personnel, navigating government regulations, finding reliable suppliers, and dealing with competitors.

Their clients have the same demands as other consumers, too. Like customers of any other industry, they seek out reviews of new products, increasingly prefer to shop online, and even demand a certain level of "corporate social responsibility" from their suppliers. When I found my way into the hidden "Dark Web" of the Internet, where drugs and weapons are anonymously bought with Bitcoins, I dealt with a trader of crystal-meth pipes who was as attentive as any Amazon representative. (Actually, I take it back. He was far more helpful.) The more I looked at the worldwide drug industry, the more I wondered what would happen if I covered it as if it were a business like any other. The result is this book.

One of the first things I noticed when I started looking at the illegal-drugs industry through the eyes of an economist was that many

of the impressive-sounding numbers quoted by the officials in charge
of fighting it simply don't make sense. Not long after I arrived in Mexico, a giant narcotic bonfire was set alight in Tijuana. Soldiers lit the
kindling and stood well back as 134 metric tons of marijuana went up
in thick, pungent smoke. The stash, which had been discovered hidden inside six shipping containers in a warehouse on the edge of the
city, represented the biggest drug bust in the country's history. The
goods had been ready for export, tightly packed into 15,000 parcels the
size of sandbags and branded with logos of animals, smiley faces, and
Homer Simpson cartoons, which traffickers use to denote where their
products are to be sent. After the packages had been tested, weighed,
and photographed, they were piled high, hosed down with diesel, and
ignited. A crowd looked on, as machine-gun-toting soldiers made
sure that no one got downwind of the mind-altering blaze. General
Alfonso Duarte Múgica, the Mexican Army's commander in the region, proudly announced that the smoldering stash had been worth 4.2
billion pesos, then equivalent to about $340 million. Some US news-
papers went even further, reporting that the haul was worth more like
half a billion dollars, based on what the drugs could have fetched in the
United States.

By any reasonable analysis, they were both wrong by a mile. General
Duarte's calculation seems to have been based on the assumption that
a gram of marijuana can be bought in Mexico for about $3. Multiply
that by a hundred tons and you come up with a total value for the stash
of around $300 million. In the United States, a gram might cost more
like $5, which is where the half-billion estimate comes from. The logic
sounds reasonable enough, even if the numbers are very rough. But it is
ludicrous. Consider another fiercely addictive Latin American export:
Argentine beef. In a Manhattan restaurant, an eight-ounce steak might
cost $50, or 22 cents per gram. By General Duarte's logic, that would
imply that a half-ton steer is worth over $100,000.

A steer has to be slaughtered, butchered, packed, shipped, seasoned,
grilled, and served before it is worth $50 per slice. For this reason, no

analyst of the beef industry would calculate the price of a live steer mooching around on the Argentine *pampa* using restaurant data from New York City. Yet this is effectively how the value of heroin seized in Afghanistan or cocaine intercepted in Colombia is sometimes estimated. In reality, drugs, like beef, have to go through a long value-adding chain before they reach their final "street price." A gram of marijuana might fetch $3 in a Mexico City nightclub, or $5 in an American college dorm. But hidden in a warehouse in Tijuana—yet to be smuggled across the border, divided into retail-size quantities, and furtively marketed to consumers—it is worth much less. The best estimates available suggest that the wholesale price of marijuana in Mexico is about $80 per kilo, or just 8 cents per gram.[3] At this price, the stash in Tijuana would have been worth more like $10 million—and probably less, because no one hiding 100 tons of an illegal product would be able to sell it by the kilogram. The Tijuana seizure was a whopper, and heads no doubt literally rolled in the cartel that lost it. But the $340 million blow to organized crime that most newspapers reported was a fantasy: the loss incurred by the criminals who owned the drugs was probably less than 3 percent of that amount.

If assumptions about the value of a single big warehouse of Tijuana marijuana could be so wildly wrong, I wondered, what else might be found out by analyzing the drug trade from a completely different perspective, applying basic economics? Look again at the cartels, and further similarities to legitimate businesses become clear. Colombian cocaine manufacturers have protected their profits by tightening control of their supply chains, along the same lines as Walmart. Mexican cartels have expanded on a franchise basis, with the same success as McDonald's. In El Salvador, the tattooed street gangs, once sworn blood-enemies, have discovered that collusion can sometimes be more profitable than competition. Caribbean criminals use the islands' fetid prisons as job centers, solving their human-resources problems. Like other big firms, drug cartels have begun to experiment with offshoring, bringing their problems to new, more vulnerable countries. They are attempting to diversify, just as most other businesses do when they reach a certain size. And they are being buffeted by the move to online shopping, exactly like other high-street retailers.

Applying economic and business analysis to drug cartels may seem outrageous. But to fail to understand the economics of the drug trade— and to go on quoting fantasy figures such as the half-billion-dollar bonfire in Tijuana—has condemned governments to pouring money and lives into policies that do not work. The world's taxpayers spend upward of $100 billion a year combating the illegal-drugs trade. The United States alone shells out some $20 billion just at the federal level, making 1.7 million drug arrests a year and sending a quarter of a million people to prison.[4] In countries that produce and traffic the drugs, military offensives against the industry have contributed to a dizzying body count. Mexico's murder rate, though fearsome, is not as high as that of some of the other countries that lie on the cocaine-trafficking route, where thousands more are murdered each year attempting to fight the drugs business. The scale of public investment is huge, and the evidence used to support it is threadbare.

As I followed the trafficking trail, I noticed four big economic mistakes that governments everywhere from La Paz to London keep on making. First, there is an overwhelming focus on suppressing the supply side of the business, when basic economics suggests that addressing demand would make more sense. Cutting supply has done more to raise prices than it has to reduce the amount of drugs consumed, resulting in a more valuable criminal market. Second, there is a constant and damaging short-termism, in which governments economize on early interventions, preferring to run up bigger bills further down the line. Prisoner rehabilitation, job creation, and treatment for addiction are among the first programs to be cut when budgets are tight, while front-line enforcement, which accomplishes the same goal at a higher cost, seems to enjoy spending without end. Third, even though the drug cartels are models of nimble, borderless global commerce, efforts to regulate them are still clumsily national in scope. The result is that the industry survives by slipping from one jurisdiction to another, easily outwitting the uncoordinated efforts of different countries. Finally, and most fundamentally, governments mistakenly equate prohibition with control. Banning drugs, which seems sensible at first, has handed the exclusive rights to a multibillion-dollar industry to the most ruthless organized crime networks in the world. The more I learned about the way the cartels do business, the more I wondered if legalization, far from being a gift to the gangsters, could be their undoing.

The following chapters will add flesh to these arguments. But the bottom line is this: predicting the cartels' next steps, and making sure that the money and lives laid down to stop them are not wasted, is easier when we recognize that they are run like other big multinational companies. This book is a business manual for drug lords. But it is also a blueprint for how to defeat them.

Chapter 1

COCAINE'S SUPPLY CHAIN

The Cockroach Effect and the 30,000 Percent Markup

"My name is bin Laden."

It's a drizzly spring day in La Paz, the headache-inducingly high capital of Bolivia, and I have been sheltering in a doorway waiting for a ride into the mountains. The car has just pulled up—a dark-gray Toyota Land Cruiser, its rear windows blacked out with dark film that is peeling at the corners—and the driver has jumped out to introduce himself. "They call me bin Laden because of this," he explains, tweaking the end of a bushy, jet-black beard that protrudes a good six inches beyond his chin. "You're the one who wants to see where we grow the coca, right?"

I am. Here in the Andes is where the cocaine trade, a global business worth something like $90 billion a year, has its roots. Cocaine is consumed in every country on earth, but virtually every speck of it starts its life in one of three countries in South America: Bolivia, Colombia, and Peru. The drug, which can be snorted as powder or smoked in the form of crystals of "crack" cocaine, is made from the coca plant, a hardy bush that is most at home in the foothills of the Andes. I have come to Bolivia to see for myself how coca is grown, and to find out more about

9

the economics at the very start of the cocaine business's long, violent, and fabulously profitable supply chain.

I jump into the back of the Land Cruiser and wonder whether to open the window, letting in the rain, or keep it closed, worsening the smell from a leaking gasoline canister in the trunk behind me. I decide to wind it down a little and then shuffle into the middle of the row of seats to stay dry. We set off, climbing from 10,000 feet to 13,000 feet, as we make our way over the top of the Bolivian altiplano, the high plateau of the Andes, which lies about three times higher than Kathmandu in the Himalayas. The car grumbles as bin Laden, who occasionally sings to himself but says very little, urges it on around bend after bend. We drive up through clouds, which when they part give glimpses of patches of snow on the other side of the valley.

Bolivia has two main areas for growing coca: the Chapare, a humid region in the center of the country where the crop has taken off in recent decades as the cocaine trade has boomed, and the Yungas, a warm area of forest northeast of the capital, where people have been growing the leaf for centuries. We are heading to the latter, and as we slowly descend the eastern slope, the air gets warmer and the bare rock of the mountainside becomes covered, first with moss and then with a thick green blanket of ferns. I focus on the view across the valley, trying to take my mind off the Yungas Road, which is utterly terrifying. Known locally as the *camino de la muerte*, or "death road," it is a narrow, gravelly track that clings to a crumbling cliff face to the right, with a ravine 1,000 feet deep on the left. As bin Laden cheerfully flings the Land Cruiser around blind corners (and, at one point, straight through a small waterfall), I edge over to the right-hand door, where I sit clutching the handle, ready to jump to safety if I feel the car start to slide into the abyss.

Fortunately, it never does. After hours on the road, some of it spent clearing a small landslide by hand, we eventually arrive at our destination. It may be because my nerves are shot from the nail-biting journey, but Trinidad Pampa, a village of about 5,000 people living mostly in homes of cinder block and corrugated iron, looks like Eden. The road into town is framed by banana trees rather than sheer drops. To the north and south, the steeply sloping sides of the valley have been carved into neat terraces, each just a few feet deep. Behind them, higher mountains recede into clouds that sit against a dark-blue sky. I jump out of the car into the warm afternoon, glad to stretch my legs, and walk over to a plantation by the verge. There is no mistaking the bushes growing there. Delicate, almond-shaped leaves on fine stalks protrude from thicker stumps that have been carefully bedded into the reddish soil. This is coca, the billion-dollar leaf for which thousands of people are murdered every year. Terrace after terrace has been cut into the mountainside for the bushes, forming a long ladder of green.

At a crossroads in the center of the village I meet Édgar Marmani, the head of the local coca-growers' union, who has come straight from the fields with muddy hands and in rubber boots. A union for drug farmers? Almost anywhere else in the world such a thing would be illegal. But Bolivia has a lighter regime than other South American countries when it comes to coca. The leaf has been consumed in the Andes since long before Europeans arrived in the Americas. Some people like to brew it in tea, whereas others simply chew the leaves in handfuls (Bolivian peasants can often be seen with one bulging cheek, sucking on a wad of leaves as they go about their business). In this form the leaf has only a mild stimulant effect, nothing like cocaine. It supposedly helps to ward off cold, hunger, and altitude sickness, all of which are tedious features of life on the altiplano. Many hotels in La Paz serve coca tea to guests on arrival—in fact, even the American embassy used to, not so long ago. I had drunk a mug of it at breakfast; to me it tasted like green tea, and not much stronger. To allow this "traditional" use of the leaf, the Bolivian government each year licenses a limited amount of land to be used for coca farming.

Marmani's drink of choice, however, is not coca but Pepsi, and we sit down on plastic chairs in a little convenience store with two plastic cups and a two-liter bottle planted between us. I start by asking him how to grow a good coca crop. "First we have to make the *wachus*," he says, pointing up into the hillsides and using the local word for the terraces. Each is dug two feet deep and cleared of stones. Every person in the community tends to a dozen of them, with the biggest landowners managing over an acre in total. The balmy weather and fertile soil of the Yungas mean that farmers can get up to three harvests a year out of their coca bushes—a much better deal than coffee, which yields a single annual harvest and is tricky to grow, requiring shade. The only difficult time, Marmani says, is the winter—July, August, and September—when there is no rain, and "*estamos jodidos*": we're screwed. Once plucked, the leaves are dried in the sun and then bundled up into *takis*, fifty-pound bags. These are loaded into a truck that bounces along to the Villa Fátima market in La Paz, one of two places in the country where coca can be legally traded. Each truck displays a license showing exactly how much coca it is carrying, and where it comes from.

Coca farmers are tolerated, or even celebrated, in Bolivia, whose president, Evo Morales, is himself a former *cocalero*, as the growers are known. Breaking all sorts of laws, he once took bags of coca to Manhattan to chew defiantly before a meeting of the United Nations, where he called for a repeal of the international conventions that outlaw the leaf. The stunt was part of a broader stand against what he sees as Western meddling in Andean affairs. In 2008, he expelled the US ambassador for interfering in local politics, kicking out the US Drug Enforcement Administration (DEA) at the same time. Despite international bans on the leaf, the Bolivian state supports various national industries that churn out all manner of coca-related products, from sweets, cookies, and drinks to coca-infused toothpaste. The industry is regulated by the Vice-Ministry of Coca, which imposes the limits on how much of the leaf can be grown. The idea is to license enough cultivation to feed the market for tea, toothpaste, and all the rest of it, without growing enough to leak into the cocaine trade. The system is far from water-tight, though: the United Nations estimates that in 2014, Bolivia had about 20,400 hectares, or 50,400 acres, of land devoted to coca cultivation, enough to produce about 33,000 tons of dried leaf. In the same year, the country's two licensed markets handled only 19,798 tons—less than two-thirds the estimated amount of coca leaf being produced.[1] It is a safe bet that the rest found its way into the illegal market, to be turned into cocaine.

Because cartels depend on coca leaf to make their cocaine, governments have targeted coca plantations as a means of cutting off the business at its source. Since the late 1980s, the coca-producing countries of South America, backed by money and expertise from the United States, have focused their counternarcotic efforts on finding and destroying illegal coca farms. The idea is a simple economic one: if you reduce the supply of a product, you increase its scarcity, driving up its price. Scarcity is what makes gold more expensive than silver, and oil more expensive than water: if lots of people want something, and there isn't enough to go around, they have to pay more to get their hands on it. Governments hope that by chipping away at the supply of coca, they will force up the price of the leaf, thereby raising the cost of making cocaine. As the price of cocaine rises, they reason, fewer people in the rich world will buy it. Just as a natural blight on cocoa crops has recently raised the international price of chocolate, causing chocoholics to cut down on their habits, destroying coca plants ought to raise the price of cocaine, persuading drug users to consume less.

Colombia and Peru, which are currently on friendlier terms with the United States than Bolivia is, have taken an especially tough line. The armies of both countries have been drafted as emergency gardening services, tasked with eliminating every trace of the coca bush. The mountainous geography has made this a fiendishly tricky task. Spotters fly up and down in light aircraft, looking out for the telltale terraces that show that coca production is under way. Farmers have gotten better at hiding their crops, but the authorities are now better at seeking them out. Nowadays the spotters' planes are helped by satellites, which take detailed images of the countryside for experts to pore over to try to tell the difference between legal plantations of bananas or coffee and illicit ones of coca. Armed with these maps, soldiers are sent to destroy the crops by hand. In Colombia, some of the eradication has been done by spraying the farmland with weed killer from light aircraft. This destroys the coca—along with many other, perfectly legitimate crops, farmers complain. In 2015, Colombia indefinitely suspended its aerial spraying program, following a warning from an agency of the World Health Organization that the weed killer may cause cancer.

The eradication campaign has been devastatingly successful, at least on the face of it. Over the past couple of decades, Bolivia, Colombia, and Peru have destroyed thousands of square miles of illegal coca plantations, eradicating more and more crops each year. Whereas in 1994 the three countries' governments destroyed about 6,000 hectares (15,000 acres) of coca,[2] in 2014 they laid waste to more than 120,000 hectares (300,000 acres), mostly by hand. It is an extraordinary feat: to picture the scale of the task, imagine every year weeding a garden fourteen times the size of Manhattan (while occasionally being shot at). By the rough calculations of the United Nations, nearly half of all the coca bushes planted in the Andes are now eradicated.

The annual loss of nearly 50 percent of production would be a crippling blow to most industries. But somehow, the cocaine market keeps bouncing back. As acre after acre of coca has been poisoned, burned, and sprayed, farmers have gone out and planted more bushes to replace the ones that have been destroyed. The result is that total output has not changed much. In 2000, following the first decade of intensive eradication measures, a total of about 220,000 hectares (545,000 acres) of land was successfully used to grow coca in South America—almost exactly the same as the amount in 1990. From time to time, individual countries have managed temporarily to drive out the coca business: Peru, for instance, cut down on its coca farming in a big way in the 1990s. But the cartels have quickly found other sources of supply. Peru's crackdown triggered a coca-growing boom in Colombia. When Colombia redoubled its efforts and drove the farmers out, the coca terraces reappeared in Peru. Western observers call this the "balloon effect": if you squeeze in one place, it bulges up somewhere else. Latin Americans have an earthier name for the same phenomenon—the "cockroach effect." Just like cockroaches, you can chase drug traffickers out of one room, but they soon take up residence somewhere else in the house.

That doesn't worry advocates of eradication, who argue that the point is not necessarily to eliminate coca farming completely but to make it more costly. For farmers to maintain high levels of output in the face of all the crop spraying, they have been forced to put in much more time in the fields. The need to create new plantations to make up for the ones destroyed by the armies imposes a significant cost on business. In the past, virtually all of the coca grown could be turned into cocaine. Nowadays nearly half goes to waste, yanked up by the roots or sprayed with weed killer by the authorities.

But even though they are having to grow twice as much coca as before to harvest the same amount of leaf, the cartels haven't had to raise their prices. In the United States, a gram of pure cocaine today costs about $180. (A typical gram bought on the street costs about half that, because it is only about 50 percent pure.)[3] That is roughly what it has cost for the past two decades, in spite of the thousands of swipes of machetes and gallons of weed killer that have been deployed. One explanation for a stable price at a time of a shock to supply would be a dip in demand. (In other words, there is less of the product to go around, but fewer people want to buy it, so the price stays the same.) But that doesn't seem to be the case. Since the 1990s, the number of people regularly using cocaine in the United States has held pretty steady at between about 1.5 million and 2 million people. Recently there has been a significant dip in US consumption, but most of that has been made up for by much higher demand in Europe. The United Nations says that worldwide demand is stable. This makes for a puzzle: constant demand and restricted supply would normally lead to an increase in price, yet cocaine remains as cheap as ever. How have the cartels managed to defy the basic laws of economics?

To understand how they have pulled off this trick, consider Walmart, which has sometimes seemed able to defy the laws of supply and demand in a similar way to the drug cartels. Walmart, the world's largest retailer, has worldwide revenues of nearly half a trillion dollars per year. Its success is built on prices that seem not to have risen much since Bud and Sam Walton opened their first store in 1962. Last Thanksgiving, shoppers could buy a turkey for 40 cents per pound and a set of nine (admittedly hideous) Thanksgiving-themed dinner plates to go with it for $1.59.

These extraordinarily low prices make Walmart wildly popular with its customers. But for the farmers and manufacturers who supply the goods, the low prices are sometimes crippling. Their complaint is that Walmart and other big chains have such a big share of the groceries market that they are able more or less to dictate terms to their suppliers. Everyone is familiar with the concept of a monopoly, in which one company is the dominant seller of a particular product and can therefore charge whatever price it likes. Critics of retailers such as Walmart accuse them of being "monopsonies"—that is, dominant *buyers* of certain products. (Just as the word *monopoly* is derived from the Greek for "single seller," *monopsony* means "single buyer.") In the same way that a monopolist can dictate prices to its consumers, who have no one else to buy from, a monopsonist can dictate prices to its suppliers, who have no one else to sell to. If you want to reach a really big audience of consumers, the theory goes, you have to be in Walmart. The store knows this and is therefore able to squeeze suppliers hard. A survey by *Forbes* magazine found that suppliers that sold a high proportion of their goods through Walmart on average had lower profit margins than those that did less business with the store. The difference was most pronounced in the apparel market: clothing manufacturers that sold less than 10 percent of their products through Walmart were able to maintain an average margin of 49 percent, whereas those that sold more than 20 percent through the store averaged only 29 percent.[4] Driving down prices and forcing suppliers to be more efficient is great for consumers, of course, and indeed it has benefits for the wider economy—a McKinsey study made the extraordinary finding that Walmart alone was responsible for 12 percent of the US economy's productivity gains in the second half of the 1990s.[5] But for suppliers, it makes life difficult. If a harvest fails and the costs of production go up, you can bet that it is the farmers, not the supermarket or its customers, that will be made to feel the squeeze.

Walmart hasn't yet opened in Colombia. But the drug traffickers in the region have applied Walmart's genius when it comes to leveraging the supply chain. To start with, the cartels are more like big-box retailers than one might imagine, playing the role of buyers rather than growers. It is tempting to imagine that the whole cocaine business is in the hands of the cartel from start to finish, with gun-toting mobsters lovingly tending their coca bushes with Baby Bio in between massacring their rivals. But that isn't usually how it works. The agricultural side of the cocaine industry is mostly handled by ordinary farmers like the ones in Trinidad Pampa, who would just as happily grow tomatoes or bananas if they paid as well as coca. Cartels play a role more like that of large supermarkets, buying produce from farmers, processing and packaging it, and then selling it on to consumers.

Are South American drug lords as single-minded as Walmart executives when it comes to managing their suppliers? A pair of economists, Jorge Gallego of New York University and Daniel Rico of the University of Maryland, decided to find out. Focusing on Colombia, they gathered information from the government about which parts of the country had undergone coca eradication, of both the manual variety and the aerial-spraying kind (detailed records of the latter are stored in planes' in-flight recorders). They cross-referenced these data with information kept by the United Nations on the price of coca leaf in different regions of the country. By combining the two data sets they were able to see the impact of coca eradication on the price that farmers charged the cartels for their coca.[6]

If the supply-reduction strategy of eradicating coca plantations were working, one would expect areas that had undergone more eradication to see a greater increase in price than those that had been spared the weed killer. Less coca should mean that, other things being equal, the local cartels would have to pay the farmers more for it. But Gallego and Rico found no such pattern. Instead, they discovered, eradication had virtually no impact on the price of coca leaf, or the various illegal refined-coca products that farmers also sometimes sell to cartels. Surprised, they ran the study again, this time allowing for a one-year lag between eradication and sale, in case it took time for the scarcity to feed through to higher prices. But again, they found that destroying crops had virtually no impact on the wholesale prices that farmers charge to cartels.

The reason, they hypothesize, is that the armed groups that control the cocaine trade in Colombia act as monopsonies. Under normal market conditions, coca farmers would be able to shop around and sell their leaves to the highest bidder. That would mean that in times of scarcity, coca buyers raised their bids, and the price of the leaf went up. But Colombia's armed conflict is such that in any given region, there is usually only one group of traffickers that holds sway. That group is the sole local buyer of coca leaf, so it dictates the price, just as Walmart is sometimes able to set the price of the produce it buys. This means that if the cost of producing the leaf goes up—owing to eradication, disease, or anything else—it will be the farmers who bear the cost, not the cartel. Just as big retailers protect themselves and their customers from price rises by forcing suppliers to take the hit, cartels keep their own costs down at the expense of coca farmers. "The shock is assumed entirely by growers, as major buyers have the ability . . . to maintain fixed prices," write Gallego and Rico.

In other words, it's not that the eradication strategy is having no effect. Rather, the problem is that its impact is felt by the wrong people. The cartels' Walmart-like grip on their supply chains means that any worsening in coca-growing conditions simply makes poor farmers even poorer, without doing much to cut the cartels' profits or raise the price of cocaine for consumers. "We're against all of this," says a farmer in Trinidad Pampa, who asks not to be named, referring to the official eradication programs that uproot any unlicensed plants. "We're always clashing with the government over it. It's infuriating for us." Even if they want nothing to do with the gangsters who control the cocaine business, growers resent being limited in what they can produce, he says. Nearby, a wall next to an overgrown field has a notice daubed on it in white paint, reading: "This plot of land has been SEIZED for eradication." Any unauthorized plantations are summarily destroyed, leaving the farmers worse off but failing to affect the bottom line of their clients, the cartels. Production remains high, retail prices stay low, and the cocaine business continues. If only it were legal, Bud and Sam Walton might have found much to admire in the drug cartels' Andean supply chain.

•   •   •

Near to where Édgar Marmani and I are drinking our giant bottle of Pepsi—which I have suddenly realized I am expected to finish and am gulping down—I can see tiny hands reaching up to grab leaves from the tops of the coca plants. In Trinidad Pampa, children work in the fields from the age of six, going to school until lunchtime and then joining their parents to help with the planting and harvesting in the afternoon. The village has no nursery, so the youngest children accompany their parents to work, tottering around on the terraces or snoozing in slings carried by their mothers. Conditions elsewhere in the Andes are no richer: the United Nations estimates that in Colombia, the average coca farmer earns little more than $2 per day. The destitution of coca growers is starkly at odds with the image of wealthy cocaine barons, posing in Ferraris and managing private zoos.

How might the cartels be forced to absorb some of these costs themselves? The root of their monopsony power is that the farmers have only one customer. So the obvious solution would be to create more competition in the coca-buying market, giving the farmers more potential buyers and forcing the cartels to pay a market rate for the product. There is just one snag: because coca is illegal in most places, governments cannot do much to increase the number of buyers in the market. So they have tried to force the price up in another way: by providing farmers with alternative ways to make a living, thereby making them less dependent on selling coca to the cartels.

Rather than using the stick of eradication to make coca farming less appealing, many policy makers suggest providing a carrot in the form of subsidies for other crops. Some European countries, whose diplomats are privately critical of the eradication-focused approach favored by the United States, have established projects to encourage other agricultural industries. The idea is that if it can be made more profitable to grow some other, legal crop than it is to grow coca, then farmers will change their focus. There is interest among *cocaleros*. Even Édgar Marmani, the local union leader, says he would consider switching to other industries if the start-up costs were lower. "Poultry, tomatoes, pork—they're all more profitable than coca, but they need investment," he complains. The European Union has put forward some cash to meet that need, funding projects in Bolivia that encourage the cultivation of bananas, coffee, and citrus fruits, among other things. Similar tactics have been tried in other parts of the world that have a problem with narco-agriculture: in Afghanistan, which grows most of the world's opium, farmers have been nudged toward growing wheat or cotton as an alternative to opium poppies.

There is some evidence that this sort of strategy can work. A recent study by the Center for Global Development (CGD), a Washington, DC–based research organization, tried to get to the bottom of how Mexican farmers decided whether to grow legal crops or illicit ones.[7] The authors focused on marijuana and opium, the country's main drug crops, and compared them with corn, the main legal one. It is hard to overstate the importance of corn to Mexicans, whose consumption of the grain is almost like a drug addiction. Corn is the main ingredient in the tortilla, the national staple, of which the average Mexican consumes two hundred pounds per year. A popular saying in the country goes, *"Sin maíz, no hay país"* ("Without corn, there is no country"). The tortilla-makers' union has as its logo a picture of a scowling Centéotl, the vengeful Aztec god of corn, to whom thousands of bloody human sacrifices were made.

For all its patriotic and practical importance, corn has been a tricky crop to make a living from in recent decades, with enormous fluctuations in price playing havoc with farmers' finances. Mexican growers saw corn's price tumble following the introduction of the North American Free Trade Agreement (NAFTA) in 1994, which opened the market up to competition from the United States. At other times its price spiked, following shortages caused by droughts north of the border. The authors of the CGD study plotted this price information alongside data on the amount of land in Mexico dedicated to the growing of marijuana and opium. How easily were corn farmers tempted into growing narco-crops, in times of low corn prices?

Quite easily, it turns out. As the price of corn fell during the 1990s, farmers started growing more marijuana, as well as more opium. The authors calculate that in areas where corn was being farmed, a 59 percent drop in the price of corn led to an 8 percent increase in cultivation of marijuana and a 5 percent increase in that of opium. But there was good news, too: as corn prices started to climb again, from 2005 onward, the amount of marijuana cultivation plummeted. There could be another explanation for this: America's legal marijuana boom has greatly reduced the incentives for Mexican farmers to grow pot (see Chapter 10). And opium-poppy production remained high, even after the price of corn bounced back. Still, the authors found that corn's price had a significant effect on farmers' willingness to dabble in illegal crops.

In other words, make it more profitable for farmers in the Andes to rear chickens or grow tomatoes, and they might grow less coca. This is effectively another way around the problem of monopsony: if the cartel

demands too low a price for coca (or marijuana, or opium, or whatever else), the farmers can simply switch to growing corn, tomatoes,
or some other crop. At the very least, the cartels will have to raise the
price that they offer for drug crops if they want to persuade farmers to
keep growing them.

This alternative-development strategy may offer more hope than
eradication. And for a while, it looked as if some progress was being
made. Since the turn of the twenty-first century, it has seemed for the
first time as if eradication and alternative-development efforts have
started to have some impact on the amount of land being devoted to
growing coca. The area of land successfully used for coca cultivation
in 2014 was about 130,000 hectares (320,000 acres), 40 percent less
than in 2000. After years in which a few hundred thousand Andean
peasants had resisted the combined efforts of three South American
armies and the DEA, it finally looked as if a breakthrough had been
made.

But just as it seemed that the tide had turned, a team of scientists
from the United Nations and the Colombian government made a startling discovery. Following nearly a year of fieldwork between 2005 and
2006, they determined that there had been something of a green revolution in the cocaine business. Whereas previously they had assumed
that one hectare of land in Colombia would enable the production of
about 4.7 kilograms of pure cocaine powder a year, they now came back
with revised estimates indicating that a hectare could in fact yield more
like 7.7 kilograms.[8] The finding was an extraordinary development: it
meant that cocaine manufacturers in Colombia had developed a way of
making 60 percent more cocaine from their coca than had previously
been thought possible.

How on earth did they do this? To find out, I go see César Guedes,
a Peruvian who works as the UN chief drugs man in Bolivia. Despite
the fairly grim field that he works in, Guedes is a cheerful soul who
frequently jumps up out of his chair to illustrate his points with quickly
drawn diagrams, accompanied by enthusiastic gesticulations. "The

cartels are permanently shopping around for what they can do better," he tells me. The process of converting coca leaves to cocaine powder is continually evolving as the *cocineros,* or "cooks," develop new recipes in their clandestine jungle laboratories. It is usually done in two steps. The first is to convert the coca leaves to a damp, cream-colored paste known as cocaine base. To do this, one ton of fresh leaves is dried out until it weighs more like 300 kilograms. The dried leaves are then chopped up into smaller pieces and mixed with a toxic brew of chemicals, including cement, fertilizer, and gasoline, which coaxes the cocaine out of the waxy leaves. The remaining plant matter is then filtered out, the chemicals removed (at least, most of them), and the remaining residue boiled down. The result is about 1 kilogram of cocaine base. To turn this paste into cocaine hydrochloride, as snortable cocaine powder is formally known, it is mixed with a solvent such as acetone, and with hydrochloric acid.[9] The resulting mixture is filtered and dried to derive just under a kilogram of pure cocaine: $C_{17}H_{21}NO_4$.

That basic process has been carried out for decades. But recently the cartels' research and development engineers have struck gold. "The process has changed dramatically. They are using new chemical precursors, and new machinery," César Guedes says. Some of the innovations are basic: rather than waste time drying leaves out in the sun, farmers cook them in ovens; chopping the dried leaves up into smaller pieces is now frequently done with the aid of a gasoline-powered hedge trimmer, which whizzes them up into tiny fragments in no time. To wring the cocaine out of the coca leaves more quickly, cartels have started using adapted washing machines as primitive centrifuges. Sometimes these laboratories are installed in the backs of trucks that constantly trundle around the back roads of the jungle, to avoid detection. All of this, and the use of new precursor chemicals, has meant that in three years, cocaine yields in Bolivia have doubled, according to Guedes.

This means that the country's role in the supply chain has also changed. Rather than sending coca paste to Colombia to be processed into cocaine, Bolivians are increasingly doing the refining themselves, before sending it over the border into neighboring Brazil for onward shipment to Europe and for local consumption. (Brazil is now the world's second-biggest market for cocaine, after the United States, and the biggest bar none for crack.) Taking control of this part of the supply chain has enriched Bolivian traffickers, Guedes says, because international smuggling is where many of the profits are found in the cocaine business. "By doing *this*"—he hops from one side of his office to another, over an imaginary border—"you double the price of your product." Getting higher yields from coca fields means that, for now at least, the small reduction in the amount of land being used to grow the plants has been in vain. According to the United Nations, the amount of land devoted to growing coca in South America fell by about one-quarter between 1990 and 2011. But, thanks to more efficient production processes, the amount of cocaine made using that smaller amount of land increased by one-third.

•   •   •

It seems that nothing is going to force the cocaine cartels of South America to raise their prices. Hampering coca cultivation mainly hurts farmers, and even successful efforts to reduce the amount of coca being grown have been instantly wiped out by basic improvements in technology.

Yet even these problems are minor when contrasted with a more fundamental weakness in the efforts to attack the cartels' cocaine supply chain. There is one way in which drug cartels are very different than big retailers like Walmart that work by selling large volumes with relatively small markups. Walmart doesn't make very much money on those Thanksgiving dinner plates, which come in at less than 18 cents each. But it sells so many of them, as well as a multitude of other cheap items, that it turns a handsome profit. Markups vary from store to store and from product to product, but most retail businesses sell their merchandise for between 10 percent and 100 percent more than the wholesale price. That may sound like a lot, but it is nothing compared with the way that cocaine's price increases as it gets closer to its market.

Look at the evolution of the price of a kilogram of the drug, as it makes its way from the Andes to Los Angeles. To make that much cocaine, one needs somewhere in the neighborhood of 350 kilograms of dried coca leaves. Based on price data from Colombia obtained by Gallego and Rico, that would cost about $385. Once this is converted into a kilo of cocaine, it can sell in Colombia for $800. According to figures pulled together by Beau Kilmer and Peter Reuter at the RAND Corporation, an American think tank, that same kilo is worth $2,200 by the time it is exported from Colombia, and it has climbed to $14,500 by the time it is imported to the United States. After being transferred to a midlevel dealer, its price climbs to $19,500. Finally, it is sold by street-level dealers for $78,000.[10] Even these soaring figures do not quite get across the scale of the markups involved in the cocaine business. At each of these stages, the drug is diluted, as traffickers and dealers "cut" the drug with other substances, to make it go further. Take this into account, and the price of a pure kilogram of cocaine at the retail end is in fact about $122,000.

That is a truly extraordinary markup. Of course, not all of it is pure profit: the reason that cocaine becomes so expensive is that shipping it around the world in secret incurs all sorts of expenses, from murdering rivals (see next chapter) to bribing officials. But the difference between the "farm gate" price of coca and the final retail price of cocaine—an increase of more than 30,000 percent—has an important implication for attempts to raise the price of coca leaf. Let's imagine that the governments of South America make a breakthrough, and that by a massive increase in eradication or by providing coca farmers with alternative job opportunities they are able to *treble* the amount that cartels have to pay to acquire coca leaf. This would mean that to buy enough coca to make a kilogram of cocaine, cartels would have to shell out about $1,155, rather than the $385 that they pay at the moment. Now let's imagine that every penny of that extra cost is pushed on to the consumer. (Again, that seems unlikely—the most probable outcome is that the cartels would force other people in the chain to absorb some of the costs, as they do with their suppliers.) It would mean that a kilogram of pure cocaine sold at the retail level in the United States would cost an extra $770—that is, $122,770, rather than $122,000. That would mean that one pure gram would cost $122.77 rather than $122: a rise of 77 cents. In sum, by trebling the price of cocaine's raw ingredient in South America—something no policy has yet gotten close to achieving—the best-case scenario is that cocaine's retail price in the United States would rise by 0.6 percent. This does not seem like a good return on the billions of dollars invested in disrupting the supply of leaves in the Andes.

Of course, the dizzying increase in cocaine's price as it moves along the supply chain is proof that supply-side interventions do work, up to a point. It is the efforts of law-enforcement agencies that mean that a simple agricultural product, which costs no more than coffee at its source, is worth more than its weight in gold by the time it arrives in Europe or the United States. But the results of the most recent coca-eradication efforts suggest that interventions at the beginning of the supply chain have reached the limit of their effectiveness. Governments are approaching the cocaine market as if it were the chocolate market, in which a rise in the price of cocoa beans leads to a corresponding rise in the price of chocolate bars. In reality, it is more like the art market, in which the tiny cost of the raw materials is insignificant compared with the high price of the finished product. Attempts to raise the price of cocaine by forcing up the cost of coca leaves is a bit like trying to drive up the price of art by raising the cost of paint. Gerhard Richter, whose canvases sell for up to $46 million, would not lose sleep if the price of the oil paints used in his works of art doubled, or even quintupled. And in the same way, as long as counternarcotics agencies focus their fire on the earliest, lowest-value stages in the cocaine supply chain, the drug cartels need not worry too much about their bottom lines.

The vast, ongoing military gardening projects taking place in the Andes are demonstrably in vain. Most of the time they serve merely to impoverish farmers; even when they do succeed in imposing a cost on the cartels, it is minuscule in comparison with the retail price that cocaine eventually fetches. Attacking the drug problem at its source sounds sensible. But economics suggests that, in fact, it is the least effective point at which to strike. It is further down the supply chain, by the United States border, that cocaine starts to become really valuable. As we shall see in the next chapter, that is also the point at which cartels consider it worth going to war.

Chapter 2

COMPETITION VS. COLLUSION

Why Merger Is Sometimes Better Than Murder

In one of the grand state rooms of Los Pinos, the presidential palace in Mexico City, Felipe Calderón brandishes a color printout of thirty-seven surly faces. It is October 2012, and Calderón has six weeks left to serve as president of Mexico. In a valedictory interview, he is trying to impress on me the progress that his government has made in putting the country's leading narcotics entrepreneurs out of business. The thirty-seven men on his sheet were designated Mexico's most wanted in 2009, in a notice published in the *Diario Oficial de la Federación*, the official gazette of the republic. Some of the photos look like prison mug shots; others look as if they could have come from family albums. Most striking of all, many of the faces have a triumphant black line slashed through them.

"On the Zetas side, one of the important ones is El Taliban," President Calderón says, referring to a mustachioed figure with the word "ARRESTED" stamped across his photo. Most of the faces belonging to members of the Zetas, one of the country's leading drug cartels, have been crossed out. "El Amarillo [The Yellow] controlled practically all of the southeast of the country for the Zetas. El Lucky controlled all of Veracruz . . . La Ardilla [The Squirrel] was among the most dangerous and bloodthirsty killers," Calderón continues. In all,

29

twenty-five of the thirty-seven faces are struck through: seventeen arrested, six killed by the police or army, and two "executed"—that is,
murdered by their business rivals. Further strikes were to follow: in
July 2013, eight months after President Calderón left office, the Zetas'
supreme leader, Miguel Ángel Treviño, was nabbed near the Texas
border. In March 2015, Mexican security forces captured his brother
and successor, Omar, in a luxury home in a suburb of the northern city
of Monterrey.

One might have expected the methodical elimination of most of
the country's leading criminal kingpins to put the cartels out of business. In fact, it did no such thing. Throughout Calderón's presidency,
the quantity of drugs being smuggled over the American border
showed little sign of diminishing, and the number of young men going
into the narcotics business remained high. The one very noticeable
change during his six years in office was that violence soared. The
mild-mannered man from Michoacán inherited Mexico with its murder rate at an all-time low. With around ten murders per 100,000 people, in 2006 Mexico was one of Latin America's safer countries. Indeed,
its murder rate was lower than that of a handful of US states. By 2012,
the rate had doubled, and Calderón left Los Pinos the most unpopular
president in Mexico's recent history. Cartoonists now depict him in an
oversized soldier's uniform, standing lost in a field of gravestones or
human skulls.

Just as Mexico's murder rate was galloping upward, the situation
in one of its closest neighbors was going in the opposite direction.
El Salvador had long had one of the world's highest rate of violence,
dwarfing that of Mexico. Its fearsome *maras*, or gangs, famous for their
head-to-toe tattoos, carry out tit-for-tat killings in the country's slums
every day. But in 2012, something extraordinary happened. Within
the space of only a few days, peace broke out. The murder rate fell by
two-thirds, after the country's two main criminal gangs, the Mara Salvatrucha and Barrio 18, agreed on an unlikely truce. The two mobs,
which had previously been deadly rivals, even held a press conference

together, in which they promised that there would be no more killings. The murder rate immediately dropped by the equivalent of about
2,000 lives a year.

Mexico's cartels and El Salvador's *maras* operate in the same region
of the world, dealing the same products, and with the same readiness
to resort to violence. Why is it then that in the space of a few years
Mexico's gangsters became so much more violent, while El Salvador's
calmed down? Or, thinking about it like an economist, why did one
market see heightened competition and the other collusion?

• • •

Ground zero for Mexico's war against the cartels is Ciudad Juárez. Like
many cities along the border with the United States, Juárez has always
been a rough-and-ready sort of place. It is not poor by Mexican standards—the bars and taco joints on some streets in the center look as
if they could have been transplanted from Texas—but on its fringes
lives a churning population of desperately hard-up workers who eke
out a living working in the *maquiladora* factories on the city's sandy
outskirts where televisions and refrigerators are assembled for export.
On a mountainside on the western edge of town someone has painted,
in huge white letters big enough to be read all over the city: "CIUDAD
JUÁREZ: THE BIBLE IS THE TRUTH. READ IT."

Until recently, some force, divine or otherwise, had more or less held
the peace. A normal year saw about 400 murders—not too dreadful
for a city of 1.5 million people, let alone a very poor one that borders
a country with free-and-easy gun laws. But in 2008, something in the
criminal underworld stirred. The level of violence rose steeply; by the
summer of 2011, bodies were piling up in the city morgue at a rate of
300 per *month*.

The murders bore the hallmarks of organized crime: many of
the victims were killed with high-caliber rounds from the muzzle of
a *cuerno de chivo*, or "goat horn," as AK-47 rifles are known, owing
to their curved magazine. Many of the dead had come from out of

town—perhaps as traveling hit men, or else as their victims, kidnapped in another state and brought to Juárez for anonymous disposal. At one point the city was classifying about fifty bodies a month as "MN" or "FN," for nonidentified male or female. More than 25,000 people simply vanished during Calderón's presidency, many of whom have ended up in the chilled cabinets of the newly enlarged Juárez morgue. On most days a small queue of families still lines up outside the tall fences of the building, in the hope of identifying a missing relative.

Why did Mexico's cartels come to fight so hard over a place like Juárez? At first glance the city doesn't look as if it should be especially important to drug cartels. It contributes nothing in terms of the supply of drugs, which are grown far south and west in the Sierra Madre in the case of marijuana and opium poppies, and way down in South America in the case of coca for cocaine. Nor is it a center of much demand: the value of the local retail market is pitiful compared with that of big American cities over the border. Yet the fight to control this city was so intense that for several years running, it had the highest murder rate in the world.

Juárez's real value to cartels, of course, lies in its role as the gateway to a much bigger market. The US Drug Enforcement Administration (DEA), the agency burdened with the task of shutting down America's favorite vice, estimates that about 70 percent of the cocaine entering the United States via Mexico crosses the border at Juárez. Plenty of non-narco contraband has always flowed through this part of the Chihuahua desert. Even before the takeoff of cocaine in the 1970s, Juárez was a favorite place for American day-trippers to come for cheap alcohol, as well as budget car repairs, dentistry, prostitutes, and just about anything else in which the low cost of labor in Mexico translates to lower prices. When you fly into the city, it is hard to tell where Juárez ends and El Paso, in Texas, begins.

To try to suffocate the cartels, the American and Mexican authorities have done their best to make the border harder to cross. Since the 9/11 attacks, in particular, US borders have become more tightly policed (to the irritation of legitimate businesspeople as well as crooks: "*El* Homeland Security—*ay, cabrón!*" a Juárez barman once complained to me, lamenting the fall in business from American day-trippers). But a perverse economic consequence of tightening up the border is that each crossing point has become more valuable. The 2,000-mile frontier between Mexico and the world's largest drug market has only forty-seven official border crossings—and of those, the largest half-dozen or so dwarf the rest in terms of the number of trucks loaded with shipping containers that they process. A cartel that fails to control at least one of these major crossings will not get far.

Competition for each crossing is therefore intense. Juárez is not the only border city to have been hit by extreme violence: places such as Tijuana, Reynosa, and Nuevo Laredo have also been cartel battlegrounds in recent years. The six Mexican states that border the United States have among the highest murder rates in Mexico. The only places that rival them are states that are home to big ports, such as Veracruz and Michoacán, which are highly prized by cartels for the same reason. Precisely because these points of entry are scarce, drug traffickers are prepared to fight tooth and nail to control them.

The conditions have always been right for competition. Why did it break out so spectacularly during Calderón's time in office? The drug trade in Juárez had long been controlled by the Carrillo Fuentes Organization, often called simply the Juárez cartel. In the 1990s, the gang was run by Amado Carrillo Fuentes, known as the "Lord of the Skies" because of the fleet of aircraft he kept to import Colombian cocaine. In a plot twist straight out of a bad gangster film, Amado died in 1997 in Mexico City while undergoing plastic surgery to disguise his appearance. No one knows quite why or how he was killed while under the knife. But a few months later, the bodies of three of the doctors who performed the botched operation were discovered encased in concrete inside sixty-six-gallon oil drums. The cartel suffered another blow when one of its main contacts in the government was unmasked. José de Jesús Gutiérrez Rebollo was an army general who had been appointed head of the National Institute for the Combat of Drugs, effectively making him Mexico's drug tsar. In fact, he was in the pay of the Juárez gang all along. (If this rings a bell, it may be because a thinly veiled portrayal of the general appeared in *Traffic*, a 2000 film about the drugs business.) With Amado dead and the corrupted drug tsar out of the game, the Juárez mob fell into decline.

Rival mafias spotted this. The steady flow of bootleg business through Juárez had always made the city a tempting target for an acquisition. All it needed now was for the right sort of corporate takeover artist to emerge. Right on cue, on a winter morning in 2001, Joaquín Guzmán, Mexico's wiliest drug trafficker, escaped from prison. Guzmán, a dumpy man from the Sinaloan Sierra Madre, is known as El Chapo, or "Shorty," on account of his five-foot-six frame. His stockiness helped with his escape from a jail on the outskirts of Mexico City, hidden in a laundry cart. Buried under prisoners' unwashed underwear, he may not have been dignified in his exit. But it did little to tarnish his reputation as Mexico's most powerful drug lord, as the leader of the Sinaloa cartel, the world's largest drug-trafficking organization. *Forbes* magazine, which has included El Chapo on its billionaires list, named him the world's sixtieth-most-powerful person in 2010. (President Calderón didn't make the list at all.)

The Sinaloa and Juárez gangs soon began to quarrel. In 2004, Rodolfo, the youngest of the Carrillo Fuentes brothers of Juárez, was murdered outside a cinema in Sinaloa. El Chapo was widely suspected of having ordered the hit. Later that year, El Chapo's brother, Arturo, was killed in prison, in what may have been retaliation. Four relatively calm years passed before one of El Chapo's sons, Édgar Guzmán, was shot dead outside a shopping center in Sinaloa. (Legend has it that on Mother's Day, two days later, the women of Sinaloa awoke to find that there were no red roses left in the state, because El Chapo, in his grief, had bought every single one.)[1] A few months later, a former girlfriend of El Chapo was found dead in a car trunk, with the logo of a rival gang carved into her body. This was war.

It is 2011 when I nervously first set foot in Juárez, at what turns out to be the peak of the fighting. Emerging from the airport, notebook in hand and nonfunctioning tracking device still redundantly stuffed down my sock, I meet Miguel, a local fixer who has agreed to drive me around for the day. Normally, on a trip like this I would take taxis, but Juárez *taxistas* have a reputation for working as lookouts for the cartels, so I have gotten in touch with Miguel through a friend. Having my own driver feels impossibly grand—until Miguel announces that his car's reverse gear is not working, so I will have to help push it out of its parking place. Not much of a getaway car, I think to myself, as we head into the city.

I can tell as soon as we hit the highway into town that something is not quite right in Juárez. Unlike in other Mexican cities, where every intersection has someone selling food, fans, or flyswatters, the streets are nearly empty. Even as the winter's day begins to warm up, everyone's car windows are still closed. People also seem to be driving very carefully. In Mexico City, the driving is dreadful (partly because the driver's test was abolished a few years back after examiners became so corrupt that it was difficult to pass without paying a bribe). In Juárez, motorists are downright courteous. I ask Miguel why he is allowing so much space between cars when he stops at traffic lights. "In case of a shootout," he shrugs. Red traffic lights are a favorite place for hit men to assassinate their targets, so having a few feet between you and the car in front could be the difference between escaping and being hemmed in.

I go to see Hugo Almada, a professor at the University of Juárez, who has tracked the ebb and flow of the drugs business in the city. Wearily, he lowers himself into a booth in Barrigas (Bellies), a gringo-style diner in the center of the city where we have agreed to meet. "The traffic of drugs is like a river," he says, miming it with one hand over the table while cutting up an enchilada with the other. "If you try to dam it"—he brings his hand down with a smack—"it just goes everywhere." Like many Mexicans, he is frustrated that President Calderón seems to have taken the war on drugs literally, sending the army to crush any sign of trafficking activity, often stirring up even more trouble. Almada grudgingly admires what he sees as the cynicism of the way the "war" is selectively fought north of the border. "We have to learn from the United States. There, drugs are moved around, the wholesale trade goes on, money is laundered—and nothing happens," he says. "But the day someone kills a policeman, they mobilize the force of the state. And the *cabrón* gets forty years in jail, and he doesn't escape. Those are the unwritten rules. Here, they [the traffickers] kill policemen as if they were lead soldiers."

There is an economic reason for the targeting of policemen, which became one of the most prominent features of the battle for Juárez. When hostilities first escalated, in 2008, Sinaloa declared war with a message that it hung on a monument in Juárez to fallen police officers. The cartel's poster, scrawled in black marker, bore the title "For those who did not believe." Under it were the names of four local policemen who had been assassinated. Beneath that list was another title: "For those who go on disbelieving," under which were the names of seventeen officers who were still alive. Soon after the list was displayed, Sinaloa methodically began to pick them off, one by one; after the first half-dozen had been killed, the rest skedaddled.

The focus on the police was no coincidence. When attempting to carry out a corporate takeover, cartels are like ordinary businesses in that they need to satisfy competition regulators that the deal should go ahead. The main regulators of the drugs industry are the police. They are the ones whose job it is to stop the business, and who can be persuaded, with enough bribery or intimidation, to allow it to go ahead. Here, El Chapo hit a problem. The Juárez cartel was skilled at wooing regulators—it had managed to corrupt the national drug tsar, remember—and the local city police were widely thought to be in its pocket.

The city's government, which has ultimate responsibility for running the force, fiercely denies this. In a bunkerlike concrete office less than a pistol shot away from the Texas border, Juárez's pugnacious mayor, Héctor Murguía Lardizábal, bristles when I ask if his city's police are up to the job of keeping the traffickers at bay. "They're more capable than yours in *Inglaterra*," he spits back, before pointedly playing with his BlackBerry throughout the rest of our interview. But there is plenty of evidence of overlap between the Juárez police and the local cartel. A former head of public security under Mayor Murguía was imprisoned in the United States after paying a bribe of $19,250 to a US border inspector in return for his agreeing to turn a blind eye to a truck crossing the border loaded with 400 kilograms of marijuana.[2] The Juárez cartel has an enforcement arm, La Linea (The Line), whose members originally came from the ranks of the city police, both retired and serving. These close links between the Juárez cartel and the city's cops spelled a dead end for El Chapo: after years of loyalty to the Carrillo Fuentes clan, the Juárez police were not for sale.

What do ordinary businesses do when regulators thwart their takeover plans? One course of action is to try a different regulator in another jurisdiction. Consider the case of a proposed merger between General Electric (GE) and Honeywell in 2000. To the horror of its competitors, GE announced that it intended to acquire Honeywell, a giant technology firm that manufactures everything from burglar alarms to helicopter parts. America's competition authorities gave the deal the go-ahead. But GE's rivals were not going to settle for that, so they went elsewhere, to the European competition authorities. Examining the same facts, the European commissioners reached a different conclusion: the deal was not in the interests of competition, they found, noting that Honeywell's jet-engine business, when combined with GE's own portfolio, could create a monopoly in some markets. GE's rivals were thus able to block the decision of one regulator by appealing to another.

Drug cartels go through a similar process. Unable to persuade Ciudad Juárez's regulator—the local police—to allow his takeover of the city's drugs business to go ahead, El Chapo appealed to a different authority. Fortunately for him, Mexico's multilayered policing system

made this possible. In Mexico, each of the 2,000-plus local governments has its own police force (at least in theory; some rural ones are
all but nonexistent). On top of that, each of the thirty-one states has its
own, separate force. The final layer is the federales (federal police), an
elite squad—all things being relative—of more heavily armed, better
trained officers, which operates around the country and was significantly expanded during the Calderón presidency.

El Chapo saw an opportunity with the federal police. The bad apples
among Juárez's city police were already playing for the Carrillo Fuentes
gang. Many of the state police were on its payroll, too. But the *federales*,
who were recruited from all corners of the country and had no particular loyalty to Juárez, might be more open to persuasion.

An absurd pattern established itself in which shootouts would take
place between the two different sets of police patrolling Juárez. Each
side would claim that the other was in cahoots with one of the warring
cartels—and both would often be proven correct. City police arrested
two federal cops found shooting up a bar; federal police broke up a kidnapping ring and discovered a city policeman among its members; and
the army arrested a group of city officers for carrying illegal weapons,
at which point the rest of the force announced that it didn't want to go
on patrol any more, for fear of being arrested. In one incident that made
international headlines in 2011, a city cop assigned to work as Mayor
Murguía's own bodyguard was shot dead by federal police officers.

Just as the United States had complained about Europe's position
on a GE takeover (which was "antithetical to the goals of antitrust-law
enforcement," in the words of the US assistant attorney general), the
local Juárez authorities complained bitterly about the *federales'* handling of the attempted Sinaloan takeover of their city. "You're nobody
to go around giving out orders in Juárez," Murguía exclaimed at one
point to a group of federal police. The fighting, now between not only
the cartels but between the rival police forces, became far more intense
after a big deployment of federal police to the city in 2008.

The Juárez cartel's reaction to the attempted takeover was similar to that of ordinary firms facing such a threat. One of its first acts was to begin a public-relations campaign against the firm trying to take it over. Advertisements painted by hand onto sheets, known as *narcomantas*—literally, "narco blankets"—began appearing all over northwestern Mexico, urging locals to resist El Chapo. Rather than being simple drug traffickers, the banners claimed, El Chapo and his Sinaloan cronies were thieves, rapists, and even double agents of the government.

And like other firms under threat of takeover, the Juárez mob needed a war chest to fund its defense. As Sinaloa tightened its grip on Juárez's drug-supply lines, the Juárez cartel found an alternative source of revenue in the form of extortion. This had a devastating effect on life in the city, as businesses were bled dry by the new "tax" demanded by the mobsters.

Walking through downtown Juárez, I feel as if I am visiting a ghost town. The El Pueblo restaurant, with giant model mariachi singers on its roof, is for rent; the nearby Hotel Olivia looks like a bomb site, its roof caved in. I walk into a bar run by one of the few local business owners willing to talk about his relationship with the mob. Inside, it takes a few seconds for my eyes to adjust from the outdoor midday glare to the gloom of the *cantina*, where I find the proprietor manning a bar that is empty save for a few bored-looking prostitutes. Paying the weekly extortion money is like having one extra employee to pay, he says. His weekly contribution is 1,500 pesos, or about $120. If you are late with the payments, "They call your house, they threaten to kidnap you." Burned out premises around the city serve as a constant reminder of what happens to those who fail to cooperate. No one is exempt: the sleek glass walls of a funeral parlor had to be replaced after being shot up; a restaurant over the road got a grenade through the window.

Slowly, bloodily, El Chapo and his allies began to get the upper hand. As well as killing local police officers, they stoked rumors that the state prosecutor's office was corruptly working for the Juárez cartel. Sinaloan hit men kidnapped the brother of the recently retired state attorney general and recorded a "confession" at gunpoint that the brother had worked as a link between the cartel and the state authorities. In the video, which was uploaded to YouTube, he named several officials as being part of the cartel, including a former police intelligence officer who had been killed a few weeks earlier (along with his brother, a retired wrestler). True or not, the forced confession helped to sap trust in the local authorities. Perhaps the decisive moment in the battle for Juárez was the arrest in 2011 of Juan Antonio Acosta, known as "El Diego," the head of La Linea. After his arrest, he claimed to have organized more than 1,500 killings. The murder rate fell, as El Chapo settled into a commanding position and the resistance from the Juárez cartel died down. With regulatory obstacles finally overcome, Sinaloa's acquisition was complete.

Mexico's multilayered policing system means that cartel takeovers have to be negotiated with several levels of government, prolonging conflicts. President Calderón often complained that his federal government was being thwarted by state and municipal authorities. Just as Juárez began quieting down, Acapulco, a glitzy bay city where John Wayne once kept a villa and Bill and Hillary Clinton honeymooned, became the target of a similar, violent takeover attempt. An exasperated Calderón complained to me that part of the problem was that the local government was not working together with the federal authorities. "Myself, I'd like nothing more than to be mayor of Acapulco. I'd have a great time, it's a city I really love," he said. "But the truth is that over there, there is a city government, and a governor in [the state], and [between them] they have 5,000 police. The desirable thing is that those police work. And while that doesn't happen, well, clearly a process of instability continues." That instability, and the unregulated competition that it creates between cartels, is thought to have cost upward of 60,000 lives during the Calderón presidency.

It has also turned Mexico into a darker, nervier place. In Juárez, tingles of fear keep me from staying put in any one place for very long, bolting down lunch in a burrito joint (called The Godfather, as if the city needed any more reminders of the mafia) and hurrying from meeting to meeting. In the evening, as we are driving back to the airport, aiming to be off the roads before dark, Miguel says quietly that he thinks someone may be following us. We press on in silence, as pickup trucks of soldiers and *federales* cruise by, their occupants staring blankly at us in the dusk through slits in their balaclavas. Eventually, with the light fading, we make it to the terminal, and later my heart lifts as the plane soars into the safety of the night sky. I never discovered who, if anyone, was tracking us that day. But on that trip, and subsequent visits to Ciudad Juárez and other border towns in northern Mexico, I never quite shook off the feeling that I was trespassing on cartel land. Even in the posh neighborhoods of Mexico City, chatter sometimes subsides when a flashy sports car pulls up outside a restaurant and a cowboy-booted foot steps onto the sidewalk. Few markets are as hotly disputed as Juárez. But everywhere is someone or other's turf.

• • •

Why are things so different in El Salvador? Like Mexico, the country is encumbered with some extremely unpleasant criminals. The two main *maras*, or street gangs, are the Mara Salvatrucha and Barrio 18, which is also known as the 18th Street Gang. Both of these mobs were founded not in El Salvador but in the prisons and poor neighborhoods of California, where young Salvadoran immigrants banded together for self-defense and to run drug and extortion rackets. The gangs were reexported to Latin America when those same Salvadoran migrants were deported. Young, jobless, and tattooed—and now with some experience of weapons and with contacts in the United States—they have continued their gangster activities back in Central America, where weaker law enforcement has allowed them to flourish as never before. The gangs are now estimated to have roughly 70,000 members in Central America,[3] about the same as the number of people directly employed by General Motors in the United States.[4] In a region whose total population is little more than 40 million, they represent a formidable force.

To find out more about how these transnational organizations work, I arrange a meeting with Carlos Mojica Lechuga, the leader of the 18th Street Gang. Mojica runs his international business from a cell in a fortress-like prison in Cojutepeque, about an hour's drive east of San Salvador, the busy capital of El Salvador. The prison must once have been a grand old building, but these days through barred windows in its stone façade, you can see daylight shining in from where there used to be a roof. Masked soldiers patrol sandbag emplacements around the perimeter of the jail, idly training their machine guns on anyone who wanders too close. Although we are right in the middle of a town, I find that I have no cell-phone reception at all. A weary nearby vendor of *pupusas*, the fried corn snacks that make El Salvador go round, explains that the blackout is caused by signal jammers designed to block prisoners' calls. He points to the spot where the signal comes back to life a little way down the road, where a gaggle of locals is waving phones around trying to pick up messages.

Inside the prison I have to give up my phone anyway, along with everything else in my pockets apart from a notebook, pen, and dictaphone. Armed guards take me into a courtyard and from there into a large, bare cell about the size of a school classroom, empty apart from a few plastic chairs. Soon Mojica is brought in. He is wearing handcuffs, but that is about his only concession to being in prison. He is decked out in a blue basketball shirt, with shiny white shorts and box-fresh, white Reebok trainers. All of it looks brand new. On his weatherbeaten bald head is a black baseball cap, embroidered with the number "18" on the front and his nickname, Viejo Lin, or "Old Lin," along the side. He is tattooed from head to toe. A large one on his neck reads "100 percent 18." Artwork down his right arm is mangled by a large scar running along his bicep. By his left eye is a tattoo of a small teardrop, and partly hidden by the peak of his cap is a phrase that runs in three lines across the entire width of his forehead: *"En Memoria De Mi Madre"* (In Memory Of My Mother).

Most gang members are young, because the chances of growing old in a *mara* are slim. In El Salvador, the murder rate in 2009 was 71 per 100,000 people, making it the most murderous country in the world, according to the United Nations. Extrapolated over the course of a lifetime, at that rate a Salvadoran man has roughly a one in ten chance of being murdered. And that's the average—for men who grow up poor, or in *mara*-linked families, the odds are far higher.

So Old Lin is unusual for his age. Just how old is he, I ask, as he pulls up a chair and sits himself down. "I'm twenty-five," he croaks, deadpan. No, he grins, he's actually fifty. He is likely to spend the rest of his life in prison, serving a sentence for beheading a pair of teenage girls who had dated members of the Mara Salvatrucha. (Reading old news reports later, I learn that he and his fellow gangsters supposedly tortured them with a floor-polishing machine before killing them.) Like many gangsters, Old Lin joined the *mara* in Los Angeles, when he was twenty-one. He has the deep voice of someone who has had too many cigarettes and not enough fresh air. Although it is a baking-hot day and I can feel my shirt sticking to my back, Lin's skin is the pale gray that comes with a life lived behind bars.

Old Lin's organization is experimenting with a business strategy completely different from that of the Mexican cartels. In March 2012, Barrio 18 agreed to a truce with its arch-rival, the Salvatrucha. Old Lin and his opposite number, an American-born gangster called Edson Zachary Eufemia (who is also imprisoned in El Salvador, in a different jail), agreed that their members would no longer seek to murder each other. "It was the result of a long reflection," Old Lin told me, slipping into CEO mode. "We don't see violence as an option anymore. We have arrived at the moment to live like brothers." The warring between the gangs killed nearly 50,000 people in the 1990s, he says. "Now we have prisons full of young people, some paying for crimes they actually committed, others not. Our families have suffered in all of this. And the country is sectorized." By that he means divided up along gang lines. In the slums of San Salvador, crossing into rival territory can be enough to provoke a killing. How much of this "sectorized" country belongs to Barrio 18? A flicker of a smile: "*Bastante.*" Plenty.

The system of "sectors" partly explains why the option of collusion made more sense to El Salvador's gangs than to their counterparts in Mexico. The point of collusion between firms, whether they are drug cartels or ordinary businesses, is to turn one big competitive market into a series of small monopolies. Imagine a country that is served by two telephone companies. If they both compete across the entire country, business will go to the firm that offers the better service at the lower price. The upshot is that neither firm is able to make much of a profit. But if the firms collude—agreeing, say, that one will cover the north of the country and the other the south—each can run its own little monopoly, charging high prices for poor service. That is why collusion is usually banned. Of course, illegal companies don't need to worry too much about antitrust rules, which is why collusion of some sort between rival gangs is more common than one might imagine.

Although it might make economic sense, Mexico's cartels have struggled to divide markets up in this way. The important border crossings and ports are scarce, and with a city such as Juárez responsible for the transit of 70 percent of northbound cocaine, coming up with a "fair" division is difficult. For the *maras,* it is different. Although they have a modest line in international drug trafficking, most of their business is done locally, dealing drugs or running extortion rackets. This domestic market is relatively easy to divide up into local monopolies. Under conditions of competition, Old Lin and his rival *mara* would have to offer ever-lower prices for their drugs, and ever-more-reasonable terms for their protection rackets (or ever-more-brutal—and therefore expensive—consequences for those who resisted). By splitting the country into uncontested "sectors," they can charge higher prices for both their drugs and their extortion businesses, thus minimizing the costs normally incurred by fighting with each other.

The truce had an extraordinary impact. Almost overnight, the murder rate fell by about two-thirds. That meant that El Salvador went from being one of the world's most violent countries to being only about as dangerous as Brazil. San Salvador, once the most murderous city on the planet, by 2012 had a murder rate slightly lower than that of Oakland, California. According to Old Lin, who is now well into his public-relations spiel, the aim was to rehabilitate the country's youth. "We want the opportunity to get jobs, to get our daily bread in a dignified way. Remember," he tells me, jabbing the air for emphasis as if the problem were nothing to do with him, "our young people have grown up in a climate of violence."

The defining feature of El Salvador's young *mareros* is their head-to-toe tattoos. Like Old Lin, nearly all gang members sport body art declaring their allegiance to either the Salvatrucha or Barrio 18. The inkings are indirectly responsible for much of the country's violence, as they effectively paint a bull's-eye on the body of any young gangster who wanders into territory controlled by rival *mara*. But they may also make collusion between the gangs more likely.

Research on the Sicilian mafia by Michele Polo, an Italian economist, found that violent competition between rival Italian gangs often took the form of attempts by one organization to poach the *soldati*, or foot soldiers, of another.[5] Polo drew up a formula to explain how mafias write "contracts" with their members to minimize the chance of defections. One element of these agreements is to set remuneration high enough to encourage loyalty. But this can get expensive, so mafias also deter defection by threatening violence against those who stray. Mexico's cartels are run along similar lines, dishing out their most horrible violence to traitors from their own ranks.

The *maras* are different in this respect. Gang membership in El Salvador is dependent not on who pays the highest wages but on where the would-be gangster is born. Once a young man has become a member

and has gotten his body covered in Salvatrucha tattoos, defecting to
join Barrio 18 is out of the question, and vice versa. Even leaving the
mara to start a new, noncriminal career is virtually impossible, as employers tend to be perturbed by job candidates who show up for an
interview with skulls and crossbones etched on their foreheads. In economic terms, this means that whereas Mexican gangbangers are highly
footloose, liable to change sides to work for whichever cartel seems to
be stronger or higher paying, the labor market for Salvadoran *mareros* is
completely illiquid. With no chance whatsoever of one gang poaching
the other's employees, the *maras* have no need to compete for talent,
which allows them to keep their wages low.

Between Old Lin's prison and the capital lies Ilopango, a suburb of
San Salvador that is divided up between the two *maras*. On my way
back to the city, I call in to meet Salvador Ruano, the recently elected
mayor of Ilopango, who seems to be greatly enjoying his new role. We
have just sat down to begin our conversation—with him speaking
through mouthfuls of a rice-and-beans concoction that he is shoveling
in from a polystyrene tray—when he jumps up to say he has to marry
a couple of people, and would I like to come? We walk out of his office and into a little conference room inside the tiny town hall, where
two couples and their families are seated around a table, excited and
smartly dressed. After a short speech on marital harmony (including
an appeal to the grooms to help around the house: "The tortilla is not
to be prepared by women alone"), he declares that the couples are now
married, and we go back to his office, where he resumes his lunch.

Mayor Ruano, who has a tendency to talk about himself in the third
person, admits that virtually every square foot of his small town is governed by either the Mara Salvatrucha or Barrio 18. "During the election campaign I went from *colonia* to *colonia*, and I came across people
with tattoos all over their body. Most of them asked: could you offer me
work?" He promised that he could, and he was duly elected. Now, he
says, offering the young gangsters jobs is helping to reduce the amount
of extortion, which was previously costing local shopkeepers $5–$10

per day. "This is a mayor who lives here, and whose children live here," he tells me, jabbing a finger into his chest for emphasis. "We all want to calm things down."

As part of the truce, the government resolved to help gang members across the country find work in the legitimate economy. A noble aim, perhaps, but it has involved the transfer of large amounts of public money to fund jobs for people who not long ago were terrorizing society. In the first year of the truce, the government promised $72 million for employment projects for former gangsters. The projects were slated to go ahead in eighteen towns, but at least forty towns said they wanted to take part in the experiment. In Ilopango, gang members have been given a small bakery to run. When I meet Mayor Ruano, he is preparing for the opening of a chicken farm the next day, which is also to be run by members of the *maras*.

The gangs' leaders seem to be doing quite well out of the truce, too. Take Old Lin. The prison I interviewed him in isn't exactly luxurious, but by Salvadoran standards it is pretty soft. Previously, he had been held in Zacatecoluca, a prison nicknamed "Zacatraz" because of its harsh regime. Just before the truce was announced, he was moved into his more comfortable digs. Edson Zachary Eufemia, the leader of the Salvatrucha, was also transferred from a tough prison to an easier-going one. The reason for the change in regime, officially, was to allow the gang leaders to negotiate the truce, by putting them in a prison where they could communicate with their organizations. "We needed to create the conditions to consult our *compañeros*," Old Lin explains. That may have been part of the reason, but the transfer to lower-security prisons surely acted as a sweetener.

The cushier conditions, as well as the public spending on job-creation projects, has made the truce deeply unpopular with the public, in spite of the much lower murder rate. People doubt the motives of the gangs, which many believe have signed the truce only to protect their businesses. They are probably right: for all Old Lin's pious talk of going straight, the falling murder rate has not been accompanied by any reduction in revenue-generating crimes. Extortion—perhaps the most hated crime of all, because it affects ordinary people and not just gangsters—has continued to flourish. "Extortion is the principal source of income of the gangs. They have said: 'We can negotiate, but not on extortion,'" says David Munguía, who was security minister at the time the pact was agreed on in 2012.

For this reason, politicians have always been uneasy about the project. When the truce was first announced, it was described as an agreement between the two gangs that had been brokered by the Catholic Church. The government welcomed the drop in the murder rate but kept its distance from the truce itself. A year after the pact had been signed, and with the murder rate still low, politicians became a little bit more willing to acknowledge their role in the policy. It became clear that the truce had been partly brokered by Raúl Mijango, a former adviser to the Ministry of Defense. After getting the Mara Salvatrucha and the 18th Street Gang to agree to the deal in March, a few months later he persuaded several smaller gangs to sign up. La Mao Mao and La Máquina (The Machine), a pair of mini-*maras*, joined the truce, as did two gangs of common criminals, La Raza (The Race) and a raggedy prison-born mob known as the M.D., for Mara de Desorden (Disorganized *Mara*).

Since then the truce has been through various wobbly incarnations. It fell apart in 2014 when a new president, Salvador Sánchez Cerén, withdrew official support for the deal, having promised on the campaign trail to crush the criminals. The murder rate duly bounced back up to pre-truce levels, as the gangs returned to their old ways of hacking each other to pieces. In a strange twist, Rudolph Giuliani, the mayor of New York City who made inroads into that city's murder rate in the 1990s, was hired by a private-sector organization to advise on how to pull off the same trick in San Salvador. His input failed to pacify the gangs, who merrily carried on their murderous ways.

Foreign governments, particularly that of the United States, remain unconvinced by the truce strategy. This has been frustrating for those in El Salvador who benefited from the dramatic fall in violence during the cease-fire. "They don't like it? Give me a different formula, then. A magic formula. If the government of the United States has another formula, tell me what it is," demands Salvador Ruano, the mayor. David Munguía acknowledges that the truce was "imperfect" but insists: "We had to stop the war between the gangs." In 2012 alone, the agreement meant that between 1,900 and 2,500 murders did not take place that, under the previous, higher murder rate, would have occurred, he calculates. In a country of 6 million, that is an incredible saving. The pact has helped to bring prisons under control, too. Shortly before I met Old Lin, El Salvador hosted a visit of José Miguel Insulza, the head of the Organization of American States. The diplomat had been taken on a tour of a jail—previously an unthinkable risk.

The gangs' collusion, mediated by the government, may have given the villains a chance to regroup. But it has given society an opportunity to take stock, too. David Blanchard, an American priest with a ministry in San Salvador where the *maras'* territories meet, is cautiously hopeful that such cease-fires might provide opportunities to put a brake on the gangs' recruitment. In a school close to the capital, he says, four sixth-grade children (that is, aged eleven or twelve) are known to be recruiters for Old Lin's 18th Street Gang. The recruiters are the most junior members; later they may graduate to picking up extortion money from shops, 9-millimeter handguns tucked into their narrow waistbands. The gangs are "like the god Baal, who demanded the sacrifice of children," he says. While the truce holds, "we are just trying to take the kids off the sacrificial altars and provide alternatives."

•   •   •

News reports on the drug war tend to give the impression that drug traffickers live in a permanent state of deadly competition. It is true that brutality is an essential part of the business: because criminal organizations cannot use the legal system, violence is the only way for them to enforce contractual agreements. But the examples of Mexico and El Salvador show that the level of violence can be altered dramatically by changes in market conditions. Looking at the two criminal

markets in economic terms reveals a few reasons that things became
so violent in Mexico and calmed down for a time in El Salvador—and
suggests how governments might keep a lid on violence in the future.

The root cause of the brutal competition for control of cities such as
Ciudad Juárez in Mexico is the necessity to control access to the limited number of border crossings. The high levels of violence in border
towns have led to calls from some people in the United States for crossings to be shut down. Yet economics suggests the opposite: by opening more of them, each would become less valuable, and less worth
fighting for. True, it would give cartels more opportunities to smuggle
their drugs into the United States. But clampdowns on supply have
tended to have little impact on the total amount of contraband being
smuggled, or on the drugs' price (see Chapter 1). Opening more border
crossings could reduce the amount of fighting, with little impact on the
American illegal-drugs market.

Mexico also shows that control of the industry's regulators—that is,
the police—is an important goal for drug traffickers. Better vetting and
higher wages for police officers would raise the cost of bribing them.
But making Mexico's police incorruptible is a long-term project, to say
the least. In the meantime, an easier reform would be to bring together
the police's multiple layers. Criminologists have long suggested doing
this in order to improve efficiency. An economic approach suggests that
it would also prevent drug traffickers from co-opting different regulators and making them fight against each other. At the moment, cartels
are able to wage proxy wars against each other at the state's expense, by
taking control of rival police forces. Amalgamating them would render
this much harder.

El Salvador offers different lessons. Although the concessions
granted to the leaders of the country's *maras* may have come perilously
close to rewarding criminal behavior, the principle of the government
acting as a mediator between warring gangs is worth pursuing. The
other reason for the *maras'* willingness to cooperate is the fact that they
operate local monopolies in separate, uncontested territories. That is
obviously not something that governments should encourage—even

though they may welcome some of the results, such as more expensive, less competitive retail drug markets.

The illiquidity of the labor market for *mareros*, born of the fact that tattooed gangsters can't easily switch from one *mara* to another, may have helped to foster the truce, by removing one element of competition. But it also tells us something about the way the *maras* are run that might make them easier to dismantle. Normally, gangs have to pay their members a reasonable wage in order to dissuade them from defecting. If the Sinaloa cartel stops paying the teenagers in Juárez slums to act as its lookouts, for example, they will find work elsewhere. By contrast, the *maras* can maintain large workforces without paying them much at all, because the barriers to exit are so high. This means that tempting *mareros* away from gang life and into ordinary jobs ought to be extremely cheap; the only thing needed is an employer willing to look beyond the tattoos. The state can play an innovative role here by paying for inmates' tattoos to be removed. A program run by the Los Angeles County Sheriff's Department in California does just that, offering to remove the tattoos of gang members who have shown a willingness to turn over a new leaf once out of jail.[6] The free service costs thousands of dollars. But the outlay is peanuts compared with the welfare payments that can be saved if it means the difference between the inmate finding work or remaining unemployed. In El Salvador, it could save lives as well as money.

Above all, the examples of Mexico and El Salvador show the difference that changing market conditions can make. More than 4,000 Salvadorans were saved by a spell of cooperation between their country's *maras*, whereas some 60,000 Mexicans died because of an increase in competition among their country's drug cartels. Neither outcome was inevitable. With stakes like that, governments should consider ways to shape these markets, rather than simply charge into battle to shut them down at any cost.

Chapter 3

THE PEOPLE PROBLEMS OF A DRUG CARTEL

When James Bond Meets Mr. Bean

It was all going so well. The deal had been agreed, the drugs were ready for collection, and the funds had been rustled up. All that was needed was for the exchange to go ahead. The leader of the operation, a high-level dealer who specialized in importing cannabis and cocaine from mainland Europe to the United Kingdom, got the cash ready: a fat bundle of £300,000 in used banknotes, equivalent to nearly half a million dollars. The notes were counted and handed over to the driver, whose job it was to travel to Belgium, meet the contact, and hand over the cash.

That was when things started to go wrong. That amount of money in crisp banknotes is quite a thing to behold. So the driver decided to deal it out—spread it around and see how it looked. It was such an impressive sight that he couldn't keep it to himself, so he invited his girlfriend over to show it off. Later, speaking to researchers from the Home Office (Britain's security ministry) in his jail cell, the boss of the operation wearily explains how the plan unraveled. "The divvy decides it would be nice to lay the money on his bed, make mad passionate love to his seventeen-year-old girlfriend and photograph it." Taking intimate selfies with the loot was probably unwise. But it gets worse: as well as having a girlfriend, the driver also had a jealous wife. The following Saturday night, before the trip to Belgium, husband and wife were out on the town when they ran into the girlfriend, who was drunk. An argument erupted during which she decided to show the X-rated photos to the driver's wife, who was not exactly pleased.

The wife decided to teach her cheating husband a lesson. Still enraged, she called the UK border police to tip them off about the upcoming drug run. The unwitting driver set off to Belgium with the £300,000 and was promptly stopped by customs officials at the port of Dover, before he had even left the country. Questioned by border agents about his big stash of cash, he cracked. "The numpty goes into meltdown," his boss sighs. The operation was blown, and the deal was off. To add insult to injury, the jealous wife—who herself had a £2,500 ($4,000)-a-week cocaine habit—came back to the boss a few months later, asking if her husband could have his job back.[1]

The narcotics game has an image of ruthless professionalism, with clinical hit men, ingenious smugglers, and logistical experts combining to outwit the police. Sometimes the business works like that. But it is also characterized by stunning incompetence. Considering the high salaries involved even at junior levels of the business—a driver can make £800 ($1,300) per day simply delivering cocaine shipments around Britain—it seems odd that the jobs are so often done by "divvies" and "numpties" (that is, idiots), to borrow the English slang used by the unlucky importer. Straightforward ineptitude is frequently the cause of drug traffickers' downfall, according to the Home Office researchers, who noted that the "soap-opera lifestyles" of dealers and their associates were often what caused them to be caught.

The mismatch between the drug business's high profits and the low capacity of its employees demonstrates perhaps the biggest problem that any drug cartel faces: human resources. Management gurus are fond of repeating the old cliché that a firm's most valuable asset is its people. But in the world of drug trafficking, it really is true. Cartels face two key problems. First, they must recruit their workers in an industry that operates under secrecy, where jobs cannot be advertised and total trust is required. This problem is compounded by the fact that drugs businesses have very high levels of staff turnover. In transit countries such as Mexico, where extreme violence is part of the job, the high mortality rate among cartel members means that replacements are continually needed. Even in the rich consumer countries of North America and Western Europe, where the body count is much lower, policing is better, meaning that employees frequently end up in jail. One British smuggler estimated that of the cocaine "mules" he sends on flights from the Caribbean to the United Kingdom, one in four will be stopped. Every arrest or death means another tedious round of hiring and vetting.

The second big human-resources headache is that the cartels must manage relations with their staff, as well as their suppliers and clients, without an easy way of enforcing contractual agreements. In a normal company, if an employee steals or if a supplier fails to provide goods that have been paid for, the firm can get redress through the courts. A drug cartel obviously can't, if a courier makes off with a stash of money or an importer fails to deliver a shipment of drugs. The one way that criminal organizations can enforce contracts is with violence, which is why a capacity to intimidate and kill is at the heart of any drug cartel's success. But deploying violence is an expensive course of action and bad for business.

These two conundrums—how to hire staff, and how to make sure they do what they are told—are what occupy drug cartels' human-resources managers. Running complex operations using an ever-churning payroll of low-skilled, unpredictable workers who are prone to sabotaging deals through sheer stupidity is no mean feat. The organizations that best accomplish it are those that are most serious about their approach to personnel.

•   •   •

In a noisy, dimly lit Spanish restaurant in Santo Domingo, the elegantly decaying capital of the Dominican Republic, some officers from the country's antidrugs squad are celebrating the end of the week by getting wildly drunk. As I pull up a chair to sit down with them, another round of beer is ordered from a long-suffering waiter, who is summoned with shouts of *"Tonto!"* ("Idiot!"). Other diners look around but don't seem eager to pick a fight.

The Dominican Republic's antidrugs squad is much busier than it used to be. Between mouthfuls of *plátano frito*, the least inebriated of the officers explains to me a disturbing trend that the country has seen in recent years: a "vertiginous" increase in the amount of narcotics being seized coming into the country. For many years the Caribbean formed a crucial stepping-stone for cocaine bound for the United States. In the "Miami Vice" years of the 1980s, speedboats would race from the Caribbean into Florida loaded with cocaine, then head back stacked with dollars. But that route was effectively shut down by the South Florida Task Force, an initiative of President Ronald Reagan that coordinated the work of the FBI, DEA, customs, tax authorities, and other federal agencies, under the command of Vice President George H. W. Bush. The task force made an immediate impact, and the Caribbean route dried up. Traffickers moved west, using Mexico as the main point of entry instead.

Lately, though, there are signs that the traffickers have come back to the islands. The result has been a sharp spike in crime. "Pressure in Mexico has caused a displacement to the east, to the Caribbean," says the officer, shuffling plates and bottles to form a map of the region on the restaurant's wooden table. The eruption of violence in Mexico and Central America has caused traffickers to look for quieter routes, and the Caribbean has come back into fashion. The big jump came in 2011, just as Mexico's drug war reached its bloodiest point. In that year the Dominican Republic seized and burned nearly nine tons of drugs, double the amount it had found a couple of years earlier. Most of the haul had come from Colombia to the brand-new port of Caucedo, on the southern Dominican coast. The majority of the drugs was destined either for Puerto Rico, and onward shipment to the mainland United States, or for ports in Spain or the Netherlands.

The interceptions are being made with the help of eight newly acquired Brazilian "Super Tucano" fighter jets, the officer tells me. (I put a question mark next to this in my notebook: investing in fighter planes to catch drug smugglers seems a bit strange. Perhaps it is. Some months after our conversation, the *Wall Street Journal* reported that Brazilian prosecutors have filed corruption charges against several employees of the jets' manufacturer, Embraer, alleging that they bribed Dominican officials to sign the deal.)[2]

Most of the smugglers arrested are locals. The sheer volume of arrests has contributed to a rapid filling up of the country's sweltering jails. In 2014, the prison population was double that of a decade earlier. The 26,000 people currently behind bars are crammed into cells built to house fewer than 15,000. The overcrowding rate of nearly 100 percent has led to miserable conditions for the inmates. A good thing, too, the officer adds: prison shouldn't be comfortable for the scumbags inside. His drunker colleague proposes a toast—to the queen of England's nether regions, apparently in my honor—and orders yet another round of drinks, at which point I call a taxi.

Many police, and many voters, welcome the fact that the country's jails are so full and so squalid. After all, the more criminals who are behind bars, the fewer there are on the streets to rob and kill, or smuggle drugs. And the grimmer the conditions, the greater the deterrent to committing crime. Most countries in the Americas seem to agree: the region has the highest rate of imprisonment in the world, led by the United States, where more than one in every 150 people is behind bars. The region's jails have some of the most hellish conditions, too. A fire at a prison in Honduras in 2012 killed more than 350 inmates; two years earlier, eighty-one prisoners died in a fire in Chile. Murder is common,

and massacre is not unusual: in northern Mexico a group of inmates
belonging to the Zetas cartel murdered forty-four rival mobsters before
escaping, apparently without much difficulty.

No one would want to be locked up in such a place. But for criminal organizations, prisons play a pivotal role in the recruitment and
training of staff. To see how, consider the story of Carlos Lehder. The
slight, studious son of a German father and Colombian mother struggled at first to fit in when he moved to the United States at age fifteen.
This was the 1960s, and cannabis was taking off in the United States,
so the young Carlos started dealing it. As he got older, he graduated
to ferrying stolen cars between Canada and the United States. All was
well until, at the age of twenty-five, he was finally busted and sent to
serve a short sentence in prison in Danbury, Connecticut. That might
have been the end of his criminal career. But in a decision that would
change the course of the international narcotics business, the prison
authorities decided to put Lehder in the same cell as George Jung. The
thirty-two-year-old Jung, a blond Bostonian, had been involved in the
drugs business on a grander scale. He was serving time for smuggling
cannabis between Mexico and the United States, for which he had used
stolen light aircraft. With nothing much else to do, the two began to
swap stories and dream up business ideas together.

It was a meeting of criminal minds. Jung knew how to import drugs
by plane; Lehder had contacts in Colombia. Until this point, cocaine,
then a relatively little-used drug in the United States, had only been
smuggled on a small scale. When Lehder and Jung were released from
prison in 1976, they set about changing that forever. Within a couple of
years they were importing the drug by the ton, hooking up with Pablo
Escobar's Medellín cartel in Colombia to send planeloads of cocaine to
the United States via Norman's Cay, a small island in the Bahamas that
they used as their base. If one person can claim to have gotten America
hooked on coke, Carlos Lehder is as good a candidate as any.

Lehder's extraordinary rise shows how criminal careers can be built
on the foundations of a stint in prison. As well as forming a working

relationship with Jung, Lehder used his time in Danbury to mix with money launderers, hit men, and people who knew how the US extradition system worked. The millionaire crook, who was eventually busted in 1988 and is now growing old behind bars in the United States, later referred to Danbury as his "college." And for many criminal gangs, that is exactly the role that jails play. Once inside, a prisoner can be recruited, trained, and given job opportunities for when he eventually leaves the system. The first human-resources problem for drug cartels is finding potential employees with the right sort of criminal background. Someone looking to solve this problem could hardly come up with a more perfect solution than a prison: a place full of criminals, with nothing much to do and no job lined up for after their release.

Meetings like the one that produced the partnership between Lehder and Jung don't happen every day. So criminal groups take a methodical approach to running their recruitment and training systems inside jails. For an especially well-organized example, consider the case of La Nuestra Familia (Our Family), a California-based prison gang. The organization was founded in the 1960s by prison inmates looking to protect themselves from another big gang, the Mexican Mafia. The Mexican Mafia had come to dominate California's jails, taxing prisoners and carrying out dozens of murders a year within the prison system. Hispanic inmates from northern California were particularly at risk from the predatory Mexicans, whose base was in the south of the state. So they decided to band together, founding their own "family" as a means of self-defense. Soon La Nuestra Familia had started its own profitable lines in extortion, robbery, and drug dealing, both inside and outside prison. Nowadays, it is thought to have something like five hundred core members, plus a further thousand or so loosely linked affiliates.[3]

La Nuestra Familia quickly faced a problem common to all criminal organizations. Although joining a gang has benefits—protection from other mobsters, a chance to earn money from criminal scams, a sense of kinship and camaraderie—it also comes with fearsome risks

for potential recruits. For one thing, gangs demand total loyalty from
their members, who have to do the bidding of their bosses without
much argument. At the root of this is the restriction on illegal groups'
communications, which leaves no room for discussion or dissent. The
New Yorker once quoted a member of the Aryan Brotherhood, another
American prison gang, lamenting the difficulty of organizing a murder
democratically: "We used to be one man one vote. . . . You damn near
had to have the whole state's okay. . . . It always got tipped off by the
time we got back to you and said, 'Yeah, dump [kill] the guy.' . . . You
can't have someone in the yard that you want to bump and let them
be out there for two or three weeks."[4] The result is an authoritarian
structure, under which the rank and file have to do as they are told,
like it or not.

Getting into gangs also has to be made reasonably difficult, in order
to sift serious recruits from time wasters. Like other membership organizations, from golf clubs to college fraternities, gangs impose an
up-front cost on new members, in the form of a payment or initiation
ritual. (In one of the most harrowing initiation ordeals, new disciples
of La Familia Michoacana, a bloodthirsty Mexican drug cartel, are
reportedly forced to read the works of John Eldredge, an American
author of Christian self-help books.) And, of course, unlike most golf
clubs, prison gangs kill those who renounce their membership. This,
too, has its own warped rationality: if life membership can be enforced,
the risk of members turning informant is greatly reduced.

Aside from getting bumped off for quitting or stepping out of line,
the biggest factor dissuading new recruits from joining up is the risk of
being abused or exploited by the gang itself. Part of the reason for all
the resentment against the Mexican Mafia was that its bosses had taken
to extorting and robbing junior recruits almost as much as they picked
on everyone else. Under the hierarchical, undemocratic structure of
a gang, it is easy for senior members to prey on the junior recruits,
who are forbidden from leaving. Although this predation is against
the interests of the gang in the long run, because it means that no new

members will want to join, it is in the individual interest of each senior member to tax what they can from the junior ones. In other words, the gang faces what economists call a collective-action problem. Everyone stands to gain if all members can agree not to exploit each other, but the individual incentives for exploiting are so strong that it is unlikely that everyone will stick to the agreement.

How do criminal gangs solve this collective-action problem? In a fascinating study in the *Journal of Law, Economics and Organization*, David Skarbek, an economist at King's College, London, analyzed La Nuestra Familia's structure. The challenge the gang faces is to align members' interests in such a way as to ensure that senior mobsters don't have an incentive to pick on the junior ones. To do this, it has come up with a complex system of rules designed to make sure that no member has an interest in exploiting another—and that if he does, he will be held accountable. All of this is set out in an elaborate "constitution," a copy of which has been obtained by the FBI. The gang has four levels of seniority. At the top is the "general," who commands up to ten "captains." They in turn manage "lieutenants," who are in charge of the lowest-ranking members, known as "soldiers." (Many of the first members of the Familia were Vietnam veterans, which may explain the military theme.) To avoid victimization of the junior ranks, the constitution establishes a mechanism whereby even the lowliest members can inform on their superiors if they find themselves being taken advantage of. Although the general has the power to fire captains, he cannot appoint them: that is the job of the rank and file. And although the general has formidable powers, he can be impeached by the unanimous agreement of the captains.

This arrangement hasn't always worked. In 1978, the general, Roberto Sosa, was impeached by his fellow gang members, after supposedly siphoning off more than $100,000—nearer $400,000 in today's terms—from the gang's funds. But he refused to go quietly. The dispute was solved the old-fashioned way, when the gang decided to kill him (they didn't quite manage, but he got the message and took off).

After that, the constitution was amended: the general was replaced by the three-man "Organizational Governing Body," which made decisions with a two-thirds majority and whose members were easier to impeach. Since then, the constitution has apparently continued more or less unchanged.

The elaborateness of the Familia's rules, which run to six articles and dozens of subsections, may say as much about the boredom of prison life as it does about the gang's organization. (The same is probably true of some of its other more Boy-Scoutish activities, which supposedly include making bombs out of match heads, writing secret messages in urine, and communicating in Náhuatl, the ancient language of the Aztecs.) But the purpose of the constitution is clear: persuading members to join gangs isn't easy, and only through a careful system of checks and balances can the organization ensure that membership is something that is likely to appeal to new recruits. As Skarbek writes: "Despite being a murderous prison gang, [La Nuestra Familia] has taken active and rational steps toward promoting effective internal governance institutions."

How can the authorities break up these institutions? Back in the Dominican Republic, I don't have much confidence after my rendezvous with the drunken antidrugs squad. But an experiment is under way in the country's prisons that at last poses a serious threat to the gangs' recruitment strategies. The story starts in what is perhaps the most magnificent lavatory in the Caribbean. The room is covered from floor to ceiling in mosaic tiles of blue, green, and white. Above the toilet, tiles in silver and purple form the outline of a jellyfish that floats among coral and weeds of red and green. Shimmering gold squares pick out the scales on a shoal of goldfish above the bath and alongside the marble basin. The bathroom, which admittedly has seen better days and could use a good scrubbing with Lysol, is in an airy hillside villa on the edge of Santo Domingo. The villa was one of the many homes of Rafael Trujillo, a murderous dictator who ruled the country for thirty-one years until his assassination in 1961 by rebels using machine guns supposedly donated by the CIA. Trujillo's rule saw the deaths of perhaps 50,000 people and the erection of countless statues of El Jefe (The Boss), as he was known. The dictator's country retreat, which includes the initials "R.T." worked into cornices in the ceilings, is arguably the most appalling of his many crimes against taste.

These grand surroundings are the unlikely headquarters of an elite new task force that has been put in charge of turning around the country's failing prisons. The glamorous headquarters, which are now used to train new prison officers, reflect the priority that the government has given to addressing the penal system, which had become a serious weak point in its campaign against organized crime. Founded by Roberto Santana, a political scientist and former rector of the University of Santo Domingo, the new prison agency takes a radical approach to offender management. Whereas under the old system prisons were deliberately made as horrible as possible, to deter people from committing crimes, Santana says he sees his jails as "schools," and his prison officers as "educators."

On a tour of the training center, Santana and his team show me how the old Trujillo banqueting rooms have been converted into libraries and classrooms to educate the next generation of Dominican jailers. Outside, I am given a demonstration of how sniffer dogs identify drugs (I repeatedly hide a small packet under one of five upturned buckets; sure enough, the dogs home in on the right one each time). As we walk around the complex, Santana, an enthusiastic lecturer who treats the country's high crime rate as an intriguing economic problem rather than a moral menace, keeps up a constant commentary on the changes he has made since being allowed to use the prisons as an academic laboratory. Everyone knew the old system was bad, with high rates of suicide, murder, and reoffending. The trouble was, he says, no other country really seemed to have cracked the problem. "The question was: where do we find an example of a good system? We looked everywhere for an answer and we didn't find it." Although a few countries, such as Norway, have experimented with radically rehabilitation-focused prison regimes, none has had to tackle anything like the crime rate seen in the Dominican Republic.

The answer was to design a new system from the bottom up, using the input of criminologists from around the world. Seventeen new "model" prisons now make up just under half of the country's total; nineteen old ones, and a unit for minors, remain under the management of the old prison authority. To see how the new system differs from the old one, I go to visit the Najayo jail, a women's prison in San Cristóbal, just west of Santo Domingo. As one walks through the front door, it becomes apparent that the prison is nothing like most of the jails in Latin America. A large plaque in the entrance displays the UN Universal Declaration of Human Rights, a charter that is routinely ignored in most of the continent's penitentiaries. Artwork by inmates hangs on the corridor walls, and in the reception area there are trophies for singing, dancing, and dominoes that prisoners have won in contests against other local jails. In a quiet room to one side, an inmate is speaking to her family and a free lawyer.

The cozy décor isn't where the differences end. Every aspect of the new regime has been designed to reduce prisoners' incentives to reoffend, thereby thwarting the cartels' capacity to recruit. It starts with the decision on which jail a newly convicted offender should be sent to. Many countries in Latin America operate an unofficial system in which prisons are allocated to particular gangs, to minimize the risk of fighting. Members of one mob will be sent to one prison, whereas members of a rival clan will go to a different one. This segregation may help to keep the peace, but it also strengthens the gangs' organizational powers. In El Salvador, Old Lin is able to run his jail like a fiefdom, because it has been reserved exclusively for members of the 18th Street Gang. A raid on a prison in Acapulco, Mexico, a few years ago discovered that inmates had managed to "smuggle in" one hundred fighting cocks, nineteen prostitutes, and two peacocks. In another Mexican prison, prisoners were found raffling off a luxury cell that they had equipped with air-conditioning, a fridge, and a DVD player. Allowing gangs to run jails in this way makes for a quiet life for prison wardens, but it greatly strengthens the criminals. If a prisoner is not a member of the 18th Street Gang when he enters Old Lin's prison, he certainly is by the time he emerges.

In the Dominican Republic's new jails, by contrast, prisons are not allocated to particular gangs. Instead, each model jail has a maximum-security area within its grounds, where gang leaders are kept, away from other inmates, preventing them from directing the show. The first thing we do as we enter the prison in Najayo is hand over our cell phones, another measure designed to limit the gangs' ability to organize. In Dominican jails, no one is allowed a phone—including the guards—meaning there is less chance of smuggling them in.

To pass the time, the 268 women locked up in the prison when I visit (who include thirty-eight foreigners, all of them drug mules) are put to work making candles, flower arrangements, and jewelry, which are sold to visitors in a prison gift shop. Part of the idea is to keep the inmates occupied and out of trouble. But there is another motive. Sixty percent of the proceeds of the sales are split between the prisoner and the jail, with the remaining 40 percent going to the prisoner's family. This is part of a wider effort to keep the inmate in touch with her relatives while inside. Part of the reason people join gangs and other criminal groups is that they have no other network to fall back on, Santana reasons. So he goes to extraordinary lengths to maintain prisoners' family links. In one case, the only family member that his staff could track down was a distant uncle who lived two hundred miles away, up a mountain. Santana dispatched an officer on a mule to track him down and bring him back to visit, which he did. At Najayo, 92 percent of the prisoners receive visitors, an especially high proportion for a women's jail. (Loneliness is a sad feature of women's imprisonment everywhere in the world; husbands are much less diligent than wives when it comes to keeping in contact during the sentence.)

Efforts are also made to line inmates up with jobs when they finish their sentences. Najayo has a bakery run by prisoners, who rise at

5:30 a.m. each day to bake 2,000 flatbreads. And everyone is taught
to read. Santana boasts that the illiteracy rate is zero: reading classes
are compulsory, and slackers have privileges withdrawn, such as phone
calls or, when that fails to work, conjugal visits. Three dozen of the
prisoners are currently enrolled in university degree courses, in law
and psychology.

Crucially, the people who staff these prisons are totally different
from the ones who run the country's other jails. Most prisons in Latin
America are run by either the army or the police. This is disastrous:
guarding a riotous prison is seen as hard, unimportant work, so it is
given to the very worst elements in those forces. The Dominican Republic has taken the opposite line: to reduce the risk of corruption,
it specifically bans anyone who has previously served in the police or
armed forces. Instead, it trains its own recruits for the best part of a
year, before starting them on salaries that are three times what their
counterparts in the old jail system earned. Higher wages mean that
they are harder to bribe.

It is expensive: the new system costs about $12 per prisoner per day,
which is more than double what the old system costs. Santana has repeatedly had to defend the notion of spending more on prisons, which
are widely seen as places where people should go to rot, not enjoy good
treatment. When I first go into his office, I find him giving a telephone
interview to a Panamanian talk-radio show, whose host is decidedly
skeptical about shelling out more money on society's most despised
members. Santana is undeterred. "It's a social investment that gives an
immense saving to society. If you don't spend those taxes on criminals,
those criminals only become more dangerous," he insists.

Some examples of how spending a few extra dollars can save thousands are ludicrously simple. In the Dominican Republic's new prisons,
inmates are provided with free meals. At first sight, this might seem
more lax than the old system, in which prisoners relied on family and
friends to bring them food and went hungry if no one came. But providing meals in-house has removed one of the biggest sources of prison

contraband: the old ruse of smuggling weapons or drugs into the jail, hidden in bags of rice or baked into loaves of bread by visiting family members. Spending a few extra cents per day to provide each prisoner with a bowl of rice and beans—an apparently "soft" measure—means that those prisoners no longer have such easy access to knives, guns, and narcotics. The taxpayer may not like paying for criminals' lunches, but beans are cheaper than metal detectors.

•   •   •

Some criminal organizations work on the basis of hiring a large staff of full-time employees. The gangs of El Salvador identify their members with tattoos; Mexican cartels sometimes commission logoed polo shirts and baseball caps. But not all drug-trafficking organizations are run on such a formal basis. In rich, well-policed countries in particular, drug-trafficking gangs tend to be fairly small and loosely organized. Their expansion is limited because with scale comes ever-greater risk of exposure: every new member of the enterprise is another potential leak, and vetting and monitoring a large group of co-conspirators is impractical. The result is that rather than being run along the principles of a "partnership," as with such gangs as La Nuestra Familia, or employing large numbers of full-time members, as do gangs like Barrio 18, rich-world traffickers often rely on a network of casual freelance workers, none of whom knows too much about the others.

Take one British trafficking outfit, which made a handsome living importing cocaine from Spain. Until it was dismantled by the police, this organization had been smuggling between 50 and 60 kilos of cocaine into the country every week. It bought the drugs from a Colombian intermediary, based in Spain, for £18,000 ($28,000) per kilo and sold them in Britain for £22,000. This generated sales of well over £1 million a week, and nearly £60 million a year. Of this, more than £10 million was profit. One might imagine that an operation this extensive, turning over the equivalent of nearly $100 million a year, would be managed by a fairly large gang of crooks. But according to interviews conducted by the Home Office, the multimillion-pound business was run by only two people.[5]

Rather than recruiting more people into their miniature "cartel," the ringleaders used a different human-resources model, hiring a large team of freelancers to work for them in various capacities. A courier would meet the Colombian smugglers in London, picking up payloads of 10 kilograms of cocaine, which he would distribute across Britain. Each of these transactions would earn him around £800. The next day the buyers would deliver cash to London to someone employed purely to collect the money, for which he was paid £250 a day. Another person was paid the same amount to count it (he would tot up as much as £220,000 in a typical day's work). A third person delivered payments to two people: a Venezuelan woman who helped the Colombians to get their money back to Spain, and a "money holder" who stored the cash earned by the enterprise. The ringleaders employed a chauffer, too, for £200 a day. In total, the pair dealt with at least half a dozen people who performed a variety of different jobs without being "members" of the gang—or seeing much of its profit.

As well as dealing with freelance contractors, cartels frequently do business with other criminal organizations. Few are the cartels that have the capacity to oversee every part of the drugs supply chain, from production to retail. A couple of Mexican cartels are currently doing their best to gain control of coca cultivation in Colombia and retailing in the United States. But they are the exceptions. Instead, most trafficking organizations specialize in one part of the chain. One gang might handle importation, after which it passes the product on to another mob that covers national distribution, before other outfits take care of the street-level dealing.

In maintaining these business-to-business relationships, people skills are vital. And surprisingly, relations between drug traffickers are more cordial than one might think. For an example of a drug trafficker with a diplomatic touch, meet Pete, who makes a living importing cocaine from South America to the Netherlands. One day he places an order for 20 kilograms of cocaine, which at wholesale prices in the Netherlands would cost somewhere upward of half a million euros (or more than $600,000). The cocaine arrives safely, sent by Pete's usual contact in Brazil. But on testing the cocaine, Pete is unhappy. Twelve kilos are good, but the remaining eight are not up to scratch, and he rings up the seller to complain about the "chalk." We know this because, unbeknownst to Pete, his phone was being tapped by the Dutch police (who, incidentally, are incorrigible snoops, with a phone-tapping order being issued for roughly one in every 1,000 working phones in the country).

At this point, were it a Hollywood film, Pete might put a henchman on the first plane to Rio to settle the score. But that isn't what happens. Instead, the export company's customer services team swings into action. The boss apologizes to Pete for the lapse in quality, which he says comes down to the fact that his usual contact failed to come up with the full 20 kilograms, meaning that he had to get the rest from another supplier. To make up for the mistake, he promises to send an "engineer" to the Netherlands to turn the chalky cocaine into something better. Pete grumbles a bit about this, but no blood is spilled.

A similar episode takes place a little later. Pete is up to his old tricks, this time using a courier who is due to fly over from South America carrying a suitcase stuffed with cocaine. The plan falls apart when the courier has a fit of nerves before boarding his flight. Instead of taking the drugs onboard, he dumps the suitcase at the airport, abandoning thousands of dollars' worth of product. He relays the news to Pete, who unsurprisingly is furious, and suspects that far from having dumped the cocaine, the courier has sold it to someone else. For a while, he seems determined to murder the courier in revenge. His cocaine supplier in Brazil—perhaps hoping to make up for the previous batch of "chalk"—even offers to do the job for him. Fortunately for the courier, Pete has a more sober brother, who decides to go to the airport himself to check out the man's story. Somehow he persuades himself that the courier is telling the truth and convinces Pete to call off the assassination. Despite losing (or quite possibly stealing) an entire suitcase-worth of cocaine, the incompetent mule lives to smuggle another day.

Pete's stories are among the cases analyzed in a highly unusual report for the European Commission on the subject of what happens when big drug deals go wrong.[6] The authors trawled through Dutch police files to extract the details on thirty-three cocaine deals that had gone awry in some way or other. All were hefty transactions, involving at least 20 kilograms of the drug, and sometimes several tons. Like the British study, it uncovers some first-class examples of incompetence. The cover is blown on one deal after incriminating details are faxed to the wrong number. A large shipment is lost after it is sent to Antwerp, when it was expected in Rotterdam. Sometimes, James Bond–style plots are undone by Mr. Bean–style pratfalls. In one deal, the smugglers set up an elaborate plan to import cocaine packed into special tubes that are attached to the hull of a ship, to be recovered by frogmen. The drugs are successfully concealed, and the ship arrives in the Dutch harbor. But the whole scheme is foiled when the divers come down with a nasty bug, leaving them unable to get into the water. The cocaine is abandoned—and may still be traveling the world, strapped to the bottom of some tanker or other.

The focus of the study is on how these disputes are resolved. What the authors find is that, like Pete the patient cocaine importer, most traffickers use nonviolent methods to settle their differences wherever possible. Of the thirty-three cases, most of which involve losses of hundreds of thousands of euros, two-thirds are sorted out without the use of violence. This might seem surprising. Drugs and violence go hand in hand because the use of force, or at least the threat of it, is the only way that drug cartels have of enforcing contracts. Drug cartels can't, as mentioned earlier, go to the courts and get their problems resolved. Although at first blush the only method they have to ensure that contracts are honored is the threat of nasty consequences, the evidence shows that, on the whole, the drug importers tend to do their best to avoid violence. Like normal firms, they react to mishaps by carrying out an investigation to find out if the problem was the result of fraud or simple bad luck. If there is evidence that someone has stolen from the organization or deliberately betrayed it, violence is not unusual. But often, people who have been negligent or grossly incompetent are given the benefit of the doubt. This, the authors write, supports the idea that "the drug trade, even at this high level, is run in a manner similar to that of any small business in which managers have to make decisions about individuals . . . that reflect the need to preserve relationships." Because of the difficulty involved in hiring new employees, and in making new contacts in the import and export game, drug traffickers may in fact be more forgiving of mistakes than legitimate firms, they suggest: "Given the impediments to information flows in these markets, relationships may be even more important than in legal markets."

What is the key to building relationships that last? Drug dealers don't generally have reputations for being diplomatic types. But smoothing over potential areas of conflict has been a factor in the success of many big cartels. Pablo Escobar devised a basic system of insurance against lost cocaine shipments, which helped to avoid disputes and persuade legitimate businesspeople in Medellín to invest in his transactions (this in turn enabled his cartel to embed itself deeper within Colombian society). Benefits for valued contractors can sometimes be surprisingly generous. The late Charles Bowden, an American observer of the *frontera*, the US-Mexico border, relates an intriguing episode in which a Mexican hit man who has been accidentally targeted by his colleagues is sent on an all-expenses-paid trip to the seaside resort of Mazatlán, by way of compensation.[7]

The names of some of the gangs mentioned in this chapter provide a clue to another way in which cartels sometimes try to maintain harmony in the ranks. La Nuestra Familia, the Mexican Mafia, and the Aryan Brotherhood all select their members on grounds of race. Prison gangs, in particular, are notorious for dividing up along racial lines. ("Just pretend it's the 1950s. It's easier to understand," explains a character in *Orange Is the New Black*, a darkly comic television drama set in an American women's prison.) Even among cartels that are less picky about skin color, it seems that cultural and linguistic ties count for a lot. Spain is the main gateway to Europe for Latin American drugs. Similarly, the studies mentioned above of Britain and the Netherlands found that a large number of the foreign subjects interviewed was from former British and Dutch colonies in the Caribbean.

Is there any advantage to the cartels in associating with people of the same race, or of a shared cultural background? The idea is anathema in the legitimate business world, where diversity is something that most firms prize. Plenty of studies suggest that a diverse workforce makes for a more creative and adaptable one—and in any case, hiring on the basis of race is illegal in most countries. Few researchers have published any evidence that there are benefits to be had from creating a monocultural workplace.[8] It seems odd, then, that so many criminal gangs seem to organize themselves on this basis. It is tempting to assume that it is simply because criminals are nasty people, to whom racism, a nasty trait, comes naturally. But that seems to go against most of what we have seen so far about criminal gangs, which so often mimic ordinary firms in doing what is best for business.

The authors of the Dutch study decided to dig a bit deeper into this question. They broke down the results by ethnicity and found that disputes that arose between parties who belonged to the same ethnic group were significantly less likely to be resolved with violence than others. Of the failed deals struck between people of the same race, 29 percent ended up leading to violence or threats. Of those disputes between people of different ethnicity, 53 percent came to blows.

It may be that the lack of violence has less to do with cultural harmony and more to do with the possibility of intimidation. Take the example of a Colombian smuggling network that was recently discovered in the Netherlands. Rather than importing cocaine, this gang was devoted to the equally tricky problem of sending large quantities of illicitly acquired cash back to Colombia without raising the suspicions of the authorities. It did this by paying amateur mules €3,000 ($3,350) each to carry suitcases containing up to €150,000 in cash back to Bogotá. (Smuggling cash out of Europe is made much easier by the existence of the €500 bill, a ludicrously high-value banknote that has made life much easier for criminals, who can hide €20,000 in a single cigarette packet. In some European countries the bills are known as "bin Ladens": everyone knows they exist, but no one apart from criminals ever sees them.) In the space of two years, the gang sent back at least €42 million ($47 million), always using Colombian nationals, who were provided with a free vacation in addition to their fee.

Always hiring Colombians was a deliberate policy on the part of the business. The woman in charge of the gang always took the precaution of getting the names and addresses of the couriers' family members, so that if a mule bolted, revenge could be taken on their nearest and dearest in Colombia. Of course, threats can be made against anyone's family, Colombian or otherwise. But carrying out violent attacks is much easier in a relatively poorly policed country than it is in Western Europe. And it is harder to pin the blame on the gang's leadership, which is based on the other side of the Atlantic. The Dutch case was by no means unique: British police, too, have identified instances of people being kidnapped in Colombia, released only when a debt is paid in Britain.

Something similar is true when it comes to the dealing of drugs in the United States. Most of America's heroin these days comes from Mexican gangs (see Chapter 9). According to officials from the Drug Enforcement Administration (DEA), much of the retailing is done by Mexican citizens who are sent over at considerable expense by their bosses in Mexico to deal the drug on America's street corners. Dispatching a Mexican task force in this way is far costlier to the cartel than simply hiring people locally, but it serves two purposes. First, running a drug-distribution cell in another country, handling small fortunes in untraceable cash, and being entrusted with large quantities of valuable drugs provides very tempting opportunities to disappear with the loot. As in the case of the Colombian cash carriers, the Mexican traffickers have an insurance policy against this, in the form of potential revenge against family members who are still in Mexico. Second, using Mexican nationals who are known to the cartel's leadership and can be reshuffled every few months makes the cells much harder to infiltrate than they would be if they relied on making local hires.

Unlike in the legitimate business world, then, race and nationality do seem to count for something when it comes to hiring—though the reason has more to do with the greater potential to carry out blackmail than with a preference for working with people of the same ethnic group. There is the odd exception to the race-based hiring approach, however. Like many other cartels, Nigerian heroin traffickers recruit mainly from among their fellow Nigerians. But when it comes to selecting mules to smuggle heroin from Europe to the United States, they make an exception. White women, they have found, are far less likely to get stopped at the airport.[9]

• • •

Penal reformers have long claimed that "prison doesn't work." This is only partly true: for drug cartels, prison works brilliantly. Jails provide a place to hire and train new members of staff, something that is normally extremely difficult for criminal organizations to do because of the constraints imposed by the illegality of their business. From kingpins such as Carlos Lehder to vulnerable young Dominicans looking for protection and employment, thousands of people every year are guided into a career in crime by a stint behind bars. How misguided it was to send low-level offenders to these universities of crime was apparent even to Richard Nixon, the first US president to declare a "war" on drugs. "To take somebody that's smoked some of this stuff [cannabis], put him into a jail with a bunch of hardened criminals . . . that's absurd. . . . There must be different ways than jail," he said in a private conversation recorded in the Oval Office in 1971.[10]

Since he made those comments, the United States, in particular, has struggled to find "different ways than jail." At the time of Nixon's remark, the country's prison population stood at about 200,000. It is now 1.6 million. Most of the criticism leveled at this policy is made on human-rights grounds, but an equally persuasive case can be made based on economics. Prison is fabulously expensive. Sending a teenager to jail costs more than it would to send him to Eton College, the private boarding school in England that educated Princes William and Harry. It seems especially odd that the United States, a country with a proud history of limited government, is so unquestioningly generous when it comes to this particular public service, on which it blows $80 billion a year. Does it really need to lock up five times as many people per capita as Britain, six times as many as Canada, and nine times as many as Germany?[11]

The case for making prisons less populous is fairly clear. Less obviously, there is also an argument for making them cushier. This flies in the face of common sense, which suggests that worse prisons provide a stronger deterrent to committing crime. But the evidence is that prisoners react to ugly, dangerous surroundings by joining criminal groups that offer them protection and privileges. "We're not a gang, we're a [labor] union," prisoners in Ciudad Juárez, Mexico, told the London *Times*.[12] Just like ordinary workers, inmates are more likely to unionize if they face bad conditions. Making jails safer removes prisoners' need for protection; providing training gives them noncriminal options when they eventually leave. The more the state fails to meet prisoners' basic needs, the greater the opportunity for criminal gangs to fill the gap.

The Dominican Republic shows how such an approach can work. The country was once addicted to high levels of incarceration, in jails that maintained dreadful standards. Under the old Dominican system, half of all inmates reoffended within three years of their release. Under the new system, fewer than 3 percent do. Both of those

figures are probably underestimates, which reflect the country's limited ability to detect and prosecute crime. But the difference is stark.
For organized-crime groups, steering inmates into criminal careers is
far easier under the older, more punitive regime. Better jails make for
worse job centers.

Making it harder for cartels to recruit people has a knock-on benefit.
The analysis of failed cocaine deals in Europe shows that when things
go wrong, drug dealers can be surprisingly forgiving people. The reason for this isn't that they are a charitable bunch; rather, it is because
they have to preserve the limited network of contacts that they have.
Hiring new people, or reaching out to new suppliers or dealers, is a
difficult, dangerous chore that risks exposing the business to possible
informants. Because of that, burning bridges with existing contacts
is used only as a last resort. In a world where networking within the
cocaine industry was easy, Pete the Dutch importer might well have
lashed out against the exporter who ripped him off with the Brazilian
"chalk," or the mule who lost the suitcase of cocaine. But because contacts like that are hard to come by, it made more sense for him to give
them both the benefit of the doubt.

The implication of this is that if one can hamper cartels' recruitment by limiting the flow of apprentices coming through prison, one
can tighten up the criminal labor market. For one thing, this will force
criminal organizations to pay their employees higher wages, cutting
into their profits. It will also deter them from violently quarrelling with
the employees they have. One can only treat members of staff as disposable if there is a steady stream of replacements lined up. In the past,
Dominican gangsters have had few qualms about bumping off uncoop-
erative associates or sending them to war against other gangs, as they
have always had new employees on tap. If prisons in the Dominican
Republic—and other places—can tighten that tap, gangs will have to
behave more like Pete the patient Dutch dealer, anxious to hang on
to what contacts they have, and more likely to resolve their problems
peacefully.

Chapter 4

PR AND THE MAD
MEN OF SINALOA

Why Cartels Care About Corporate
Social Responsibility

There is a carnival atmosphere in Culiacán, the capital city of Sinaloa, a drug-war-plagued Mexican state. Men, women, and children fill the streets, marching and chanting as trumpets and trombones play in the background. It is February 2014, and Mexico has just seen the news that many thought would never happen: Joaquín Guzmán, the leader of the Sinaloa cartel and one of the most wanted men in the world, is finally behind bars. El Chapo ("Shorty"), as the cartel kingpin is known, had presided over a long reign of terror, ordering the murders of thousands of people in Sinaloa and far beyond. For years he evaded capture, somehow always slipping away just before the army's helicopter gunships arrived. But eventually his luck ran out. After a dramatic chase through the sewers of Culiacán, into which he escaped via a hidden door under a bathtub in a safe house, he fled to the coastal resort of Mazatlán. There, in a cheap hotel, he was finally discovered and arrested at gunpoint, before being taken to Mexico City to be paraded before television cameras that beamed the news to millions of astonished Mexicans.

The reaction in his home state was immediate. Within days, flyers were dropped around the cities of Sinaloa, calling on citizens to take to the streets to mark the momentous occasion. Sinaloans duly came out to march. But there was a surprising feature about the parades that followed Shorty's arrest. If you looked closer at the people marching—a mixture of young and old, men and women, teenagers and families—you could see that they were wearing T-shirts and waving banners bearing some unexpected slogans. "Shorty is more loved and respected than many politicians!" read one banner. "Sinaloa is yours, Shorty," said the words emblazoned on a T-shirt. Others wore clothes bearing the number 701, Guzmán's position in the latest billionaires' ranking compiled by *Forbes* magazine. "Shorty, make me a baby," read the slogan on a tight-fitting top worn by one young woman. The crowds had come out not to condemn the vicious drug trafficker, but to celebrate him. Around the streets, as the march progressed—unimpeded by police, who apparently had other things to do—a cry was repeated: "*Que viva el Chapo!*"

With thousands of murders to his name, Shorty Guzmán ought to be the most hated man in Mexico. But in a few parts of the country where his malign influence is strongest, people's feelings are decidedly mixed. Although some of those marching in his support in Culiacán were no doubt there under duress, others were genuine admirers. A nationwide opinion poll carried out by the *Reforma* newspaper found that only 53 percent of respondents approved of his arrest, with 28 percent saying they actively disapproved.[1] Mexican drug traffickers are celebrated in *narcocorridos*, bouncy trombone-and-accordion ballads that tell of their exploits and their skill in outwitting the police. In homage to Shorty Guzmán, José Eulogio Hernández, a Stetson-wearing crooner better known as the Colt of Sinaloa, declares:

> *From his feet up to his head he's a little short in stature*
> *But from his head up to the sky is how I calculate his height.*[2]

Guzmán's imprisonment did not last long: in July 2015, little more than a year after his capture, the Mexican government announced that he had slipped through their fingers yet again. Closed-circuit TV (CCTV) footage of the kingpin's prison cell, later released by red-faced officials, shows Shorty pacing around before walking around the corner into his personal bathroom—and never coming back. Prison wardens discovered a hole in the bottom of his shower, leading to a professionally built, mile-long tunnel, complete with primitive ventilation pipes and a motorbike mounted on rails, used to move earth and rubble. Shorty had apparently run away down the escape tunnel, smashing lightbulbs as he went, before vanishing into the countryside. Within hours, the first *narcocorridos* celebrating his audacious escape had been uploaded to YouTube. One, by Lupillo Rivera, jauntily explained:

> *Tons [of drugs] have been moved by water and air*
> *A well-planned tunnel can emerge anywhere.*

Shorty is not alone in his relative popularity. A curious feature of the drug-trafficking business is that the people at the top of the game manage to enjoy a reputation that is better than that of most criminals—and indeed, many politicians (the US Congress would love to have the popularity rating that El Chapo enjoys). Traffickers even spark fashion trends: after Édgar Valdez Villareal, a beefy cartel henchman incongruously known as the Barbie Doll, on account of his blond hair, was arrested wearing a distinctive green Ralph Lauren polo shirt, clothes stalls around Mexico City quickly started selling copies to young men who wanted to mimic the look.

Something similar happens in Western countries, where drug traffickers are often portrayed in a romantic way that glosses over their crimes. Johnny Depp played a lovable Colombian American capo in *Blow,* a movie about the rise of Pablo Escobar's Medellín cartel. Escobar's son, Juan Pablo, has written a book about his dad, in which he describes his father's early criminal business selling fake diplomas to his high-school friends. Howard Marks, a convicted drug trafficker from

Britain, wrote an autobiography entitled *Mr. Nice* (one of his pseud-
onyms) and made a living giving talks in which he described his criminal career as a grand adventure.

There is nothing romantic about what the cartels do. Under the direction of Shorty Guzmán, the Sinaloa mob has murdered and muti-
lated anyone who stands in its path. Its victims have been tortured,
burned alive, and publicly hanged—and not in the name of revolu-
tionary struggle but simply to enable the cartel's members to make
money. People such as the "nice" Howard Marks may not have per-
sonally bumped anyone off, but it is their money that pays the wages
of those who do. The business is as grubby as they come. Yet far from
being viewed with disgust, the people who run it enjoy a reputation
as semirespectable outlaws, in both their home countries and abroad.
Their transformation in the popular imagination, from seedy, brutal
thugs to lovable rogues, is one of the most dramatic public-relations
(PR) coups in the business world. How did the cartels pull it off?

•   •   •

"TO ALL CITIZENS," begins the notice, written entirely in capital
letters. "Through this medium I wish to clarify that I do not order the
killing of children and women. I do not condone extortion or kidnapping. Those that are responsible for totally destroying the state are the
members of La Linea. . . . The rules are clear: no children, no women,
no innocent people, no extortion, no kidnapping. La Linea kills for just
1,000 pesos [about $70] in extortion payments."[3]

This message, professionally printed in black and red on a large
white banner, appeared in the early hours of the morning one day in
Ciudad Juárez, where it dangled from a footbridge in a busy part of the
city. It was 2010, and the battle that pitted Shorty Guzmán's Sinaloa
gang against the local Juárez cartel and La Linea, its contract-killing
department, was heating up. The banner, signed by Shorty himself,
was one of dozens of *narcomantas*—literally, drug-blankets—that

began popping up all over town. As the level of violence rose, so did the amount of advertising.

Marketing may not seem like the sort of thing drug cartels would worry about much. Although the reputation of advertising executives is not much higher than the one enjoyed by drug dealers ("legalized lying" is how H. G. Wells described the advertising business; "the rattling of a stick inside a swill bucket" was George Orwell's take), the communications game isn't something that one would expect mobsters to be particularly interested in. In fact, they take their marketing, particularly PR and advertising, extremely seriously. Maintaining some measure of support among the public is the only way that fugitives such as Shorty Guzmán can stay on the run without having their whereabouts reported to the police. For this reason the cartels employ a variety of elaborate methods to polish their public image.

Their brazen campaigns can be seen all over northern Mexico. The traditional method is to hang a sheet or plastic banner from a highway bridge and alert local photographers before the authorities can cut the ad down. Sometimes the messages are amateurishly daubed onto old bedsheets; often they are professionally designed and produced. Their purposes vary. In Nuevo Laredo, on the Texas border, the Zetas once kicked off a recruitment drive with a banner proclaiming: "The Zetas operations group wants you, soldier or ex-soldier. We offer you a good salary, food, and benefits for your family. Don't suffer mistreatment, don't suffer hunger—we won't feed you Maruchan soup [a brand of instant noodles]." More commonly, they take the form of attack ads, bad-mouthing or issuing threats to rival gangs (in which case the messages are sometimes accompanied by hanging bodies), or messages that reassure citizens that the cartel is on their side: engaged in drug trafficking, but not in crimes such as extortion that affect ordinary people.

This kind of primitive outdoor advertising may work insofar as it demonstrates to local people that a particular cartel has enough local clout to be able to hang up such a banner in a public place, implying a degree of control over the local police. But their power to persuade is dubious. All over the world, in both the legal and illegal economy, advertising is going through something of a crisis. Generations ago, consumers might have believed the "legalized lies" that were written on Madison Avenue and printed in trusted newspapers and magazines. These days, with a deluge of free online and offline media, consumers are harder to convince, and especially skeptical about paid-for advertisements written by the very people who are trying to sell the product. It is hard to imagine anyone being taken in nowadays by the health claims made in cigarette advertisements in the 1950s. The insistence of Shorty and the Zetas that they are fair dealers and good employers rings equally hollow.

Instead, marketing professionals are directing their energies elsewhere—and so are the cartels. A decade ago the branding gurus Al and Laura Ries argued that traditional advertising had lost its power and that it was becoming easier to change consumers' perceptions through advertising's cousin, PR.[4] More recently, social media have allowed firms instantly to spread their PR messages online through what David Meerman Scott calls "newsjacking." Unlike advertising, PR ignores the paid-for advertising space in newspapers and on air, and instead focuses on influencing the much more valuable realm of editorial column inches and TV news spots. An admiring article in a newspaper carries more weight than a paid-for ad on the opposite page. *PR Daily*, a US trade paper, estimates that editorial space is worth three times as much as paid-for advertising space. Companies are jostling to get their messages into this sought-after area, lobbying journalists as never before to mention their clients in articles. In Britain, the number of people working in PR (47,800) now exceeds the number of journalists (45,000).[5]

Selling off bits of editorial space is appealing to news organizations, whose own industry is on the rocks. For low-paid reporters, it is tempting to write kind articles about companies that offer free-flowing hospitality or complimentary goodies. In the newspaper business it is becoming more common to offer "native advertising," sponsored content that lies somewhere between an article and a paid-for advertisement. These items, which at first glance look more or less like ordinary stories but in fact may be written or approved by advertisers, offer a way for companies to get their message into something that looks like editorial content but isn't. Most journalists feel uneasy about advertising leaking into news coverage. But advertisers are willing to pay far more for this powerful new means of persuasion. Readers may not trust slogans in advertisements, but if a company can get a newspaper or TV channel to repeat the same idea in its own words, that really means something. The same is true for drug cartels, which in recent years have dramatically, and often brutally, upped their lobbying of the media.

That is how I end up in northern Mexico one May morning, driving as fast as I dare through the desert as the sun begins to peep over the horizon, my journalist's ID hidden deep inside my suitcase in a bag of old socks. It is still mild outside before the daily furnace really fires up, and I have been awake since the early hours, surprising hotel workers who were still taking the nighttime covers off the canaries' cages in the lobby as I came down to breakfast. I am heading east on Highway 40 out of Monterrey, a big, wealthy city near the US border. As local cartels try to raise funds for their latest turf war, being kidnapped has become a serious risk for anyone who looks like his or her family might be able to afford a juicy ransom. A rich friend in the city who had previously rolled around in a gleaming new Range Rover had earlier stopped by my hotel in a much shabbier, older car, explaining: "You don't want to attract anyone's attention these days."

Monterrey's problems with violence are well publicized. Its newspapers are full of headlines about shootouts and killings, as are those in many other cities in the north. But while chatting with businesspeople in the city, many of whom had moved their families to safety in the United States, I heard rumors of something even stranger and more sinister that was happening in another northern town. One hundred and fifty miles or so to the east lies a place where the public debate about the drug war has been very quiet. Reynosa, which sits across the border from McAllen, Texas, looks much like any other frontier town, with *maquiladora* factories, cut-price health clinics, and a seedy red-light district called "Boys' Town." Like most other places along the border, it functions as a smuggling point for narcotics. But in spite of the ramping up of violence all over northern Mexico, very few reports of cartel killings are coming out of Reynosa. The city somehow never seems to be mentioned in television or newspaper reports about the drug war. Murders are never written up, and bodies are not photographed. Politicians don't seem to talk about it. It is as if Reynosa has been cut off from the rest of the country: a town with no news. I decide to pay a visit.

In the early morning the road is virtually deserted, and I make speedy progress along Highway 40. No one wants to spend too much time on this particular stretch, because the route between Monterrey and Reynosa has become known for shootouts between the Gulf cartel and the Zetas, former allies who are now in deadly competition for control of Mexico's northeast. Halfway there I pass Los Ahijados (The Godchildren), a restaurant where a couple of months earlier, just before Easter, there was a two-hour battle between fifty soldiers and forty cartel gunmen. The shootout had left the cheerfully painted building riddled with bullets, its walls looking like a cheese grater.

In Reynosa, the intimidation of journalists has resulted in a press that is almost totally under the control of the local mobs. In the past two months, I read, one local journalist has been murdered and five have vanished. Two visiting reporters from Mexico City were kidnapped there and beaten up. An American journalist sniffing around was approached by an unknown man in the street and told in no uncertain terms to leave town, which he did.

After parking my rental car, I make my way to the *palacio municipal*, or city hall, hugging the shady side of the street and walking as briskly as I can without breaking into a jog. My nerves haven't been helped by the fact that my first interviewee, an employee at the council, has had to change the time of our meeting on short notice—because, he explains matter-of-factly, a colleague has just been murdered, and so things have been rather busy. No one is quite sure why the victim, a junior council worker, was killed the previous day. He had been sitting in his car at a traffic light five blocks from the *palacio* when gunmen drew up and shot him dead. The death has not been covered anywhere in the press, and when I drive past the crime scene later on, it seems that the local authorities have already done a very efficient cleanup job—miraculous in a city that often doesn't even collect the garbage on time.

No one is likely to report the murder because journalists in Reynosa have been given strict instructions by the local cartel to obey a total blackout of drug-war news. In the absence of any reporting whatsoever, the city government has set up a Twitter feed to provide the most basic information about ongoing battles, to help citizens to stay safe. From his desktop computer, my interviewee—to whom, for safety's sake, we'll give the pseudonym Alfredo—runs @GobiernoReynosa, an account that provides local residents with a drip of essential news about security matters. Those monitoring the feed see messages such as: "SITUATION OF RISK. Various points of the city are blocked. Drive with care and do not go out if not necessary," and "It is reported that the SITUATION OF RISK ON THE HIGHWAY TO MONTER-REY HAS ENDED. Traffic slow on the ring road. Be patient." The account is run between 6:00 a.m. and 11:00 p.m., updated every hour or so, or more frequently if something is going on. "The newspapers, radio, and TV haven't had reports for two years now," says Alfredo, who remarks that he was given the idea by his Internet-savvy daughter. No reporter who lives locally wants to put his name on a story about crime. Sometimes media in other cities have better updates than local ones. "Papers in Monterrey publish news from here, and our papers publish news from there," Alfredo says.

Mexico's cartels have invested a lot of time and money in persuading journalists to tame their coverage. Persuasion takes the traditional form of *plata o plomo*—"silver or lead," meaning a bribe or a bullet—which the gangs use to get their way in other areas of public life. Reporters are routinely threatened and, if that doesn't do the trick, murdered, in a way designed to send a warning to others. To take one example from the dozens of recent cases, consider José Bladimir Antuna, a crime reporter on *El Tiempo de Durango*, who was found killed with a note by his body reading: "This happened to me for passing information to soldiers and for writing what shouldn't be written. Check your words carefully before filing a story." Antuna had been investigating the earlier murder of a colleague on the same newspaper and had strayed into reporting on the corrupt links between the local police and organized crime.

As the drug war has escalated, so too has the pressure on journalists. In the ten years up to 2004, a relatively peaceful period, thirteen reporters were killed in Mexico. In the following ten years, up to 2014, sixty were killed. Criminal investigations are so poor that it isn't always possible to establish a motive for the killings (and some victims died in cross fire, rather than being targeted). But it seems that most of the reporters were not chosen at random: eight out of ten of the victims covered the crime beat, according to the Committee to Protect Journalists, an American nongovernmental organization (NGO). The cartels' tactics have worked, up to a point. In 2010, the deadliest year to date, five Mexican newspapers publicly announced that they would no longer cover drug-war crimes at all, such was the risk to their journalists. In some cases, cartels have even managed to plant their own stories in the media. After four of its staff were kidnapped, the Milenio television channel was told that the staff would be executed if the channel did not run a report accusing a rival cartel of colluding with corrupt cops. Milenio reluctantly complied (though it ran the item only on its regional channel, and not on its national network).

Cartels have two audiences in mind. One is the general public. If people can be convinced that Shorty Guzmán's Sinaloa mob, for instance, is the more honorable cartel, and that it doesn't carry out extortion or murder children, they may be less likely to pass on intelligence to the police and will instead inform on its rivals, whom it claims to be much worse. Similarly, cartels' propaganda often accuses local police or prosecutors of being corrupt, with the aim of discouraging the public from sharing information with them.

The other audience that the cartels are aware of is the government. Whenever there are reports of violence, the authorities respond by sending large numbers of heavily armed police or soldiers to the troubled area, to keep a lid on things. This thicker presence of law enforcers makes it harder for the cartels to do business. So preventing reports of violence is extremely important: if no news gets out about last night's massacre, no extra troops will be dispatched the following week, and business can continue as usual. Following shootouts, cartels sometimes even drag away their dead, partly in order to bury them but also to minimize the appearance of violence and thus reduce the risk of a strong response from the army. Bodies are dumped in wells, old mines, or hidden desert graves. For local people, cartel warfare can be a disorienting experience: gunshots, sirens, and helicopters will be heard outside, and the next day there will be little sign that anything happened—and certainly no mention of it in the newspaper.

Why, then, do the cartels so often court publicity with their gruesome executions? Many of their killings seem designed for a mass audience, filmed and promoted online using similar techniques to terrorist groups such as the Islamic State. In Ciudad Juárez, a pathologist once told me that the most dangerous time to step outside was at 5:45 p.m., because that was when the cartels would carry out their murders in order to lead the 6:00 p.m. evening news. The reason is often because one gang is seeking to cause trouble on the patch of a rival. If a dozen dead bodies are dumped in a public place, the government tends to respond by sending a shock force of troops to the area, making it much harder to do business for a few weeks. Cartels will sometimes deliberately "heat up" a rival cartel's patch—*calentar la plaza*, as it is known—precisely in order to provoke such a crackdown. This also requires the cooperation of the media, which are sometimes ordered to give a particular story plenty of column inches.

Told by one cartel to shut up, and by another to splash the news on a big scale, reporters cannot win. In a front-page editorial that was republished around the world in 2010, *El Diario de Juárez* addressed the local mafia directly, following the murder of two newspaper employees. Entitled "What do you want from us?" it began: "Gentlemen of the different organizations that are fighting over the territory of Juárez . . . We bring to your attention that we are communicators, not mind-readers. For that reason, as information workers, we want you to explain what you want from us, what you want us to publish or stop publishing, so that we know what to stick to. You are, at the moment, the de facto authorities in this city, because the legally instituted powers have been able to do nothing to prevent our colleagues from continuing to fall."[6]

The iron grip that drug cartels have on the local media slips somewhat on the Internet. Like ordinary companies, organized-crime groups have struggled to control their image online. The @GobiernoReynosa Twitter account has remained very unspecific in its bulletins, limiting the details to descriptions of "situations of risk." But some amateur reporters have used the anonymity provided by the Internet to go into far greater detail than most newspapers dare. Sites with names such as *El Blog del Narco* have gained large audiences by publishing news that cannot be read in print (along with pictures and videos that are too gruesome even for Mexico's bloodthirsty press). Some journalists say they submit stories to these blogs that are too risky to publish under their own bylines. To the cartels, this leakage of information online represents a threat to their control of the news.

There are signs that they are already trying to muzzle online reporters with the tactics previously reserved for the mainstream media. The first known instance of people being killed by cartels for their use of social networks was in 2011, when two dead bodies were strung up from a bridge in Nuevo Laredo, another border town in Mexico's northeast, with a sign warning that the same fate awaited all "Internet gossips."

Shortly after that, a prominent blogger was identified and killed, her body left alongside a computer keyboard.

Cartels are willing to pay large amounts to silence even amateur reporters. In 2013, leaflets were distributed all over the state of Tamaulipas, where Reynosa lies, offering a reward of 600,000 pesos (about $40,000) for information leading to the identity of the people who ran *Valor por Tamaulipas* (Courage for Tamaulipas), an anonymous local news website. The following year, the Twitter account of one of its contributors, who called herself "Felina," or Catwoman, was hijacked. "Friends and family, my real name is Maria del Rosario Fuentes Rubio, I'm a doctor and today, my life has come to an end," the first tweet said. A couple of tweets later came a final message: "Close your accounts, don't risk your families the way I did, I ask you all for forgiveness." This was accompanied by a picture of the woman's dead body. Astonishingly, despite the risks, *Valor por Tamaulipas* and a few sites like it are still going. But the cartels' ruthless PR campaigns have often protected the gangs and their collaborators from being exposed in the way that they deserve.

·   ·   ·

A longer-term strategy that cartels use to launder their reputations is to invest in the mysterious world of corporate social responsibility. CSR, as it is known in management jargon, is often seen as a modern fad. But it has a long history. In the eighteenth century, citizens began to organize boycotts of companies that were involved in the slave trade, thereby causing more responsibly minded firms to trumpet their "humane" approaches to people management (needless to say, some of these claims were more genuine than others). One hundred years later, Victorian factory owners built "model villages" for their workers, with the aim that they should live secure, comfortable lives. Near where I grew up in northern England is the town of Saltaire, created by Sir Titus Salt, a Victorian wool magnate who believed so strongly in temperance that the town was built without a single pub. (The principle has been undermined in recent years by the opening of a bar called Don't Tell Titus.) The distinctive feature of CSR, and the reason it attracts suspicion in many quarters, is that it is partly guided by ethical zeal and partly by self-interest. Saltaire's lack of pubs may have made for healthier residents, but it probably created more punctual workers, too.

A boom in CSR as a serious business strategy took place in the 1990s. Most big firms now dedicate large amounts of time and money to demonstrating their commitment to global citizenship, sustainability, triple bottom-lines, and other responsible-sounding, if rather hard to define, objectives. It might not always be clear what the ideas mean, but they certainly aren't cheap: despite choppy economic conditions, in 2014 the 128 American firms in the Fortune Global 500 managed to find nearly $12 billion to spend on CSR initiatives.[7]

Not everyone thinks that the do-gooding is worth it. Many shareholders wonder what spending on philanthropic ventures—protecting the environment, feeding the poor, saving the whale—really does to improve the value of a company. A survey by the Tippie College of Business at the University of Iowa found that firms that shelled out for CSR did better than others during downturns, because, the authors speculated, their clients were more loyal and less likely to abandon them when money was tight. But others argue that the causation may work the other way: firms that are stable and successful are more likely than wobbly ones to have spare cash to lavish on nonessential projects.

In recent years managementologists have cooled a little on CSR. Its remaining supporters are confounded by the fact that some of today's most successful firms have not been harmed by their lack of interest in sustainability, corporate citizenship, and so on. Ryanair, a budget airline based in Ireland, has conquered the European flight market despite being widely loathed and not seeming to care. Unlike other airlines, which offer passengers the chance to "offset" their pollution by buying carbon credits, Ryanair has no time for green campaigners. "We want to annoy the fuckers whenever we can. The best thing you can do with environmentalists is shoot them," Michael O'Leary, its pugnacious boss, has said. Carlos Slim became the world's richest man by milking his telecoms concessions for all they were worth, and giving away less of his fortune than other billionaires.

But even though CSR seems to be flagging in some legitimate industries, it is thriving in the underworld. Some high-rolling criminals have acquired a reputation for carrying out ostentatious acts of philanthropy. Shorty Guzmán, who liked to strut around the poshest restaurants of Sinaloa, was known for the thousand-dollar tips he gave to waiters. Pablo Escobar gave out Christmas presents to the children of Medellín, built roller-skating rinks, and even housing for the poor. La Familia Michoacana provides cheap loans to businesses, and an informal "dispute resolution" service (which no one tends to question). Many drug lords have paid for the construction of churches. Mexicans even have a word for this: *narcolimosnas*, or drug alms. On a small chapel in the state of Hidalgo there is a brass plaque that reads: "Donated by Heriberto Lazcano Lazcano," followed by a quote from Psalms. Lazcano, also known as "The Executioner," was the leader of the Zetas cartel and reportedly enjoyed feeding his victims to pet lions and tigers. (He met a more ordinary end, shot dead by marines in 2012.)

Some priests seem happy to accept donations from such people. In an interview with local journalists in 2005, the late Ramón Godínez Flores, a bishop from the state of Aguascalientes, reasoned thus: "Did [our Lord] not receive a tribute from [Mary Magdalene], when she anointed his feet with a very expensive perfume? Jesus didn't ask her, 'Where did you buy that expensive perfume?' He didn't mind where the money came from: he simply received the tribute." But what if a priest suspects that the funds were ill-gotten, the surprised reporters asked. Not a problem, Father Godínez reassured them: "Money can be purified when the person has good intentions. You don't have to burn money just because its origins are bad; you have to transform it. All money can be transformed, just as a person who has been corrupted can transform himself."[8] Some drug lords have used philanthropy

to acquire an almost saintly status. After he was killed by the police
in 2010, shrines popped up in Michoacán to commemorate Nazario
Moreno González, the leader of La Familia Michoacana. His holy status was cemented when he "rose again," to be killed by the police in
2014. The government admitted that he apparently hadn't died in 2010
after all; this time, ministers promised, it really was him.

The reason for CSR's popularity among drug traffickers is straightforward: whereas it isn't immediately obvious how General Motors'
shareholders are enriched by the company's donating money to the Detroit Opera House, the benefit to drug lords of being good corporate
citizens is very clear. As Ryanair, the Slim empire, and countless others
show, it is perfectly possible to run a successful business without being
very popular. In the criminal world, however, entrepreneurs' freedom
depends on their maintaining a basic level of support among the people
in whose communities they operate. If the Sinaloa cartel goes out of
business, the monthly pensions supposedly given out to the elderly in
some parts of the sierra will cease. That isn't to say that the cartels are
good for society: the corruption, violence, and fear that they generate
have held Mexico back for decades and have dissuaded far more inward
investment than drugs have ever generated. But the larger the constituency of people who feel they have something to lose if the cartel goes
down, the less likely that is to happen.

Dishing out money to the poor or building chapels with their names
on them are two blunt ways that drug barons have engaged in corporate
social responsibility. But there is another, more sophisticated way in
which they have invested in CSR for their own benefit. Tarun Khanna
and Krishna Palepu of Harvard Business School have written extensively about the "institutional voids" that exist in emerging markets.
Developing countries lack all sorts of basic infrastructure that firms
in the rich world take for granted: decent roads, reliable legal systems,
good schools, free health care, and so on. In order to smooth their own
operations, and to curry favor with the communities in which they do

business, large companies sometimes go about providing services that the state has failed to produce.

To understand how the thugs of the drug world have managed to earn the approval, or at least the cautious acceptance, of ordinary people, I pay a visit to an elderly lady whom we'll call Rosa. She greets me in an airy, modern apartment in La Condesa, a rich neighborhood of Mexico City where in the local park even some of the pedigreed dogs are clad in designer outfits. As I leave the elevator and walk into the apartment's gleaming kitchen-dining room, a delicious smell is in the air. Rosa, a barrel-shaped seventy-year-old who cannot be taller than about four feet six, has been frying blueberry pancakes, and she offers me a plate stacked high with them. The swanky apartment isn't hers: it belongs to a Mexican business consultant, whom I know through work. Rosa is his *muchacha*—literally, "girl"—the old-fashioned term Mexicans use for women old or young who work as cleaners, cooks, and all-purpose home help. He has invited me around to meet Rosa because he thinks she might have an interesting story to tell. Her news is that, in between mopping floors and making blueberry pancakes, she is plotting a murder.

Rosa lives in a poor neighborhood in Mexico state, a vast suburban ring around the capital that is home to 17 million people. Life in her barrio is tough, and lately it has been getting tougher, thanks to a crime wave that has gone unpunished by the hopeless local police. Three months ago, one of her sixteen grandchildren came home with her husband to find two burglars in the middle of ransacking their house. The robbers escaped but later came back to give the husband a vicious beating with an axe handle, as a warning not to report them. "He still walks like this," Rosa says, mimicking the awkward swing of his fractured arms. In another recent case, an elderly man living alone was robbed. Neighbors answered his calls for help and dragged the burglars to court. But somehow they paid their way out—through bail or bribe, Rosa isn't sure. The old man died a couple of months later of a heart attack, caused by the anger and shock, she says. A few years ago, the same bandits had murdered two people in a raid on a chicken farm, to steal just a couple of thousand dollars.

"They enter the houses, they take whatever they want, they threaten people. They scare us," Rosa says, banging a tiny fist on the kitchen table. "We don't have lots of things, we're poor. They steal televisions, stereos, sheep, cattle, clothes, even electrical cables." And the police are doing nothing about all this. "Honestly, I don't trust them," Rosa says. "If the authorities don't do anything, what are we left with? One can't live like this anymore. We can't live with the fear that at any moment they can enter our house and kill us." Recently, something happened that made her see how the problem might be solved. She was traveling home on a bus when the bus was attacked by robbers on a lonely stretch of road. This time, however, the passengers fought back—giving them a good *golpiza*, or walloping. "But then a patrol car arrived. It didn't give them time to finish them off," Rosa says, disappointedly.

That has given Rosa and her neighbors an idea. They are saving up to pay for someone to get rid of the robbers who are menacing them, once and for all. The idea is to give them a *golpiza*, she says. Is that all? "Well . . . " Rosa looks for the right words to describe what she is undertaking. "Let's say that if they overdo it . . . so what." They will look for someone to do the job in Pachuca, a nearby city. She has in mind a man, in his forties, ex-army, who has a gun and has done similar jobs in the past. "There are people there who lend themselves to that. They do *revenges*," she says, widening her eyes a little as she mouths the word.

Dark purple patches have soaked into my napkin from the blueberry pancakes, which suddenly don't seem so appetizing. I make my excuses and head home, wondering what my own cleaning lady gets up to in her spare time. Rosa's story may be horrifying, but it is not as unusual as it sounds. Where the state is weak, people find unorthodox and sometimes extralegal ways of solving problems that ought to be fixed by public authorities. One of the first signs of state failure is when people begin to take the law into their own hands. In the weak, chaotic countries of Central America, for instance, the local newspapers are full of stories of towns that have rounded up local thieves or rapists and given them a public beating, or worse. Even in rich countries, organized crime sometimes provides sinister "public services" that aren't offered by the legitimate authorities. In Northern Ireland, the Irish Republican Army (IRA) used to shoot the kneecaps of people accused of dealing drugs or committing other crimes that were considered beyond the pale. The principle was the same as in the case of Rosa: a criminal group claimed to be filling an "institutional void," thus winning the approval of some members of society for its warped "socially responsible" work (which provided a convenient synergy with its core business of meting out violence to rival armed groups).

Many organized criminal groups provide this sort of "protection." Pablo Escobar funded a gang of thugs to do his dirty work, calling them "Muerte a Secuestradores" (Death to Kidnappers), in a weak attempt to convince people that they only targeted wrongdoers. Along identical lines, the Sinaloa cartel created a hit squad called the "Matazetas," or "Zeta Killers," which claimed in a series of online videos: "Our only objective is the Zetas cartel." The group would work "always to benefit Mexico's people," its balaclava-wearing members claimed.

Do these acts of criminal corporate social responsibility ever really benefit society? Herschel Grossman, an American economist, created a model of mafia-provided public services and found that in some cases, competition between the state and the mob could result in public services that were better than those offered when the state alone provided them.[9] In Grossman's model, mafias extort money and provide services in much the same way that governments levy taxes to fund public spending. The higher the rate of taxation, and the worse the public services provided by the state, the more people and businesses will lean toward relying on the black market to fill their needs. The mafia faces the same dilemma: the higher the extortion payments it demands, and the less it provides in return, the more people will turn to the state. This form of competition can potentially be beneficial, Grossman argues, because it prevents the state from charging high taxes and delivering little in return. "According to this analysis, the existence of the mafia harms only the members of the ruling class or political establishment whose main source of income is political rent," Grossman writes (acknowledging, in the deadpan style of an economist, that there exists "the possibility that the mafia's activities are socially disruptive").

This is fairly silly. Few societies were ever improved by organized crime. But there are times when cartels perform services useful to some. A classic organized criminal ruse is for competing firms to agree to rig their bids for contracts. One of the earliest studies of this phenomenon was carried out in 1876 by Leopoldo Franchetti, an Italian politician and economist who visited Sicily to write a report on its "Political and Administrative Conditions."[10] Fans of The Sopranos will be pleased to hear that the earliest formal study of the Italian mafia was all about food. Franchetti examined two professional societies of millers based near Palermo, the island's capital. Under normal market conditions, the millers would have competed with each other on the price and quality of their flour. Customers would have bought the flour that was cheapest and of the highest quality. But the millers soon realized that there was an easier way to run their industry. Rather than compete, they decided to collude, taking turns to cut back on their production in order to create scarcity, charging higher prices than they would otherwise have been able to do. In other words, they formed a classic cartel. The plan was perfect, except that it was too difficult to ensure that the millers really did restrict their production and keep their prices high. There would be a strong incentive for each one of them to overproduce and sell its product a fraction cheaper than the agreed price, thus grabbing the whole market. The courts couldn't be called upon to enforce the agreement, as price-fixing is illegal. So the millers decided to employ what Franchetti calls "powerful Mafiosi" to enforce the agreement. Everyone was happy: the millers made more money for doing less work and the mafia presumably collected a cut.

Only the poor consumer was worse off, paying higher prices for bad flour and enduring second-rate spaghetti.

Organized criminal groups have provided similar services ever since, acting as the enforcers of contracts between businesses that cannot use the courts because they are selling an illegal product, such as drugs, or taking part in an illegal activity, such as price-fixing. In a classic essay[11] in which they build on the work of Franchetti, Diego Gambetta and Peter Reuter give a host of examples of how the mafia has performed similar services in Italy and in New York City. In Palermo and Naples, the unregulated traffic-light windshield-washing industry was regulated by the mafia. In Rome, by contrast, there was no mafia involvement. The outcomes were very different. Whereas in Palermo and Naples the mafia ensured that the squeegee men stuck to their agreed territories, in Rome the window washers came to blows over who worked at the most profitable junctions. Soon the Roman police got involved and made life much harder for all operators. In the cities where the mafia regulated the industry, business continued as usual.

In New York City, the mafia was long involved in the garbage-collection business. It hardly sounds very profitable—certainly less glamorous than the international cocaine trade—but by fixing the prices charged for waste collection, garbage-disposal firms could dramatically increase their profits. The problem was that, as with the millers in nineteenth-century Sicily, the agreement would break down if one firm put in a competitive bid in order to steal the contract. The solution was to enlist the mafia to make sure that all sides kept the bargain. Bringing in the mob had the other useful (to the garbage-disposal firms) side effect of deterring new entrants to the market, Gambetta and Reuter note. This was vividly demonstrated when, in 1972, the Brooklyn District Attorney's Office set up a new waste-collection business as part of an undercover investigation into the mafia. It wasn't long before the new business's trucks were destroyed by mobsters.

For businesspeople who want to make a bit of extra money and don't mind breaking competition rules, organized criminal gangs thus provide a useful service in enforcing contracts. The evidence is that they charge quite reasonable prices for doing so: witnesses say that the New York mafia's fee for fixing prices in the concrete industry was only 2 percent of the contract price; in Sicily, the construction industry reportedly paid 5 percent to the mafia (of which it kept 3 percent and used the remaining 2 percent to pay bribes to politicians). If the price-fixing agreement means that a firm can jack up its rates substantially, these fees are well worth it. (And it seems they can: a study in the 1980s by the RAND Corporation found that residential customers on Long Island were paying 15 percent more for their garbage collection than they would in a competitive market, and commercial customers were paying 50 percent more.)[12] The agreements were so robust that garbage-collection firms were even able to buy and sell "contracts" to serve particular customers or neighborhoods, with the exclusive rights guaranteed by the mafia. As Gambetta and Reuter write: "The suppression of competition is a near-universal dream of established entrepreneurs. The mafia is one of the few non-governmental institutions that can help accomplish this goal." By acting as a useful guarantor of corrupt agreements between companies, organized-crime gangs can win support in the business community, further enlarging the segment of society that has a stake in the mob's remaining in business.

•   •   •

The world ought to be outraged by the appalling acts of cruelty perpetrated by drug cartels. Most people are. But through tactics borrowed from the legitimate business world, the cartels have managed to win just enough support in a few key areas to lessen their chances of being reported and convicted. By making flashy donations to charitable or religious causes, they have softened their images. Stepping in to provide public services where the state has failed, they have come to be seen in some poor areas as alternatives to the legitimately elected authorities.

By guaranteeing corrupt agreements between firms, they have forged links with the business class. By deploying advertising, mastering online media, and intimidating journalists, they have ensured that all of this is presented to the public in the most positive light possible.

How can governments sabotage the cartels' public-relations machine? The single-most-effective way to undermine gangsters' "charitable" efforts is for the state to up its own game in the provision of basic public services. If the police and courts in Mexico City's violent suburbs had been doing their job properly, Rosa the septuagenarian killer-cleaner would not have dreamed of looking for a hit man to do the job for her. If the government of Medellín had spent a bit more on parks, swimming pools, or youth clubs, Colombians would have been less impressed by Pablo Escobar's roller-skating rinks. If the government of Mexico provided proper pensions to the elderly, no one would line up to receive handouts from Shorty Guzmán's henchmen. And if Mexican banks were less stingy with their credit (they lend half as much as their counterparts in Brazil, and one-third as much as those in Chile),[13] households and businesses would be less likely to borrow money from the mob. When analysts talk about drug cartels taking over territory where there is a vacuum of power, they envisage territory where the government has neglected to send enough police or soldiers. More often than not, there is another problem: these are places where the government has not bothered to provide any public services, from recreation to rubbish collection and microcredit. In short, the more responsible the state is, the less scope there is for the mob to show off its own phony "responsible" side.

How can anyone undermine the role that cartels play as a guarantor of illegal agreements? Unlike other services, this is one that the state cannot provide, as price-fixing and bid rigging are rightly illegal. The evidence from Sicily and New York City is that mafia involvement in these industries has weakened. One reason is better investigation of competition. New York's garbage-disposal business is now overseen by the Business Integrity Commission, which seems to have stamped out most of the mob's involvement in the industry in the city (though it continues in the suburbs to some extent). Another reason is globalization. It may be easy enough for the mafia to maintain price-fixing among local millers in Sicily, but it is a taller order to sign up big firms from other regions of Italy, or indeed other parts of the world. As small, local firms are replaced by big, international ones, enforcing price-fixing agreements becomes harder.

When it comes to scrambling the cartels' public messages, there are two things that governments could do. First, they should wise up to the gangs' strategy of trying to *calentar la plaza*, or heat up each other's territory. If a threatening advertisement or a big, public dump of bodies takes place somewhere, the reflex of the government is to send reinforcements to that city, to keep the peace. That is understandable, but often it is exactly what the criminals want. What the government should do is change the incentive structure by sending reinforcements to a city run by the *other* cartel. Attempting to heat up another cartel's *plaza* would then be likely to backfire, as it would result in a shock force of troops being dispatched to the home turf of the cartel deemed responsible.

Second, as for the cartels' sinister "PR" campaigns, the answer is to offer better protection to journalists. Easier said than done, of course. An aide to Felipe Calderón, Mexico's president from 2006 to 2012, once scoffed when I told him this. "What are we supposed to do—give a bodyguard to every journalist in northern Mexico?" he asked. Clearly not, but better investigations of murders would remove the impunity that currently exists for anyone who fancies bumping off a reporter, a crime that is currently highly unlikely to result in a conviction. Countries could consider ramping up sentences for those who kill journalists, much as the sentence for murdering a police officer is higher than that for killing an ordinary citizen in many countries. As a last resort, news organizations can agree among themselves to publish the same version of reports on particularly sensitive subjects, giving them safety in numbers. For a while in the 1990s, Colombian newspapers did this.

It is an unattractive strategy for a host of reasons: it eliminates competition, reduces the likelihood of mistakes being corrected, and introduces the dangerous notion of an "official" account of events. But it may be better than the total silence that currently exists in some cartel-run hotspots.

Finally, governments in wealthy countries should do a better job of educating the drug-buying public about how its money ends up being spent. Public-education films in the rich world have historically focused on the risks to health caused by taking drugs. Several decades later, those campaigns don't seem to have made much of an impact—and that is not surprising, given that the chances of dying of an overdose are fairly slim. The truth is that buying and taking illegal drugs probably won't kill you. But it may very well kill someone else. Cocaine, for instance, is manufactured and exported exclusively by cartels that use murder and torture as part of their business model. (The "fair-trade cocaine," which some dealers have recently started hawking online— see Chapter 8—is bogus.) Buy cocaine in Europe or the United States and it is an uncomfortable certainty that you have helped to pay for someone to be tortured to death in a place like Reynosa. People ought to know this. It is a testament to the success of cartels in laundering their images that millions of consumers buy drugs each year without giving a moment's thought to the fact that they are funding unimaginable suffering.

Chapter 5

OFFSHORING

The Perks of Doing Business
on the Mosquito Coast

If you were washed up on the rugged Caribbean shores of Honduras, west of the wilderness known as the Mosquito Coast, you might think you were in the lost world. Off the beach and a little way inland begins a thick and humid jungle, where butterflies dart through the air and the hum of the undergrowth is broken only by the squawk of parrots. It is hard to remember what century you are in, let alone what country. Yet ten miles or so from the sea, you would stumble upon an unexpected sight: a colossal mountain of underpants. From boxer shorts to skimpy briefs and billowing bloomers, thousands upon thousands of pairs of undergarments are stitched together in giant factories on the edge of the tropical city of San Pedro Sula and stacked up in crates to be exported around the globe. Honduras is now the number-one supplier of cotton socks and underwear to the United States. The low cost of labor in Honduras—average income per person is about $45 a week—has made the country a natural base for companies looking to lower their costs by setting up outposts overseas. Factories in its northern jungle now churn out a bewildering array of products to be shipped to consumers all over the world.

"Offshoring"—the practice of moving business operations to a foreign country, and sometimes outsourcing them to another company—was one of the biggest business trends of the late twentieth century. International transportation became quicker and cheaper, just at the same time as communications got easier. An international fashion for free trade saw many countries open up their economic borders through grand deals such as NAFTA, initiated by Canada, Mexico, and the United States in 1994, which was followed by the European Union's eastern enlargement in the early 2000s. With these barriers broken down, companies assembling products in the United States and Europe wondered why they were paying rich-world salaries to local workers, and rich-world rents for local premises, when the job could be done just as well a few hundred miles away in a country where wages, property, and everything else were far cheaper. There began a great migration of manufacturing power to Latin America, North Africa, and the Far East. In 2000–2003, foreign companies built 60,000 factories in China alone. In San Pedro Sula, the textile factories sit alongside car-part production lines, fruit-packing warehouses, and air-conditioned call-centers, where English-speaking locals handle inquiries from customers in the United States.

The offshoring boom has delighted Western consumers, who have found themselves paying less for their Honduran socks and Chinese computers. (It has horrified some Western workers, meanwhile, who have seen their jobs go south and east.) Alan Blinder, a former vice chair of the Federal Reserve, has predicted that offshoring will be "the next Industrial Revolution," with 30–40 million service-sector jobs in the United States eventually ripe for the offshoring treatment.[1] As wages in the developing world catch up with those in the West, there are signs that the movement is slowing down a little. But the change has already been immense: nearly one-quarter of American employees now work at an organization that has moved at least some of its business processes overseas.[2]

The advantages of offshoring have not been lost on the drugs industry. Like other firms, cartels want to reduce their costs. And even more than legitimate companies, they have reason to shop around for the most relaxed regulatory environment in which to operate. In Central America, you don't need to go far to see that the conditions that have lured the textile and car factories to the region have also proved irresistible to the drugs business. In recent years, the cheap, poorly governed countries of Central America have been discovering growing evidence that a certain set of Mexican multinationals has moved in. Around San Pedro Sula, socks are not the only things being made at a discount in the jungle.

• • •

The great continents of North and South America are linked by a slender isthmus that is just thirty miles wide at its narrowest point, forever looking as if it is about to snap. Central America is smaller in area than Texas, and yet it is home to seven tiny countries, most of them prone to coups and needless wars over minute patches of swamp. The region literally seethes: fly over it and you cross more than twenty active volcanoes, several of them reliably huffing and puffing and occasionally spitting lava.

Central Americans describe their region as a "trampoline," for the way it is used to bounce shipments of drugs from South America to the great market of the United States. The US State Department calculates that as much as 80 percent of all the cocaine in the United States makes a stop on the isthmus at some point in its journey north, usually being sent from Colombia or Venezuela by boat or light aircraft and then moved on to Mexico. The trampoline has been getting heavier use since the old Caribbean smuggling route was effectively shut down in the 1980s, forcing traffickers to find a different path from South to North America. And lately, a new pattern has emerged. Rather than simply bouncing on Central America, Mexican traffickers are putting down roots.

Their footprints keep appearing. In 2011, Honduran police discovered for the first time a large cocaine-processing laboratory, which they calculated had the capacity to turn 400 kilos of cocaine paste into pure cocaine powder every week. Evidence gathered by investigators pointed to the fact that the lab was being run by the Sinaloa cartel of Joaquín "Shorty" Guzmán. A few months later, Guatemala made an even more frightening discovery: on a ranch called The Coconuts in the north of the country, near the Mexican border, twenty-seven people were found decapitated, their heads left scattered around the surrounding fields. A message written in blood on the wall of the farm, apparently using the severed leg of one of the victims, was signed by "Z200," a local leader of the Zetas.

Like the firms making underwear and car stereos in San Pedro Sula, the cartels have discovered that offshoring parts of their business has many advantages. First among them is the abundant supply of cheap labor. In a large, run-down building in the center of Guatemala City, I meet a young man we'll call José. He is only eighteen, with a baby face and a mop of fluffy dark hair. But he has the hard, tired eyes of someone decades older. He already has several years under his belt working as a hit man for a local gang. It may be more accurate to say hit boy than hit man, because when he began this career he was only eight years old. Another gang had murdered his father, stabbing him in the street and then coming back to finish him off when they learned that the initial attack had failed to kill him. José started his criminal life by killing the man who had murdered his dad. "I enjoyed it," he says, his face expressionless.

The crumbling old building where we have met is the headquarters of La Ceiba, an NGO that provides refuge and training to troubled youths in the capital. In one room, teenagers are being shown how to put together a PowerPoint presentation; off a corridor are quiet rooms where they can speak to counselors—"like confessionals," says one member of the staff. Here, José is now trying to turn his life around. Leaving the gang will be difficult, he says: they have sworn to kill a member of La Ceiba if he abandons his criminal career. For a man who has murdered so many others, he is a slip of a thing, not much over five feet tall with a skinny, pale body. Stunted growth is one effect of chronic malnutrition, which is common among children in Guatemala. José's innocent appearance is jarringly at odds with the life he describes. As he relates his father's murder, describes the time he was shot in the chest (he shows the jagged scar), and demonstrates how he can hardly move his beaten right arm any more, he shuffles his feet in tiny, child-size shoes, with Velcro straps.

José's story of stolen youth is utterly chilling. But it is music to the ears of the drug cartels' talent scouts, who, like other entrepreneurs, are keen to tap into Central America's cheap labor market. Like many countries in the region, Guatemala has a large population of poor, marginalized young men and boys, who are easier to persuade to begin a life of crime than their richer neighbors. Average income per head in Guatemala is only $3,500 a year; in Nicaragua it is less than $2,000. In Mexico, it is more than $10,000. Just as clothing manufacturers can offer lower wages in Central America than they can in Mexico, so can drug cartels. Even more highly prized by the cartels are members of Guatemala's special forces, known as the Kaibiles, a name derived from that of an indigenous leader who outwitted the Spanish conquistadors. The Kaibiles were responsible for some of the worst human-rights abuses of the country's gruesome civil war in the 1980s and 1990s. Guatemalan mothers scare their children by warning them about a visit from the feared commandos—killers, cannibals, men who bite the heads off live chickens, it is said. Nowadays, out of work, some of those ex-soldiers have found employment with the drug runners.

The man charged with fighting back this unwanted inward investment works in the grandest and most gloriously hideous of Central America's presidential palaces. Designed as a sort of neocolonial mansion-cum-fortress, Guatemala's Palacio de Gobierno is made of a local stone with an unfortunate greenish tinge, a fitting metaphor for the rottenness of much of Guatemalan public life. On my way into the palace,

I have to elbow through a herd of goats that has been parked by the side entrance, apparently as part of a farmers' protest. It is 2011, and I am in town to meet the then president, Álvaro Colom. He is a thin, rather gray, very softly spoken man, whose words come out somewhere between a croak and a whisper. His understated appearance is accentuated by the fact that beside his desk is a dazzling stuffed quetzal bird, Guatemala's unofficial mascot, a sort of miniature tropical peacock with magnificent bright green and blue tail-feathers. Few creatures can compete with the quetzal's luminous looks; Colom, unfortunately, is not one of them.

He has spent his presidency trying to maintain a grip on a state that has been gradually hollowed out. Following the end of the country's ruinous civil war in 1996, the army was greatly reduced in size. That might have been a good idea, had the soldiers been replaced with a civilian police force. But they were not. The country has seen "a systematic destruction of the security system," Colom says. The army now numbers 10,000 men, down from more than 30,000. For one thing, that means that 20,000 former soldiers are now looking for work, which the cartels are happy to provide. For another, it has left the country very poorly defended. At one point there were only thirty-two soldiers policing a two-hundred-mile stretch of the six-hundred-mile Mexican border. The cartels have set up bases in northern Guatemala and have been "using it like an international airport," the president says. An aide says that in the Laguna del Tigre (Tiger Lagoon), a patch of wilderness in the north, there is a "cemetery" of thirty or forty light aircraft that have been flown in by drug traffickers and then abandoned.

The inability of the government to hold large swathes of its own territory points to another feature that cartels see as an asset: a hopelessly weak state. Mexico may sometimes seem lawless, but it is like Switzerland compared with some parts of Central America. An American diplomat in Guatemala City recommends that I take a car back to my hotel after visiting the embassy, though it is only a ten-minute walk through the center of town in broad daylight. This seems absurd, until a couple of days later an economist from a big bank tells me that his own organization forbids visiting employees from traveling more than a block on foot beyond their hotel, ever since a colleague died in a shootout in a restaurant. I have one close call myself, after unwisely flashing my iPhone around in a shady neighborhood. A man grabs me by the collar and starts dragging me down the street, until apparently thinking better of it and allowing me to wriggle free. "Ciudad Juárez: the country," is how one journalist friend describes Guatemala. He is right. About 40 percent of the murders in the country are the work of drug cartels, President Colom says.

Although it is poor by Western standards, Guatemala is classified by the International Monetary Fund (IMF) as a middle-income country; the average person is about 50 percent wealthier than in next-door Honduras. In spite of this, the state has repeatedly proved incapable of meeting the most basic needs of the population. Like José the teenage hit man, many of the country's children are slowly starving: half of those under five suffer from chronic malnutrition, the fourth-highest rate in the world. Nowhere in Latin America comes close to this figure: in Haiti, which is the region's closest thing to a failed state, the rate is half as high. The reason the government has failed to fix this and other problems is that it collects pitifully small amounts of tax. Public spending amounts to only about 12 percent of gross domestic product, the lowest in Latin America, where the average is over 20 percent.[3] Successive presidents have tried to raise taxes, each time having their reforms blocked or diluted by a private sector that seems allergic to paying its fair share. Guatemala has turned into a do-it-yourself economy, in which public services have withered away and have been replaced by private contractors.

This applies even in public security. A cheerful man with a gleaming gold tooth and an even shinier pump-action shotgun guards the hotel where I am staying, hoisting his weapon up onto his shoulder to open the door for guests as they come and go. Down the road, a teenager brandishes a rifle that looks older than he is, as he stands guard outside a florist shop. Although the crime rate is sky high, it is rare to see police

patrols, even in the capital. What you do see absolutely everywhere are
heavily armed private security guards. A few blocks from where I am
staying, a gun shop, Armsa, advertises its wares on a billboard featuring a giant Glock handgun, which points directly into the building next
door, a brightly painted nursery for children aged between two and six.
Across the country, private security guards outnumber the police by
five to one. Anyone with money can buy more than enough firepower
to outgun the authorities.

   As the cartels increase their influence in Guatemala, there are worries that they are getting deeper into its politics. At the time of my
meeting with President Colom, elections are coming up. In a strange
twist, the president has just announced that he is divorcing his wife,
in order to allow her to run for office. The constitution forbids close
relatives of the president from succeeding him. So Colom and his wife,
Sandra Torres, have decided to part company. The president is aware
the colorful Ms. Torres could inspire more excitement on the campaign trail than him. "I'm not a great generator of passion," he admits,
with a thin smile. Alongside the soap opera of the presidential divorce,
the election season has seen stories about drug money entering every
side of the race. Is Colom worried about the possibility of infiltration
of his party? He thinks for a moment and then says, barely audibly: "All
the political parties must be careful. It's the *country* that is infiltrated."[4]

·   ·   ·

For criminals looking for an offshore base in the Americas, Guatemala
has a lot to offer. But it faces stiff competition from its southern neigh-
bor, Honduras. Guatemala arguably leads the way in terms of its slack
labor market and dysfunctional state, but Honduras can claim an edge
in a factor that is perhaps even more valuable to organized crime: ac-
commodating government.

   It was 1994 when Alan Rosen, an American businessman, heard
about a very unusual business opportunity while on a trip to Honduras.
Through a friend, he learned that a retired colonel from the Honduran

army was seeking to sell a piece of moon rock, for the proposed sum of $1 million. When Rosen left the country the "opportunity" still puzzled him, but his interest had been piqued. Back in the United States, he discovered in his research that moon rocks could fetch much higher prices. So the following year he returned to Honduras, where he managed to arrange a meeting with the colonel, who by this time seemed very anxious to close a deal. It emerged that the rock—really more of a pebble, weighing little more than a gram—had been given to the people of Honduras in 1973 as a goodwill gesture by Richard Nixon, then the president of the United States. The rock was encased in acrylic and mounted on a wooden plaque, along with the Honduran flag. The colonel insisted that he had the right to sell it, and Rosen eventually bartered him down from $1 million to just $50,000. Not only that: he persuaded the colonel to let him walk away with the rock for a down payment of only $10,000, plus a refrigerated truck, which he claimed was worth $15,000.

Back in the United States, Rosen got the rock tested by a Harvard professor, who confirmed that it had indeed come from the moon. With this expert certification in hand, Rosen began searching for a collector to whom he could sell it. A few years later, after placing a few carefully worded newspaper advertisements, he thought he had found a buyer. But when he turned up to meet him, in Miami, the collector turned out to be an undercover cop. The rock was seized and given back to the government of Honduras. The full details of the strange tale are recorded in what is perhaps the weirdest case name in American legal history: *United States of America v. One Lucite Ball Containing Lunar Material (One Moon Rock) and One Ten Inch by Fourteen Inch Wooden Plaque.*[5]

If senior members of the armed forces are prepared to sell even chunks of the moon, what else might they be prepared to give up if the price is right? One of the most important factors for drug cartels to consider when choosing an offshore location is the openness of the government to welcoming the sort of foreign direct investment that they offer. Friends in high places are vital if a cartel is to set up a serious presence. Establishing a factory, clearing a landing strip, or moving groups of heavily armed paramilitaries around the countryside is much easier if a contact in the defense ministry can ensure that a certain region is never patrolled, or that the radar is switched off at a certain time. For this reason, maintaining good relations with the government matters even more to illegal businesses than it does to legitimate ones.

When it comes to corruption in the public sector, Honduras has a track record that few can rival. It was the original "banana republic," so called because its politicians were so easily bribed and bossed around by the foreign fruit companies that arrived in the nineteenth century. The president of the day was ousted in 1974 after it emerged that he had accepted $1.25 million from the United Fruit Company in return for lowering certain export tariffs. In recent decades, the corruption has involved drugs rather than fruit. Various high-ranking soldiers have been convicted of drug-smuggling offenses, and senior members of the government have been caught turning a blind eye to trafficking—or sometimes even playing an active part in it. In 1988, for example, the Honduran ambassador to Panama was arrested at Miami International Airport carrying nearly 12 kilograms of cocaine in his luggage.

Political instability has helped to encourage this criminality in politics. Honduras has experienced three military coups in the past half century, each time leading to a new, temporary government, some of whose members are out to make a fast buck, whether through dealing drugs, tapping social-security funds, or selling pieces of moon. From the point of view of the cartels, it is a highly promising place in which to forge relations with the government.

On a sweltering day in Tegucigalpa, the higgledy-piggledy capital, I go to see Pompeyo Bonilla Reyes, a former military man who is now Honduras's overworked security minister. Tegucigalpa is built on top of a rabbit warren of old silver mines, its neighborhoods scattered over hillsides and jammed into deep gullies. Inside the *casa presidencial* I make my way through a crowd of brightly clothed Garifuna women, from Honduras's English-speaking Caribbean coast, to a room just off a shady courtyard, where I meet Bonilla. These days he wears a suit rather than a military uniform, but he maintains the upright posture of the parade ground. Above a square jaw and flattened nose are the serious eyes of a man who knows he must stay several steps ahead of the cartels in order to stay alive, let alone in his job. A few years earlier, Honduras's drug tsar, Julián Aristides González, was shot dead by two men on a motorbike as he dropped his daughter off at school. He had been due to retire two months later and was planning to move his family to safety in Canada. The Sinaloa cartel was blamed.

At the time of my meeting with Bonilla, the Honduran police force is going through yet another round of *depuración*, or vetting, in an attempt to purge it of corrupt officers. Although the crackdown is code-named Operation Lightning, progress is slow: a few months into the purge they have evaluated only 570 officers out of a total force of 14,000. Of those who have been vetted, 150 have been thrown out, an unpromising ratio of bad apples to good. How did the Honduran state become so rotten? "It's due to our geographic situation," the minister says. Honduras sits smack in the middle of Central America, sandwiched between the cocaine-producing countries of South America and the insatiable consumers of the United States. "We are between those who consume drugs and those who produce them. So logically, we are a corridor of traffic," Bonilla says.

Ventures such as the recently discovered cocaine laboratory are hard to get off the ground without the cooperation of the local police, who, hopeless though they may be, would probably notice if a large drug factory were set up under their noses. One reason that organized crime thrives in Honduras is that officers' salaries are very low, making it cheap for criminals to pay them to switch their allegiance. Just as gangsters find it cheaper to corrupt policemen in Mexico than in the United States, it is slightly cheaper still to corrupt them in Honduras than it is in Mexico. A Honduran police officer makes less than $300 per month, a rate that the cartels can easily top up in return for the officer's looking the other way when they move their drugs or carry out their hits.

If police officers or soldiers resist this sort of pressure, it is also cheap to murder them. As part of their move offshore, the Mexicans have started to pay their local contractors not in cash but in drugs, which they then sell to local *pandillas*, or street gangs. Just as Roman soldiers were paid their "salaries" in salt—an easy-to-transport, high-value item whose worth was understood across borders—traffickers have found it convenient to pay their troops today in cocaine, which fulfills the same criteria. The emergence of this modern-day salary—a "cocary," perhaps it should be called—has created a violent local retail market, as gangs hawk their drugs on street corners. The murder rate has soared as the local *pandillas* engage in tit-for-tat killings—"adjusting their accounts," as the businesslike Spanish phrase has it. In 2013, nearly one in every thousand people in Honduras was killed, the highest murder rate in the world, according to the United Nations. The scale of the violence is unbelievable: after working out the probability of a man's being murdered over the course of his lifetime, I run the numbers past the *Economist*'s research department, suspecting that I have miscalculated. They turned out to be correct after all: at the current rate, for an average Honduran man the odds of being murdered over the course of a lifetime are a staggering one in nine.[6] The sheer number of killings leaves detectives little chance of clearing many of them up.

Bonilla insists that the government is winning the battle and that the country is not yet a failed state, a phrase that is mentioned increasingly frequently regarding Honduras. "Crime isn't in control here," he says. The gangs "run things very well in certain zones. But in no municipality of Honduras has the state lost its authority."

As in Guatemala, that is debatable. According to estimates from the US State Department, in 2012 three-quarters of all cocaine-smuggling flights originating in South America landed in Honduras.[7] The flights began in earnest following the country's latest coup, in 2009, when the president was marched out of his home in the early hours of the morning, still in his pajamas, and put on a one-way flight to Costa Rica. When protests against the coup began the next day, the country's police were ordered to scramble to the capital to keep the peace. This meant that the rural Mosquito Coast was even less closely watched than before, allowing smugglers to sneak in under the radar.

Some cocaine deliveries are made by boat. Local fishermen use GPS technology to collect offshore caches of "white lobster," as the drug is jokily referred to on the coast. Other deliveries are made by light aircraft, often Cessna Conquests or Beechcraft Dukes, which land on primitive strips of clearing in the jungle that local farmers keep mown and hidden for a small fee.[8] Air-traffic data from the United States show swarms of flights originating in Venezuela and heading to Honduras's desolate Caribbean coast, following the 2009 coup. The landing strips are bumpy, and the planes frequently make crash-landings. With aircraft costing several hundred thousand dollars, this might seem like a serious loss. But the economics of the cocaine business is such that it hardly matters. Just as eradicating a field of coca in the Andes makes little impact on retail prices in the United States, a crashed plane here or there does not make much of a dent in the cartels' bottom lines. The loss of a half-million-dollar aircraft will add an extra $1,000 to the cost of smuggling each of the 500 or so kilos that it can carry. Those kilograms retail for more than $100,000 once they reach the United States. So the retail price of the drug will be pushed up by less than 1 percent, even if the cartels have to crash and abandon a plane on every shipment.[9]

An interesting study in Guatemala hinted at the extent of the clandestine runway business. Miguel Castillo of Guatemala's Francisco Marroquín University carried out a study of land ownership in Petén, Guatemala's northernmost department, a jungle wilderness where the cartels have been spotted more than anywhere else. He found that someone—no one is quite sure who—has been buying up land in Petén at an astonishing rate. In the municipality of Sayaxche, 90 percent of the land changed hands between 2005 and 2010. In San José, nearby, the figure was 75 percent, and in La Libertad (where the massacre at The Coconuts ranch took place), the figure was 69 percent.[10] As well as providing a base for landing strips, processing labs, and training camps, buying up large chunks of land is a useful method of money laundering. And because much of the land in the area is occupied by peasants who have no legitimate legal documents to prove their claim, persuading people to sell is not difficult—even before using terror tactics of the sort seen at The Coconuts.

•   •   •

The offshoring boom has completely changed the way that chief executives see their companies. Whereas once upon a time firms were anchored to a particular country, or at least a continent, today's corporations are willing to go wherever in the world offers the best business conditions. Jack Welch, a former head of General Electric, has mused that it would be handy for a firm to have its factories on giant barges, so that they could be floated around the world, docking in whichever country offered the best economic conditions at the time. Carl Gerstacker, a former chair of Dow Chemical, had a similar idea: "I have long dreamed of buying an island owned by no nation and of establishing the world headquarters of the Dow company on the truly neutral ground of such an island, beholden to no nation or society," he once said. For the big-thinking executive, national borders belong in the twentieth century.

In this area, of course, drug cartels are some way ahead of ordinary companies. International borders have never meant much to smugglers, whose entire business model revolves around ignoring them. Carl Gerstacker's fantasy of a private island, free of national laws and governments, has already been tried out by Carlos Lehder, the Colombian American ally of Pablo Escobar, who bought an island in the Bahamas that he used for several years from 1978 as his base for flying cocaine into the United States. Even before the age of offshoring, the narcotics trade was an early standard-bearer of globalization, with prim Victorians enthusiastically trading drugs along with tea and spices as world trade opened up in the nineteenth century. Britain twice went to war with China to keep the international opium trade alive. Meanwhile, Western consumers began to develop a taste for imported narcotics. Charles Dickens was supposedly a fan of opium; in Vienna, Sigmund Freud devoured line after line of cocaine, causing him to write giddy letters to his girlfriend, Martha Bernays ("Woe to you my little Princess, when I come. I will kiss you quite red and feed you until you are plump. And if you are forward you shall see who is the stronger, a gentle little girl who doesn't eat enough, or a big wild man with cocaine in his body.")[11]

Drug barons have long seen the world as their oyster. But how do they determine exactly where to set up shop? As we have seen, countries such as Guatemala and Honduras have plenty going for them. Still, choosing between them, and their Central American neighbors, isn't easy.

Ordinary multinationals face the same decision, and they take it after poring over detailed country-by-country analysis. Perhaps the most influential study, awaited anxiously by bureaucrats and business-people everywhere, is one that is published each year by the World Bank. "Doing Business" is a three-hundred-page document of tables and charts that looks rather dry but has the power to cause elation and despair in boardrooms and finance ministries around the world. In "Doing Business," the World Bank's experts rank nearly two hundred countries on how easy they make it for companies to operate. The report shows, for instance, how long it takes to register a new firm (from just half a day in New Zealand to 144 days in Venezuela), and how many forms a company must fill out if it wants to import something (only two in Ireland, compared with a headache-inducing seventeen in the Central African Republic). A good score in "Doing Business" means a rush of inward investment. A bad score means foreign firms may flee. Governments love to crow about how their country has jumped ahead of its regional rivals: if you visit Mexico on a business trip, someone is

quite likely to tell you before you even leave the airport that the country has a higher ranking than Brazil. The report has spawned many imitators: the World Economic Forum (WEF), for instance, publishes its
own "Global Competitiveness Report," an even more detailed ranking
that works in a similar way.

These indices are minutely studied by multinationals trying to
decide where in the world they should strike out next. Consider the
American underwear magnate, poised to open his next great work-
shop. He knows that Central America offers cheap wages and proximity to the United States. But which of its countries should he go for?
"Doing Business" will tell him that getting a permit to build his factory
will take 158 days in Guatemala, 115 days in El Salvador, and only 82
days in Honduras. Filing taxes will take 320 hours a year in El Salvador,
256 hours in Guatemala, and 224 in Honduras. The relative ease of
doing business in Honduras, according to some measures at least, helps
to explain why the jungle around San Pedro Sula is fast being nibbled
away by new foreign-owned factories.

Drug cartels' priorities are sometimes different, of course—they
don't worry much about how long it takes to file taxes, for instance.
But curiously, indices such as those produced by the World Bank and
World Economic Forum provide some useful clues as to where they are
likely to set up shop next. You just have to read them backward.

Take the "Global Competitiveness Report." The first section on its
scorecard is devoted to assessing the strength of public institutions.
For ordinary firms, strong state institutions—courts of law, police
forces, parliaments, and so on—are a desirable thing in a host country.
Business is slowed down if firms keep being bothered for bribes every
time they apply for planning permission; enforcing contracts is made
impossible if rival companies can secretly persuade judges to rule in
their favor. For cartels it is just the opposite: countries with weak institutions make ideal places to set up shop. The World Economic Forum's
rankings could almost have been designed with drug cartels in mind.
Its analysts helpfully rate countries according to things such as how

widely accepted bribery is, how corruptible judges are, how reliable the police force is, and even what presence organized crime already has in the country. Drug cartels wanting to know where they are going to find it easiest to outgun the local cops, bribe the judges, and get the business community to launder their cash only need read the index.

I decided to do a little experiment and compile a makeshift "Cartel Competitiveness Report," using the World Economic Forum's data. I chose nine of the qualities that it assesses that seemed to be of the most interest to organized-crime groups: diversion of public funds, trust in politicians, bribery, judicial independence, favoritism in decisions by government, business costs of crime and violence, presence of organized crime, reliability of the police, and ethical behavior of firms. In each of these categories, the WEF gives countries a score between one and seven. Ordinarily, seven would be the best, and one the worst. For cartels—which find it useful to bribe politicians, intimidate judges, outwit the police, and so on—it is the other way around.

Applying this analysis to Central America, some wide variations are apparent (see Figure 5.1). The worst place for organized crime to do business is Costa Rica, which stands out for its boringly independent judges and reliable police. Next door, Panama is a fairly awkward home for criminals, too: it also has an annoyingly good police force, and its companies are hard to corrupt. Nicaragua is similarly unpromising, with a private sector that reports not having to spend much on security. The places where criminal companies ought to feel more at home are Guatemala and Honduras, which both score below three points, on average. Guatemala stands out for having among the least-trusted politicians in the world, and Honduran businesses report that they incur huge costs from crime and violence. A Mexican cartel looking for an offshore base would be well advised to try these two countries first.

Does experience bear this out? Measuring exactly how much narcotic offshoring goes on in each country is tricky. But one proxy measurement of criminal activity is violence, which tends to flare up when the cartels move in. Looking at the murder rate, it seems that crime

FIGURE 5.1 Cartel Competitiveness Report

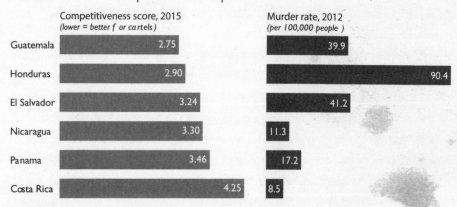

NOTE: Belize, with a population of just 300,000, is excluded, as the World Economic Forum does not collect data from there.

SOURCES: Data from World Economic Forum 2015; UNODC 2012.

has indeed flourished in the countries where it is easiest for the gangs to do business. Costa Rica, Panama, and Nicaragua have murder rates that are fairly low by regional standards, suggesting a fairly limited cartel presence. El Salvador, Guatemala, and Honduras, by contrast, have dramatically higher rates of violence.[12]

•   •   •

Putting a brake on drug cartels' offshore activity is hard, and subverting the World Economic Forum's figures may be slightly frivolous. But there is a serious point to it. Indices such as the World Bank's "Doing Business" report have made a huge difference in the way that countries are run, by providing a simple, cheap, and achievable road map and rewarding those countries that follow it. Why not do something similar in the field of security?

A few organizations already compile studies a bit like this: Transparency International, for instance, publishes an annual "corruption perceptions index," which shames countries into doing more to stamp out graft. But it is based on surveys of businesspeople, and it is not clear exactly what countries ought to do to make things better. "Doing Business," in comparison, measures hard facts (such as how many forms one has to fill out to arrange an electricity connection) and makes simple, doable recommendations.

It wouldn't be difficult to do something more like "Doing Business" devoted to the subject of security. Such an index could record things like the number of police per capita, officers' salaries as a percentage of the national average, whether laws have been passed to allow things such as extradition and wire-tapping, and how tight the gun-control rules are. Some of the attractions of Central America to criminals will only be solved over time, such as the big, cheap labor market. But others can be fixed more easily. After a long ban, Honduras recently began allowing the extradition of its citizens, who now face the fearsome threat of American justice and jails, rather than just the feeble local prosecutors. Guatemala has started using polygraphs when hiring cops, a small step toward tackling corruption. Plenty of low-hanging fruit remains to be picked: gun laws remain extremely lax in much of the region, for instance. Recording, adding up, and publicizing this information would give an incentive for countries to improve their performance, as well as provide a useful to-do list for them to follow.

In the meantime, the abuse of regions such as Central America by international drug gangs is leading to calls for a new approach to the drug problem from a growing constituency of countries. A year after my meeting with Álvaro Colom, I meet his successor as president of Guatemala, Otto Pérez Molina, who cuts a very different figure. In contrast to Colom's shuffling, mumbling demeanor, Pérez Molina, a former director of military intelligence, strides around purposefully and speaks with a clear, loud voice. During the election campaign, his piercing gaze looked down on the country from bright-orange posters all around the country. His promise was that he would attack crime with a *mano dura*—an "iron fist"—which is also, I discovered, an apt description of his handshake. I first see him in action at a meeting of the World Economic Forum in Mexico, not long after his inauguration. It is a speech that stuns the audience.

The *mano dura* campaign led many people to assume that Pérez Molina would take a hard line against the drugs trade. To everyone's astonishment, following his inauguration the president did an about-face, announcing that, in fact, he was in favor of the legalization of all drugs. As a military man who has devoted years of his life to attempting to stamp out the traffickers by force, his calls for a cease fire had real weight. "Twenty years ago, I was director of intelligence in Guatemala. . . . We had great successes. A lot of cocaine was captured. Plantations of marijuana were destroyed. Also at that time many drug-trafficking bosses were captured. Twenty years later, I assume the presidency of the country—and I find that the drug-trafficking organizations are bigger," he told the WEF. Policy makers in the West have to acknowledge that the current approach of suppressing drugs by force is causing casualties well beyond the people who take them, he tells me later. "Today more people are dying in Central America through drug trafficking, and the violence it generates, than are dying in the United States through the consumption of drugs," he says. His calls have been echoed in neighboring countries: Costa Rica has decriminalized marijuana and called for international rethinking of the approach to other drugs. Pérez Molina's presidency ended in scandal in 2015, when he resigned after being charged with corruption, apparently unrelated to narcotics. But his impact on the drugs debate in the region has been a lasting one, showing that calls for rethinking of the war on drugs can come from the right as well as from the left.

In the short term, offshoring has provided cartels with a useful way of cutting their costs, using the cheap labor and relaxed regulatory environment on offer in Central America. But just like offshoring in the legitimate economy, the practice is having political repercussions. The soaring levels of violence in newly afflicted countries has amplified calls for a new approach in the West to the drug problem. A new group of countries, some of them with very outspoken governments, is pushing for radical changes to the way the business is regulated. Meanwhile, the effortless move by organized crime from Mexico to Central America has forced even advocates of the war on drugs to recognize that suppressing the trade in one place can have the effect of simply pushing it up somewhere else. In the long run, the narcotics industry's move offshore could have profoundly disruptive consequences for the cartels.

"Bin Laden," the author's driver, peers over the edge of the *camino de la muerte* (death road) on the way to a coca plantation in the Bolivian Andes (Chapter 1).

© Tom Wainwright

Carlos Mojica Lechuga, leader of Barrio 18, a gang in El Salvador, pictured with fellow mobsters in Cojutepeque prison (Chapter 2).
© Edgardo Ayala

Joaquín "El Chapo" ("Shorty") Guzmán, leader of the Sinaloa cartel. Captured in 2014, he escaped after little more than a year (Chapter 4).
© Agence France-Presse

A federal police officer on patrol in Acapulco, Mexico, where a cartel takeover battle has flared up in recent years (Chapter 6).

© Keith Dannemiller

Matt Bowden, a New Zealander who made a fortune selling legal highs and now spends his time performing as Starboy, a glam-metal act (Chapter 7).
© James Niland

Assorted fake IDs used by Ross William Ulbricht, aka "Dread Pirate Roberts,"
who ran the Silk Road, the Amazon.com of narcotics (Chapter 8).
© New York Times/Redux/Eyevine

Mexican president Felipe Calderón's hit list of cartel kingpins. He put more
than half of them out of business, but violence increased (Chapter 2).
© Tom Wainwright

The fence separating Tijuana, Mexico, from California. Cartels have diversified from drug smuggling into people smuggling (Chapter 9).

© Getty Images

A technician examines marijuana plants in a facility belonging to Medicine Man, a legal cannabis company, in Denver, Colorado (Chapter 10).
© Medicine Man

Chapter 6

THE PROMISE AND PERILS OF FRANCHISING

How the Mob Has Borrowed from McDonald's

"Look, asshole, we're going to make things really clear for you."

The message that flashed up on Ricardo's Facebook page came from his daughter's account. But his daughter clearly wasn't the one doing the writing.

"We've been watching your little princess. We know where she lives, and when she goes to school." The threat went on, listing details that made clear that the authors had indeed been keeping tabs on the girl's movements. The message ended with a demand that Ricardo deposit 20,000 pesos, or about $1,350, into a Mexican bank account. If he failed to comply, it warned, "I'm going to tell my guys who are parked over the road watching your girl to go in and get her, and you know you won't see her again."[1]

Extortion attempts like this used to be carried out via "poison pen" letters, slipped under doors in the dead of night. Anonymous phone calls were the next stage in the crime's evolution. Now, such threats are often made via social media, which offers the same anonymity with the nasty twist that the extortionist has access to personal details and photos of the victim's family and friends.

Whether the threat is made on paper, over the phone, or online, the tactics have always been the same. The victim knows that the perpetrator is likely to be bluffing, but also that such threats are sometimes carried out. More than a thousand kidnappings are recorded each year in Mexico, and many thousands more go unreported.[2] Most people, including Ricardo, hold their nerve, call the police, and never hear from the extortionists again. But a few are not so brave.

The extortion industry flourishes because the cost of making the threat is so low that the response rate doesn't have to be very high for the business to remain viable. Sending a Facebook message is free, and making phone calls is cheap, often done by banks of prisoners who are employed to make the calls from prison using smuggled cell phones. Meanwhile, the risk of prosecution is minimal (Ricardo reported the extortionists' bank details to the Mexico City police, who still failed to catch the culprits). Even a low response rate therefore makes the business successful.

In this way the extortion game is similar to the economics of sending spam e-mail. When receiving an e-mail promising a share of a lost Nigerian inheritance or cheap Viagra, nearly everyone clicks delete. But a tiny number takes the bait. Computer scientists at the University of California–Berkeley and UC–San Diego hijacked a working spam network to see how the business operated. They found that the spammers, who were selling fake "herbal aphrodisiacs," made only one sale for every 12.5 million e-mails they sent: a response rate of 0.00001 percent. Each sale was worth an average of less than $100. It doesn't look like much of a business. But sending out the e-mails was so cheap and easy—it was done using a network of hijacked PCs, which the fraudsters used free of charge—that the spammers made a healthy profit. Pumping out hundreds of millions of e-mails a day, they had a daily income of about $7,000, or more than $2.5 million a year, the researchers figured.[3]

Extortionists' costs are somewhat higher than those of spammers, and the risks they face are greater, hopeless though the Mexican police may be. So the response rate to their demands has to be higher, in order to make the enterprise profitable. Achieving a high response rate depends on making their threats seem credible: if people fear the extortionists, they are more likely to cough up. So in order to show their targets that they mean business, the small-time crooks who run extortion rackets are always on the lookout for ways to make themselves sound more fearsome.

It is here that organized crime steps in. What the local gangsters need is a recognized brand, to strike terror into the hearts of their victims and convince them to pay. At the same time, ambitious drug cartels are in the market for cheap and quick ways to expand their empires. It is a perfect match: the local thugs get to use the cartel's name, and the cartel benefits from a bit of extra manpower. The simplest way for small-time gangsters and big-time organized crime to come together like this, some have found, is by drawing up a franchise agreement.

.   .   .

The first franchising "royalties" were literally paid to monarchs. Franchises, whose name comes from the French word *franche*, meaning "free" or "exempt," were granted by medieval kings, who would give a person the right to carry out some service or other—building a road, organizing a market, collecting taxes—and in return levy a fee. Franchising as we now understand it first became prominent in the business world in the nineteenth century, when the Singer sewing machine company gave salesmen the exclusive right to sell their machines in particular regions of the United States, in return for a cut of their sales. The idea really took off in the 1950s, when big American chains such as McDonald's and Burger King used franchising as a way to grow rapidly, taking advantage of the post–World War II economic boom. These days, there are about half a million franchisee-run businesses in the United States. Car dealerships, gas stations, retailers, and, of course, restaurants are the biggest sectors of the franchising industry.[4]

To that list, we can now add organized crime. Criminal businesses have usually been run on very different principles from franchises. Historically, drug cartels have been rigidly managed from the top down, with a single, all-powerful boss sitting proudly at the top of an obedient pyramid of underlings. But recently some Mexican cartels have begun a radical process of decentralization. Like burger chains after World War II, Mexico's drug traffickers have gone through an extraordinary period of expansion over the past two decades. In the 1990s, they were merely assistants to the Colombian cartels, which employed the Mexicans to transport drugs over their territory and into the United States. But following a crackdown on crime in Colombia in the 1990s and the deaths of many of the country's capos, including Pablo Escobar, the Mexicans managed to grab a larger part of the value chain. Rather than merely doing the bidding of the Colombians, they have come to oversee the whole operation, from production to distribution.

No group has grown more quickly than the Zetas. Until as recently as 2010, the Zetas were scarcely considered a cartel in their own right, instead functioning as a paramilitary group that carried out enforcement operations for the Gulf cartel. But since a split with the Gulf in 2010, they have grown at dizzying speed, spreading across eastern Mexico, along the Caribbean coast of Central America, and, according to some recent reports, establishing links with the 'Ndrangheta mafia in Italy. Truly, they are the McDonald's of organized crime, with a branch in every city in some regions.

In order to finance this turbo-charged growth, the Zetas have employed a version of franchising. According to a recent analysis[5] by the regional head of the UN's Office on Drugs and Crime, the Zetas have decided not to send their own representatives into new markets to set up criminal outposts from scratch and instead have adopted local gangsters into their club, as franchisees. Zeta scouts go to new areas and identify the most promising local criminals, "to whom the mother cell offers a kind of franchise on the use of the Zetas' criminal marque," the UN report says. As part of the "affiliation package," the Zetas' central command provides the franchisees with military training, and in some cases arms. In return, franchisees share a slice of their revenues with the central organization and agree to form a "solidarity pact," an agreement that they will fight for the Zetas if a war breaks out with another cartel.

The benefits to both parties are similar to those that accrue to franchiser and franchisee in the ordinary business world. For the franchising company, it means rapid, self-financing growth. McDonald's requires its franchisees to buy the restaurants that they run, stipulating that they must have at least $750,000 at their disposal before they are even considered for taking on a franchise. This allows the business to grow quickly in terms of revenues, without needing to shell out for new assets (85 percent of McDonald's 35,000 restaurants around the world are owned by franchisees, not by McDonald's). For the Zetas, this principle is even more important. As an illegal business, its access to credit is severely limited, meaning that self-financing growth holds special appeal.

In addition, the franchiser is able to take advantage of the franchisee's entrepreneurial dynamism. Rather than being a mere employee, a cog in a vast machine, a Zeta franchisee has responsibility for wringing the most money possible out of the particular patch that he has been given. With this responsibility comes what Peter Drucker, perhaps the most influential of all management gurus, described as the "managerial attitude"—more important than pay or skill, he argued, this attitude "makes the individual see his job, his work, and his product the way a manager sees them, that is, in relation to the group and the product as a whole."[6] Franchisees also bring local knowledge. This is as valuable in the criminal game as it is in the burger business—perhaps more so, as corrupt connections with local law enforcement, a crucial condition for success, are more easily forged by local operators. Correspondingly, the franchisee can make use of the mother organization's expertise. Part of the deal is that the franchiser passes on its "recipe" for success, whether it concerns cooking french fries or making car bombs.

Perhaps most important, there is the brand. McDonald's hasn't conquered the world by making food that tastes delicious: it has done so by making food that tastes reliably the same. A Big Mac bought in Bangkok or Beijing is more or less identical to one bought in Oak Brook, Illinois, where the company is headquartered. It certainly isn't the nicest meal you can have in any one of those cities, and it probably isn't even the best value. But consumers know that any restaurant displaying the famous golden arches is going to meet a basic level of quality. Franchisees are buying a reputation they would otherwise have to earn. And when McDonald's sponsors the Olympics or hires Justin Timberlake to endorse its food, every franchise benefits from the advertising message, too.

For an illustration of how this works in the underworld, visit the cool surroundings of the Roxy *nevería,* an ice-cream parlor in a tony suburb of Mexico City. The Roxy is a Mexican institution: founded in 1946, it looks as if it hasn't changed very much since then in terms of its décor, which includes swiveling bar stools and candy-striped awnings. Not so long ago, the Roxy was the victim of an extortion attempt. A man arrived in a taxi and delivered an envelope containing a tape recorder, which held a recorded message demanding a payment of 250,000 pesos ($17,000). If the sum wasn't paid, the tape promised, the manager's family would be hurt, or worse. The warning might not have been taken seriously—or have made the city newspapers—had it not been for the fact that it was signed by "Comandante Juan Ballesteros," who claimed to be a local representative of La Familia Michoacana.

The mention of the name La Familia Michoacana gave an immediate weight to the threat. The extortionist may not have looked particularly tough or have been carrying an assault rifle. But La Familia's reputation—as a gang that once rolled five severed heads onto a nightclub dance floor in Michoacán—meant that the people at Roxy knew what they were dealing with. Allying himself to the famous brand of La Familia was intended to increase the response rate to the extortionist's threats and make his business more profitable. (In the case of the Roxy, it backfired: bravely, and unusually, the ice-cream parlor's owners took the story to the media and to the police, who for once managed to round up the alleged perpetrators.)

The franchise model also explains why the Zetas, in particular, engage in such appalling acts of brutality. They are the ones who, more than any other Mexican mob, take care to photograph and video their atrocities, from beheadings to hangings. A gruesome murder carried out by the Zetas in northern Mexico hardens the image of its franchises all over the world, just as an advertising campaign by McDonald's at the World Cup in Brazil strengthens the appeal of its outlets everywhere else.

Of course, there is the danger of free riding. Many robbers and extortionists claim to be allied with the Zetas, La Familia, or some other cartel, despite having nothing to do with them. For the franchising system to work, criminal gangs have to protect their trademarks just as ferociously as legitimate firms do. The UN report notes that "new cells are responsible for preserving the 'good name' of the Zetas by chastising with violence (death) the use of the Zetas' trademark by unauthorized criminal operators." Talk of "trademarks" and "brands" isn't just metaphorical. Cartels often have their own logos, which appear on uniforms and equipment issued to franchisees. Baseball caps and backpacks branded with a Zetas logo—a shield split into three segments, containing outline maps of Mexico, the gang's home state of Tamaulipas, and a letter Z—have been discovered in Zeta-affiliated hideouts around Mexico and Central America. All of this gear, from armored vests to weapons, ammunition, vehicles, and so on, is cheaper and easier to acquire in bulk, another benefit to being part of a franchise. Just as McDonald's can order its ovens, fryers, cash registers, tables, and chairs by the thousand, the Zetas can buy or steal large quantities of equipment to distribute among their franchisees, who would otherwise be left paying more for inferior, homemade gear.

On a hot day in a city in northern Mexico, in a restaurant attached to an upscale mall, I have an appointment with a man who was once a franchisee of sorts with the Sinaloa cartel. The franchisee—we'll call him Miguel—is now in his fifties, a short, wiry mountain man with an ingrained frown that comes from a lifetime squinting into the sun. He is a man of few words, and he scans the restaurant's clientele cautiously as we talk over lunch at a table outside. Miguel comes from Sinaloa and, as a young man, became an "associate" of the local cartel. He didn't work for it directly, he emphasizes, with professional pride—rather, he operated under a sort of license from the main organization. Sinaloa has worked in this way for a long time, so much so that it is often called the Sinaloa Federation, rather than cartel. Miguel would get up in the middle of the night to walk up into the mountains to collect marijuana from farmers there, then bring it back to Culiacán, the state capital. There, he would get it ready to be smuggled over the border, compressing it into tiny packages using a hydraulic pump before wrapping it in polythene and dipping it in wax, in order to disguise the drug's pungent smell.

The franchise arrangement gave Miguel and his fellow traffickers the freedom to go about their business as they chose, dealing with their favorite farmers, setting their own quantities and prices, and generally working in whatever way they preferred. A similar setup seems to be under way at the moment in the southern Mexican state of Guerrero, where the business of growing and processing opium poppies for heroin production has been handed over to independent entrepreneurs, who operate small patches for the cartels on a franchise-like basis. Lately, it seems, there has been feuding among these groups—something that Miguel says has changed since his day, when there were few if any run-ins with rival traffickers. "There was always the danger of being captured by the police or the army," he says (and indeed, that was what eventually happened to him—a spell in prison was enough to put him off the game when he got out). "But in Sinaloa we had no problems with the other cartels. It was easier to work with them than to kill them." He pushes some food around his plate. "Today they don't understand that."

Since Miguel's time running marijuana in the Sierra Madre, the boom in franchising has caused a restructuring of the industry. Historically, drug-trafficking organizations aimed simply to control the supply of drugs, getting them from A to B along whatever path worked best. The Zetas have a different model: rather than controlling routes, they try to control territory. Once they have granted a franchise in a particular area—it could be a small town or a whole state—they expect their local representatives to control all of the criminal activity that takes place there, sending a cut of the loot back to Zeta central command. As well as moving drugs, Zeta cells use their territorial control to engage in many other types of criminal enterprises, using the same local connections. Extortion is one lucrative business; kidnapping is another. Local drug-dealing makes up a growing part of their income. A curious side effect of this is that taxi drivers have become targeted for employment by the cartels. Taxis, as mobile, private vehicles with an excuse to stop anywhere and carry anyone, make ideal vessels for ferrying drugs and kidnap victims around. Control of a city's taxis is thus a prize worth fighting for, and taxi drivers are frequently subjected to intimidation. "You can run but you can't hide: we're coming for you and your families," read a note recently posted in the men's bathroom of a taxi-drivers' union in Playa del Carmen, apparently written by Sinaloa mobsters to drivers who were signed up to the Zetas.

In Mexico's northeast, Zeta franchises have been known to deal "Z"-branded whisky, which they force local bars to sell. They have also got into the pirate DVD business, branding their products with little "Z" sticky labels. Rodrigo Canales, a Mexican professor at Yale University's school of management, believes that one reason for this diversification is that the Zetas don't have first-class connections in the international drugs business. The gang was "founded in treason," he notes, when it betrayed its former employer, the Gulf cartel. In doing so, the Zetas lost their links to American drugs markets, and so they have had to rely on other means of income instead.[7]

Lately, some of the worst violence in Mexico has been in Guerrero. A sprawling, poor state that stretches from the dusty center of the country down to the lush Pacific coast, it has long been a rough-and-ready place where the government's power has a limited reach. The very word *guerrero* means "warrior"; the state flag portrays a pre-Columbian soldier wearing a jaguar skin and wielding a spiked club. In recent years the state's tough reputation has been borne out. In the past decade the murder rate has trebled,[8] clearing tourists out of Acapulco, where human heads now occasionally roll up on the beach. Even the recorded murder figures may understate the true extent of the violence, as the warring factions have a habit of hiding the dead bodies. In 2015, police were alerted to a nasty smell coming from an abandoned crematorium, where inside they discovered sixty-one rotting corpses. One of the most talked-about recent episodes of violence in Guerrero was the disappearance of forty-three trainee-teachers in 2014 in the town of Iguala, a crime that still hasn't been solved and probably never will be.

There is evidence that Guerrero's recent descent into chaos may be an example of what can happen when criminal franchising agreements break up. In the ordinary business world, one of the most common causes of complaints among franchisees is the belief that they are having to battle for turf against rival franchisees of the same company. Ordinarily, if a competitor opens up shop nearby, a company can try to outdo it in terms of quality or undercut it in terms of price. In the case of franchising, this isn't really possible: if a McDonald's restaurant is doing a roaring trade in a neighborhood where it is the only branch, and suddenly the parent company announces that it is going to open two more franchises in the area, the restaurant will lose revenue to competitors against whom it cannot compete, because they are selling the same products at the same price.

The question of territory, and the proximity of other branches belonging to the same brand, becomes crucial to the success or failure of a franchisee. To the franchiser, however, it isn't so important. The mother brand makes its money by taking a cut of franchisees' sales, not of their profits. Opening more branches will always lead to an increase in *total* sales, even if each new branch cannibalizes some of the business of existing outlets. The interests of franchiser and franchisee are therefore not very well aligned, making the question of territory a subject ripe for conflict. Local managers have frequently taken their bosses to court over "encroachment" by new franchisees. Burger King, Mc-Donald's, Sheraton hotels, and America's Favorite Chicken Company (which owns Popeyes) are among the chains that have been sued by franchisees who were unhappy about new branches opening too close to their existing patch.[9] Judges have taken different sides in different cases, sometimes recognizing an implied agreement by the franchiser not to open other branches in the vicinity, and other times saying that it is tough luck for the franchisee.

In the world of criminal franchises, of course, there is no recourse to the courts. So when a cartel franchise overstretches itself, disputes are solved in the traditional manner, with spiked clubs and other weapons. It seems that in Guerrero, something like that may have been happening. The case of the missing forty-three students remains murky, but it appears likely that the people responsible for the students' fate were from a gang called Guerreros Unidos (Warriors United). According to most analysts, this gang began as a local franchise of the Beltrán Leyva Organization, a big-time cartel that managed the international smuggling of multiple types of drugs. The Beltrán Leyvas, a family led by Arturo, known as "The Beard," employed several different gangs all over their territory, which was centered in the Guerrero region. But it seems they may have taken on too many franchisees. As well as the Guerreros Unidos, who managed the northern *tierra caliente*, or "hot country," the Beltrán Leyvas were employing gangs such as the Rojos (Reds), who looked after the center of the state, and a mob that called itself the Independent Cartel of Acapulco, which managed the port. It also sometimes drafted in help from gangs such as the Ardillos (Squirrels) and the Granados.[10]

All of these Beltrán Leyva franchises were operating in Guerrero. It seems that it may all have gotten a bit too competitive. After the Beltrán Leyva Organization was weakened, following the death of Arturo the Beard, its various franchisees began to scrap with each other. The Guerreros Unidos, Rojos, and Independents of Acapulco have lately all been at each others' throats, as well as fighting off gangs belonging to other criminal franchises. This is the cause of much of Guerrero's awful violence. And it may have been the cause of the disappearance of the forty-three students: one theory is that the Guerreros Unidos thought that the students, who were traveling in a stolen bus to attend a demonstration in Mexico City, were members of one of the state's many other small criminal bands, using the bus to transport heroin. Franchising overreach has ruined the efficiency of the drug-smuggling operation in central Mexico, as rival franchisees spend their time murdering each other (and innocent civilians), rather than getting on with the business of trafficking drugs.

This isn't the only drawback to franchise arrangements. Local, territorially based franchises are much less mobile than teams that are led from the top down. In the ongoing war between the Zetas and the Sinaloa cartel, Sinaloa has often proved more capable of striking at the Zetas in their heartlands. During one flare-up in hostilities, it dispatched a hit squad of "Matazetas," or Zeta Killers, to the state of Veracruz, where the gang did just what its name suggests, murdering scores of local members of the rival cartel. With a model that involves co-opting locally rooted thugs, the Zetas are much less capable of responding in this way.

Finally, although decentralized leadership has its benefits, it also means that the cartel gives up some control to local managers, who may make mistakes. And if a major blunder is made by a local branch, it can have consequences for the entire brand. Again, consider the dangers faced in this regard by ordinary franchises. McDonald's has some 30,000 branches run by franchisees, who are trained and made to follow a rule book but are given certain leeway in how they run their businesses. The chain's extraordinary success shows how well the model can work. But looser reins may sometimes allow lapses in quality control that tarnish the whole brand's image. In 2014, a McDonald's restaurant in Japan managed to serve a customer a batch of french fries containing a human tooth, a story that made diners around the world think twice about biting into their Big Macs.

The same risk is faced by the cartels. With a decentralized system of management, errors by inexperienced or poorly monitored local bosses are more likely than in a top-down system. And a mistake by a local affiliate can have devastating consequences for the whole brand. Consider the case of Jaime Zapata, a special agent with US Immigration and Customs Enforcement who was murdered by cartel henchmen in Mexico in 2011. Zapata and a colleague were driving an armored Chevy Suburban from Monterrey to Mexico City when they were forced off the road in an ambush by armed men, just south of the city of San Luis Potosí. Their $160,000 armored car was able to deflect the nearly ninety bullets fired at it by the cartels. But in stopping the car, Zapata put the car into "park" mode, causing the doors automatically to unlock. The mobsters were able to open the door and shoot the two agents, wounding Zapata fatally.

It later emerged that the gunmen were local members of the Zetas who had probably spotted Zapata and his colleague earlier when they stopped to buy a sandwich by the side of the road. It seems that the mobsters thought that the two burly Latino men were rival cartel members, not American agents. One member of the gang later told the American authorities that he and his fellow Zeta affiliates had a "standing order from the Zetas leadership to steal vehicles deemed valuable to the cartel." Murdering Zapata broke a serious unwritten rule of Mexico's cartels: never kill Americans, and especially not American cops. In spite of the endemic violence in the country and the high level of involvement of American agents in Mexican affairs, Zapata is believed to have been the first American law-enforcement official to die in the line of duty in Mexico since 1985.

This was a very serious miscalculation, and it provoked a strong response from the United States. The week after Zapata's murder, federal agents arrested more than one hundred drug-trafficking suspects in a

coordinated sweep across the United States. The leader of the gang
that killed Zapata was arrested in Mexico and extradited to Washington, DC. This was only the beginning: in 2012, the leader of the Zetas,
Heriberto Lazcano, was shot dead by Mexican marines. The following
year, the new leader, Miguel Treviño, was captured. The cartel continues, but it has been weakened, and its senior leaders paid a heavy price
for the incompetence of one small group of affiliates. Just as a single
blunder in a restaurant kitchen can tarnish a company's global brand, a
single dire mistake by a group of Zetas affiliates triggered devastating
strikes against the cartel's top leadership. Licensing your brand comes
with serious risks attached.

•   •   •

The franchising of criminal brands has been a successful strategy for
drug cartels, but it represents a dangerous development for everyone
else. It has allowed a few criminal organizations to expand very rapidly,
while diversifying their revenue stream from simple drug trafficking
into a whole spectrum of illegal activity. Their incomes are increased
by the fact that local cells have instant brand recognition, enabling
them better to extort and intimidate. Equipment is easier and cheaper
to acquire in bulk, meaning that local members are better equipped
than they would otherwise be. Advertising is more effective, as one
atrocity enhances the notoriety of all franchisees. Meanwhile, territorial squabbling between local branches means more violence than
before.

Is there any silver lining in all of this? One positive development
is that franchised organizations generally seem to be less professional
than cartels that are dedicated purely to the business of trafficking
drugs. Gangs such as the Zetas, which get their money by taxing the
earnings of local bands of thugs, have proved less adept than other cartels at corrupting or intimidating senior members of the government.
In its prime, the Juárez cartel's employees included Mexico's drug tsar.
In its terror campaign against the Colombian state, the Medellín cartel

brought down a passenger airliner, killing 107 people onboard. Organizations like these represented an existential threat to the state itself. The same is not true of networks of thugs like the Zetas, for all the violence they cause.

They may also be simpler to pacify, in the long run. Old-school cartels like Sinaloa exist everywhere and nowhere, their business based on smuggling goods rather than holding territory. Drive them out of Mexico, and they set up shop in Central America; put the heat on them in Colombia, and they scuttle over the border to Peru. A franchise like the Zetas, by contrast, lives or dies by the territory it controls. Force it off a particular patch, and its income from that area is lost. So far, the local police in Mexico have proved largely incapable of doing this. But hounding a gang of bandits out of town is at least a simpler target than dismantling a complex international business.

Franchises' tendency to slide toward infighting may mean that the Zetas' model of expansion ultimately causes it to unravel. In drug trafficking as in burger flipping, franchisees, who are not truly part of the company, are never going to be quite as loyal to the brand as regular staff. *Entrepreneur* magazine has pointed out that franchises tend to have a weaker "core community" of employees than do top-down organizations. The same is true of criminal gangs. No one knows this better than the Zetas, who started out as the armed bodyguards of the Gulf cartel. Within a few years the Zetas had become too ambitious for their limited role, at which point they turned against their Gulf employers, all but destroying them. As they take on more and more franchisees, the Zetas take on more and more risk. The franchising model that has powered the cartel's growth could yet prove to be its undoing.

Chapter 7

INNOVATING AHEAD
OF THE LAW

Research and Development in
the "Legal Highs" Industry

Between a beauty salon and a fish-and-chip shop on a busy road in
north London is a narrow little store with a greenish light shining
through its steamed-up windows. Inside, psychedelic trance music
plays softly in the background. Along one wall is a row of illuminated
cabinets displaying the goods on offer. There are pipes and bongs, in
all kinds of novelty shapes: a gun, a gas mask, a big pair of porcelain
breasts. A clothing rail is loaded up with cannabis-themed T-shirts.
One cupboard holds various innocuous-looking containers, including cans of beer and tubes of Pringles, which unscrew to reveal hidden compartments in which to secrete one's "stash" (of what, the shop
does not suggest). People with things to hide can also buy a working
computer mouse that contains a tiny, hidden safe.

Head shops like this one are just about tolerated in most countries
on the basis that the "lifestyle accessories" they sell are, in theory, not
supposed to be used with drugs. The many and varied bongs and pipes
"are sold on the understanding that they will not be used as a means
of smoking illegal substances," the company says on its website. As far

as the managers are concerned, consumers will presumably sit back in their cannabis-leaf patterned T-shirts and use their cannabis-patterned lighters to spark up a Bob Marley–themed bong filled with . . . tobacco.

The authorities seldom kick up a fuss because head shops don't supply the drugs themselves. But nowadays, this is changing. On sale online and in almost any major city, from London to Los Angeles, are psychoactive substances in a new class, known variously as "legal highs" or "designer drugs." Concocted in laboratories rather than on Andean hillsides or in Afghan poppy fields, these synthetic drugs mimic the effects of more mainstream narcotics. Some are close cousins of MDMA, also known as ecstasy. Others claim to have an effect closer to that of cannabis. The game-changing difference is that in most jurisdictions these fast-evolving chemical highs are completely legal to sell, possess, and consume.

I ask the friendly, bearded young man behind the counter if he has any legal highs for sale. "Well, they're not 'highs,' because they're not for human consumption," he says, his freckled young face completely inscrutable. "But"—and he raises an eyebrow very slightly—"I do have some *aromatherapy incense*, if you would like to see that." I ask to examine a selection, and he brings out five packets of what he says are the most popular ones ("I can't actually recommend any, obviously") from under the counter. The glossy, plastic packets are about the size and thickness of a pack of baseball cards. Each costs £10 ($15) and contains one gram of "incense," or whatever one wants to call the substance inside. One packet, "Jammin' Joker," shows a dreadlocked smiley face in sunglasses wearing a Rastafarian-style hat; another, "Psy-clone," has swirls of colors, its letters in a back-to-front jumble. "Clockwork Orange" has a manically staring, orange eyeball in the shape of a clock face.

The shop assistant declines to say anything about the respective qualities of the different mixtures, instead suggesting I do some research online. A quick look around the Web turns up some distinctly mixed reviews. "Goooood . . . got me going for 76 hours straight!!!!!!"

says one five-star rating of Clockwork Orange. Another user of the same substance says that he "spent the last of this Hell I was trapped in wrapped round the toilet silently crying and waiting for my head to stop throbbing." Either way, it appears that most people are not using the little packets for aromatherapy.

The legal highs business has the potential to turn the drugs industry upside down. How has this new category of narcotics managed to escape prohibition, and what does its emergence mean for dealers of other drugs?

•　　•　　•

To understand how legal highs soared into a commanding position in the international drugs market, start in New Zealand. The beautiful Pacific archipelago, where Hobbits frolic, may seem like just about the least likely place in the world to become a hub for the narcotics trade. If you were an international exporter of cocaine or heroin, would you bother to ship drugs to New Zealand? The country has a population of only 4.5 million, about the same as Kentucky. It lies in the middle of nowhere, 1,000 miles off the southern tip of Australia. If you wanted to ship cocaine from the coast of Peru, the nearest serious coca-growing country, it would mean a voyage of more than 6,000 miles. There are no direct flights to Auckland, its largest city, from any cocaine-producing country. The upshot is that imported drugs are incredibly hard to get hold of in New Zealand. Only about one in every two hundred adults reports having taken cocaine in the past year, a very low rate for a rich country (in the United States, for instance, the figure is about one in forty-five). Heroin is vanishingly rare: rates of usage are one-sixth what they are in the United States and one-eighth their level in Britain.

But the Kiwis are only human, and they like to take drugs just as much as people in other countries. Indeed, when it comes to drugs that they *can* get hold of, they consume them in prodigious quantities. Consider cannabis, which can be grown just as easily in the lush New

Zealand countryside as it can in Morocco or Mexico. Kiwis grow and
smoke masses of it—in fact, according to the United Nations, no country in the world smokes more marijuana per person than New Zealand, where one in seven adults claims to have gotten stoned in the past
year. But it isn't only pot: New Zealand also has the second-highest
consumption of amphetamines,[1] which are made locally, in small laboratories dotted all over the islands. Despite its tiny population, New
Zealand shuts down more crystal-meth labs each year than any country in the world apart from the United States and Ukraine.[2] Getting
drugs into the country may be hard, but that has only made the Kiwis
experts in producing and consuming narcotics of their own.

New Zealand's love affair with synthetic drugs began around the
turn of the millennium, when methamphetamine first became popular. Meth was made using precursor chemicals smuggled in from
China, supposedly intended to be used in cold and flu medicines. The
drug has taken off all over Asia, where cocaine is relatively scarce and
access to precursors is easy. (In Thailand, where meth has caught on
in a big way, it is known simply as *yaa baa*, the "madness drug.") With
rates of addiction soaring, the government of New Zealand launched a
crackdown on methamphetamine, intercepting more precursor drugs
and ordering more raids on the "kitchens" where it was being cooked.
It wasn't long before Kiwis began to look for an alternative.

This was when a young narco-entrepreneur named Matt Bowden
entered the scene. If the world's top international traffickers were ever
to hold a conference—a sort of Davos of drugs—then Bowden would
stand out. First, there is the hair: long, blond, and blow-dried to feathery
perfection in a way that would make Jennifer Aniston jealous. This is
complemented by a wardrobe including black-and-white leopard-print
suits and military-style greatcoats with oversized epaulettes in gleaming metallic silver. To top off the look, he is often to be seen wearing
lashings of makeup: thick black eyeliner, sometimes surrounded by
elaborate patterns in white or silver, and set off with colored contact
lenses. The macho *narcotraficantes* of Latin America might curl their

mustachioed lips in disgust at his appearance. But Bowden once ran a multimillion-dollar drug-dealing empire.

A native of New Zealand, he made one of the most unusual fortunes in drug dealing. He has sold drugs to thousands of partygoers worldwide, raking in millions of dollars in revenue. These days he has taken a step back from the narcotics business, instead spending much of his time touring the world performing rock concerts under the stage name "Starboy." His shows mix the glamorous with the Gothic, with bright lights and feather-boa-wearing dancers bopping in the background. As Starboy, he has had a top-ten hit in New Zealand and has now spun off a range of clothing, based on what he calls "Steampunk Burlesque Circus Express." His Twitter profile describes him as "an interdimensional traveller, redefining the boundaries of psychedelic rock music and progressive drug policy." All this means that he is by no means your typical drug baron. Yet the strangest thing about Bowden is this: although the Starboy empire was founded on drug money—piles of it—he has done it all without breaking the law.

He came into the drugs business as a consumer, with past addictions to various substances under his belt. After a family member died of an ecstasy overdose, Bowden became determined to come up with a safer, legal alternative to the drugs that were causing people harm. The drug that he settled on was benzylpiperazine, or BZP. A boring looking off-white powder, BZP was initially developed in the 1940s as a worming tablet for cattle. But tests revealed that it also had the side effect of giving people a euphoric rush, similar to that provided by amphetamines. Bowden began selling the drug as "party pills," via his company, Stargate International, which styled its products as "social tonics." In so doing, Bowden and Stargate became the most prominent ambassadors of an industry selling millions of legal, recreational drugs to young partygoers in the nightclubs of New Zealand.

The drug became wildly popular. By some estimates, up to 5 million BZP-laced "party pills" were being sold in New Zealand every year, equivalent to more than one dose for every person in the country.

Surveys showed that nearly one-quarter of Kiwis had tried the drug. It soon took off in other countries, becoming popular in Europe from around 2004 (in the United States it did less well, having been outlawed since 2002). As Bowden had promised, some people did indeed seem to be using BZP as a safer alternative to methamphetamine—in fact, one academic study suggested that rather than being a "gateway drug" to harder substances, it was offering some people a gateway out.[3] The existence of a new legal-highs industry meant that the drugs lost contact with organized crime, were less likely to be contaminated, and lost much of the stigma associated with addiction or adverse reactions, says Bowden now, when I catch him in between his tour dates. Regulating the drugs was better than simply banning them, he says: "The message was 'keep off the rocks,' not 'don't swim.'"

But although few medical problems were reported, there were worries about people mixing the drug with other substances. People taking BZP often seemed to combine it with the binge-drinking of alcohol, which created the social problems for which drink is well known. And without proper regulation, the "party pills" were on sale all over the place, especially in New Zealand, where they could be found in corner shops and gas stations, without age restrictions or adequate health warnings. "It was a cowboy industry—the drugs were being sold alongside sweets and ice cream," says Ross Bell, of the New Zealand Drug Foundation, an NGO. The government grew suspicious of the new craze, and although there had still not been a single recorded death from BZP, in 2008 it was banned in New Zealand. Most countries where it was still on sale quickly followed suit.

The ban on BZP looked like the end for legal highs. In fact, looking back now, it is clear that it was really the beginning of the industry. As soon as BZP was outlawed, the local narcotics industry quickly got to work developing alternative legal highs. Within days, replacement drugs such as trifluoromethylphenylpiperazine (TFMPP) and methylhexanamine (DMAA) hit the shelves. Like BZP, they were perfectly legal—in the sense they had not yet been banned—and there was nothing to prevent consumers from buying them, apart from their unpronounceable names. More bans followed, only for new varieties to be synthesized. Ever since the clampdown on BZP, a game of cat-and-mouse has been played out between the manufacturers and the authorities. A new synthetic narcotic is developed, becomes popular, is identified by the government, and gets banned—by which time the narco-chemists have come up with a slightly different variation, which immediately goes on sale. The speed at which they are modified means that these constantly evolving new strains of synthetic narcotics remain a step ahead of the law.

The new generations of legal highs have spread far beyond New Zealand. In the United States and Europe, they are sometimes coyly marketed as "bath salts." Like the head shops selling "aromatherapy incense," manufacturers believe that by marketing them as such, they further protect themselves from prosecution, should a substance be banned without them realizing it. Similar products are sold online, with disclaimers that the drugs are to be used as "plant food," "chemical supplies," or "novelty items." One website, OfficialBenzoFury.com, notes in tiny print that its products are "not for human consumption." Instead, it makes a point of referring to them all as "research chemicals." Consumers who leave reviews on the site go along with the charade, referring to their drug taking as scientific research. "Vibes were amazing in the lab rat cage," says one five-star review of methoxphenidine powder, marketed by the seller as "sure to be a very popular research chemical." Other vendors don't even bother to hide the fact that the substances are intended for getting high. Herbal Express, a website serving the British market, promises: "Today, you will no longer have to risk yourself spending years in jail just because you want that high. If you want legal weed, legal speed or legal ecstasy, why not buy legal highs online sold as research chemicals, party pills and herbal incense? It is the safe way to purchase these substances, and try a new experience in your life."

New drugs are being churned out at an extraordinary rate. The UN's Office on Drugs and Crime says that in 2013, it was alerted to ninety-seven new synthetic drugs. It now monitors 350 and counting of these "new psychoactive substances" around the world. The agency, usually upbeat about progress in the war on drugs, admits that "given the almost infinite scope to alter the chemical structure of [new psychoactive substances], new formulations are outpacing efforts to impose international control."[4] In Britain, the government's list of banned substances extends to more than six hundred drugs.[5] Household names like heroin and cocaine are outnumbered by scores of minutely different synthetic chemicals, from alphamethylphenethylhydroxylamine to zaleplon, ziperol, and zopiclone.

Police officers, who have the unenviable task of distinguishing one white powder from another, struggle to stay on top of the developing market. So do policy makers, whose job it is to monitor, test, and ultimately ban the endless cascade of new drugs. David Amess, a British member of Parliament, was tricked by a satirical television show into raising concerns in Parliament about an alarming new drug nicknamed "cake" (which, he advised viewers, was a "bisturbile cranabolic amphetamoid," which also went by the street name of "chronic Basildon donuts"). It was entirely fictitious.[6]

"Legal highs" sound safer than illegal drugs. In fact, they are often riskier. When it comes to older, plant-based drugs, such as marijuana, cocaine, and even heroin, users at least know roughly what they are getting. Smoking a joint of cannabis is less hazardous than smoking crack, which in turn is probably a bit safer than smoking heroin. By contrast, a legal high, which may have been on the market for only a matter of days, is an unknown quantity. The mystery white powder could be very strong or very weak, and there is no way of knowing until taking it. The number of cases of people being harmed after taking legal drugs is growing. Richard Philips, a twenty-six-year-old British man, was left brain damaged after taking a psychedelic substance called "N-Bomb" (better known to chemists as $C_{18}H_{22}INO_3$). A few weeks later, Jake Harris, a twenty-one-year-old from Manchester, stabbed himself through the neck while apparently tripping on the same drug. N-Bomb was perfectly legal in Britain at the time; the government banned it a few days after Harris's death.

Back in the London head shop, I try to get some advice from the man behind the counter. Are the best-sellers that he has laid out for me fairly similar in their effects, I ask? "No. They're not," he says firmly, in a way that suggests they are very different indeed. "I can't elaborate for obvious legal reasons. It would be a lot easier for everyone if I could, but there we are," he shrugs. Looking up the drugs online, the news isn't especially encouraging. There is one story about a man in Bolton who died a few minutes after smoking Psy-clone. Three fifteen-year-olds from Northumberland were hospitalized after they vomited blood after taking Clockwork Orange. Even some of the people selling the substances seem wary of them. "There's a lot better stuff out there than these," the shop assistant tells me, pointing at the packets he has offered me. "These ones are only legal because they haven't had reason not to be legal, if you see what I mean." In other words, because they haven't been proven to kill anyone—yet—they are still on sale, even though they could well be more harmful than a drug such as ecstasy, which is already banned.

Perversely, the rules that govern the legal-highs market are likely to encourage ever-more-dangerous drugs to be developed. Under ordinary market conditions, manufacturers would have an incentive to produce drugs that got people high and were also safe. No one would buy harmful ones if there were healthier alternatives available that did the same job. Ordinarily, competition would encourage this sort of innovation, with each firm adapting its recipe until it came up with a chemical high that left the user euphoric and unharmed. In other markets, this is basically what happens: in the drinks industry, wines that cause raging hangovers tend to be outsold by smoother ones; "low tar" and "light" cigarettes have increased their share of the market in recent years, dubious though their claims may be.

The legal-highs industry works in the opposite way. The cat-and-mouse game between manufacturers and the police means that the priority for drug developers is to keep tweaking their products to make them different from substances that have already been banned. The research-and-development teams in drug-makers' laboratories are not trying to come up with products that are better, or safer. Instead, they are simply trying to devise something that is new enough to be allowed on sale. If it turns out to be rough on the user, never mind— by the time anyone realizes, it will be banned anyway, and it will be time to release the latest variety. These perverse incentives mean that legal highs are being made with less and less concern for safety. Most new ones now are "synthetic cannabinoids," which claim to mimic the effects of cannabis. A few years ago, this claim may have been more or less accurate. But as generation after generation of the drugs has been banned, manufacturers have formulated iteration upon iteration, and the effects have become further and further removed from those associated with an ordinary joint. The endless tinkering with the chemical composition has created "Frankenstein drugs," says Ross Bell of the New Zealand Drug Foundation, who claims that the compounds in the current crop of legal highs are more likely than past versions to cause anxiety, increased heart rate, hallucinations, and depression.

Some countries have attempted to pass blanket bans on legal highs, automatically outlawing all new psychoactive substances that come onto the market. In 2015, Britain announced plans to impose such a prohibition, modeled on an Irish initiative of a few years earlier. But such bans have the same weakness as the old system: new substances have to be proved to be "psychoactive" before they can be outlawed, and in the time it takes for that to happen, manufacturers can do a brisk trade. The Irish ban has succeeded in reducing the number of head shops, but that seems simply to have pushed the business online. The proportion of young Irish people using legal highs has risen slightly since the ban, according to a survey by the European Commission.[7]

For the companies that make them, the legal highs have proved handily profitable. Most of the manufacturers in New Zealand import their chemicals from laboratories in China, at a cost of between $1,000

and $1,500 per kilogram. In their labs in New Zealand, the manu-
facturers spray the chemicals onto dried plant material, resulting in
a smokable product that looks a bit like natural cannabis or tobacco,
belying its synthetic origins. The impregnated plant mixture is then divided into portions of a couple of grams each, and stuffed into brightly
colored packets before going on sale. A single kilo of pure chemical
base is enough to fill about 10,000 of these packs. Each one is sold for
about $7.50 to retailers, who market them for $15 each to consumers.
According to an analysis by the New Zealand Treasury, the total average cost of making each packet is between 75 cents and $1.50, meaning
that manufacturers enjoy a profit margin in excess of 500 percent—or
double that, if they sell directly to the consumer online, as many do.[8]

How have they been able to protect such extraordinary profits? In
an industry where there is apparently so much easy money to be made,
one might expect new competitors to enter the market, eventually
driving prices down. The legal-highs business certainly seems to have
room for more players. One recent estimate by the Treasury indicated
that New Zealand's domestic market alone was worth a little over $100
million per year, with annual sales of 7 million packets. Yet at that time
the country had only nine serious manufacturers, with the lion's share
of the market controlled by just two: Matt Bowden's Stargate and another firm called Lightyears Ahead.

To see why the market has remained so concentrated, look at its
cousin, the pharmaceuticals industry. It, too, is a vast business with
pretty healthy profits. Margins average around 30 percent, according to
the World Health Organization[9]—not as high as in the Kiwi legal-highs
club, but pretty good by the standards of the conventional business
world. One might think that there was room for more start-ups. Yet
the pharmaceuticals industry is dominated by fewer than a dozen giant
companies.

One reason is that success requires terrifyingly steep investment in
research and development. The cost to pharmaceutical companies of
developing a new medicine and shepherding it through the necessary

trials is generally estimated to be somewhere north of $1 billion (a study by Tufts University in 2014 came up with the startlingly high figure of $2.6 billion).[10] And companies need to budget for failures as well as successes. "Torcetrapib," a treatment for high cholesterol, was abandoned by Pfizer in 2006 after the firm had spent $800 million on its development.[11] What's more, firms that can afford to develop drugs in several new areas at once are better protected against the risk of one project collapsing. Deep pockets are required for all this research investment; small firms struggle to find the money to take part.

A second reason is that pharmaceutical companies need to navigate fiendishly complex legal regulations. Even pharma giants sometimes get into hot water for failing to follow the maze of rules laid down to protect patients. In 2012, GlaxoSmithKline agreed to pay $3.3 billion, America's biggest-ever health-care fraud settlement, after it admitted wrongly branding an antidepression drug as being suitable for under-eighteen-year-olds and failing to disclose safety information about a diabetes treatment. Johnson & Johnson and Pfizer have recently been forced to reach similar multibillion-dollar settlements.[12] Staying on top of the law—and paying the consequences if its rules are broken—is also something that big firms, not surprisingly, are skilled at, possessing the financial resources to deal with penalties far more easily than start-ups or smaller businesses can.

The legal-highs industry mirrors both of these features. Commissioning a new chemical from China isn't all that expensive, but the drug may survive only a few months on the market before being banned, meaning that it is profitable only if the manufacturer is able to shift a large amount very quickly. Again, some drugs prove to be duds, and the companies best placed to survive these failures are those that can hedge their bets by investing in several different products at once. This, too, gets expensive. And just like pharmaceutical companies, legal-high peddlers need to stay on top of fast-evolving regulation. Accidentally cooking up a batch of one of the hundreds of substances that are already banned would mean a substantial fine, or even time in

jail. Big companies have the legal resources to jump through the regulatory hoops required of them, and the financial resources to survive
if they slip up.

All of this means that the legal-highs market favors big firms over
small firms, making it quite different from conventional narcotics markets that, as we saw in Chapter 3, tend to remain quite small in countries with good police forces, in order to limit the risk of discovery. In
the upside-down world of legal highs, the companies that survive are
the ones that have the muscle to innovate and stay on top of the law.

• • •

Trying to suppress the drugs business is tricky at the best of times. The
cartels are experts in finding ways to flout whatever bans governments
announce. But the legal-highs phenomenon presents a new sort of problem. Usually the difficulty lies in tracking down and prosecuting those
who break the law. But in this particular corner of the narco-economy,
the people selling the drugs do not break the law at all: rather, they stay
ahead of it. How can the business be policed?

Regulators always struggle when it comes to industries that are
based on innovation. In the tech business, new services and inventions
created by the likes of Google and Facebook present legal and moral
dilemmas about privacy and data protection faster than courts can rule
on them. In the banking industry, the pace of financial innovation in
the run-up to the meltdown of 2007 made it hard for the authorities to
notice that the pileup of credit-default swaps, collateralized-debt obli-
gations, and other inventive products represented an accident waiting
to happen. Even now, the regulators lag far behind the financial inno-
vators. The Dodd-Frank Act, a mammoth piece of legislation designed
to prevent bankers from taking the kinds of risks that nearly capsized
the world economy in 2007, had still not been fully implemented five
years after it was passed in 2010. In the meantime, the whiz kids of
Wall Street have zoomed ahead with complex new financial products,
of unknown riskiness.

Regulators' lives are made much easier when they can assess new innovations before they are put on the market, rather than after the event. In practice, this is often impossible: the tech industry would move at a snail's pace if the courts had to approve every new Google invention before it was released into the wild, and finance would grind to a halt if regulators forbade banks from launching new products without prior approval. But in other industries, the risks to the public are so great that this is precisely how regulation works. Before putting new medicines on sale, drug companies must subject them to exhaustive testing, until they gain approval by government bodies—the US Food and Drug Administration (FDA), for instance, or the European Medicines Agency. Mistakes are still sometimes made, of course. But on the whole, premarket testing means that potentially harmful drugs are weeded out before they have had the chance to hurt anyone.

Why not do this with legal highs? The current system is one in which regulators are constantly playing catch-up with drug manufacturers. Chasing reports of new potions here and overdoses there, they are doomed always to be late to spot harmful substances. What would happen if someone set up an FDA of narcotics?

In 2013, New Zealand attempted to do exactly that. Its Parliament passed the Psychoactive Substances Act, upending the logic of the legal-highs business. Rather than allow manufacturers to put their products on the market and then ban them once they had been proven harmful, the government turned the tables and established a system under which pill makers would have to prove that their product was safe before they were allowed to sell it. The manufacturers' claims would be assessed by a new Psychoactive Substances Regulatory Authority, which would have powers similar to the bodies that regulate medicines. In effect, the reform reversed the burden of proof: instead of the government constantly chasing after new products that had gone on sale, it would force manufacturers to prove that their drugs met basic standards before they were allowed to put them anywhere near consumers.

The move sounds sensible enough, but it was highly controversial. What it meant, in effect, was that New Zealand had voted to establish the world's first legal, regulated market in synthetic drugs. The Psychoactive Substances Authority would not ban drugs if they got people high; only if they were dangerous. To everyone's surprise, the law passed almost unopposed (the one member of Parliament who voted against it did so because he was against plans for the drugs to be tested on animals).

At a stroke, some useful rules were imposed on the industry. Selling the drugs to under-eighteens was banned, and so was advertising at the point of sale. Firms needed licenses to sell the products, meaning that the number of retail outlets was slashed from more than 3,000 to fewer than two hundred. Manufacturers had to register their products, giving users a clearer idea of what they were taking. For instance, potential drug takers could see that if they took a dose of "illusion Connoisseur," they would be receiving 45 milligrams per gram of the active ingredient, PB22-5F. If they wanted a bit less, they could try the "illusion Massif," which contained the same ingredient in a lower concentration. In all, the number of products on offer dropped from more than two hundred to fewer than fifty.[13] Manufacturers had to list their names and addresses, giving an interesting insight into how the industry operated—some of the business addresses were ordinary homes, whereas others were in swanky business parks.

The new regime has gotten off to a bumpy start. For one thing, the regulatory authority has struggled with its vast new job, doing things more slowly and clumsily than had been hoped. An initial transition period, during which existing legal highs were allowed to remain on sale while the government hammered out the details on how the new certifying regime would work, meant that harmful drugs were allowed to stay on the market for longer than they should have. This increased the worry that under the new system, the government was condoning the sale of dangerous substances.

A bigger problem was that the reform came too late. Most of the least harmful highs had already been banned years before. The ones still on sale were true "Frankenstein" drugs, repeatedly modified in order to get around previous bans, to the point where many of them did users far more harm than good. The government appeared to have a crisis of confidence, and in 2014, with an election looming, it passed a hasty amendment revoking all the temporary licenses that it had granted. Taking the drugs off the market until they had been properly assessed might not have been such a bad idea. But the amendment also included a curious clause that the drugs could not be tested on animals. Without such tests, no drug is likely to be licensed for use by humans. And so at the time of writing, the reform is effectively suspended: the Psychoactive Substances Regulatory Authority stands ready to grant licenses to drugs that can be proved safe, but manufacturers are forbidden by law from carrying out the experiments necessary to do so. In May 2015, Matt Bowden, the original legal-highs entrepreneur, put his company, Stargate, into liquidation. "This has been the most difficult time of my life," he told New Zealand's 3 News. "Dealing with this has been more difficult than dealing with meth addiction." He had even had to sell his Audi to pay the bills.[14] When I catch up with him a few months later, he is in the middle of moving, his three properties having been repossessed. "I am probably going to have to leave the country," he tells me in a hurried e-mail.

Botched though it was, New Zealand's reform suggests a different approach to regulating the new generation of synthetic drugs, which have proved so difficult to suppress using conventional means. Keeping up with the chemists who turn out a different, new "legal high" every week has been all but impossible. Testing the drugs before they go on sale—and licensing the ones that do the least harm—is extremely controversial, as it gives official blessing to substances that get their users high. But the alternative, as countries are beginning to realize, is a spiral of new, ever-more-dangerous alterations.

A bonus effect of this sort of regulation is that it changes the incentives for manufacturers. At the moment, they are driven by the need to synthesize new varieties that avoid existing bans, with little care for whether the resulting product is safe. Under a regulated market, the incentives would be different. Manufacturers would have a powerful motive to perfect (and patent) drugs that were less harmful and more satisfying to customers. Some are already thinking along these lines. Bowden says that if he ever gets his business back up and running, he would like to develop a synthetic substitute for another drug: alcohol. He believes that in time, his pharmacologists could come up with something that got people as drunk as booze, but without causing addiction, cirrhosis, or hangovers. It is a strange reflection on our existing drug laws that under the present system, such a product would instantly be banned.

Chapter 8

ORDERING A LINE ONLINE

How Internet Shopping Has Improved
Drug Dealers' Customer Service

The first time anybody bought something on the Worldwide Web was in 1994. Exactly who got there first is the subject of much debate online. Some maintain that the first sale was a copy of an album by Sting, *Ten Summoner's Tales*, which was bought on the website NetMarket for $12.48 plus shipping. A rival claim has been made by Pizza Hut, which says that it got there slightly earlier, selling a large pizza with pepperoni, mushrooms, and extra cheese to an online customer. Its old black-and-white pizza-ordering website, PizzaNet, has been preserved for posterity in a hidden corner of Pizza Hut's current website.[1]

These may have been the first sales ever made on the web. But delve back to the earliest days of the Internet, before the Worldwide Web had been spun, and an even older transaction is said to have taken place online. In either 1971 or 1972—the precise date seems to have been lost to history—students at Stanford University's Artificial Intelligence Laboratory used Arpanet, an ancestor of the modern Internet, to arrange a deal with students on the other side of the United States, at the Massachusetts Institute of Technology. The subject of the transaction was, perhaps inevitably, a bag of marijuana.

167

Since the first tentative trades on PizzaNet and its ilk, online retailing has boomed. As broadband has spread to people's homes and
to their smartphones (and soon, perhaps, to their glasses and their
watches), going online to search for and buy anything from homes to
holidays has become part of life in the rich world and is fast spreading to emerging economies, too. By most accounts, e-commerce now
makes up more than one-tenth of all retailing in developed countries,
and its share is rising. In some well-established industries, such as the
book trade, online sales are on the brink of surpassing offline ones.
Meanwhile, the online economy is pushing into ever more markets,
revolutionizing them as it goes: home delivery of groceries is back in
fashion for the first time since the 1950s, and mobile apps such as Uber
have shaken up the taxi business (at least in those countries where
taxi-drivers' unions have not managed to ban it).

To the long list of industries that have been turned upside down by
the Internet, it may soon be time to add the narcotics business. Ever
since the Stanford marijuana purchase, illicit drugs have been a part
of the online-shopping revolution. And as e-commerce has grown, so
too has the online trade in drugs. The electronic paper-trails left by
conventional web browsers, and the indelible nature of credit-card his-
tories, make it harder to shop online for illegal products. But people
are managing to overcome these obstacles. In October 2013, the FBI
announced that it had arrested the man believed to be behind the Silk
Road, an online marketplace selling hundreds of millions of dollars'
worth of drugs, as well as other sorts of contraband. The scale of the
site—it included thousands of listings from across the entire phar-
macopoeia, being shipped to customers all over the world—opened
people's eyes for the first time to the fact that as conventional online
retailing had boomed, so had the illegal sort. Just like ordinary retailers, drug dealers have been able to cut their costs by selling online.
And just like other consumers, drug users enjoy the convenience of
online browsing and home delivery. Could there ever be an Amazon of

amphetamines, or an eBay of ecstasy? And if so, how would it change the drugs business?

•   •   •

Even for the most dedicated shopaholic, buying drugs has never been a very enjoyable consumer experience. Transactions are nervous and hurried, with money hastily counted out and grubby plastic bags exchanged in dark corners of nightclubs or in lonely parks at unsociable hours. Drugs' illegality means that the threat of being spotted by police—or being beaten up, or robbed, or ripped off, and with no way to report it—is never far away, for either buyer or seller. Customer service is abysmal. "He's never early, he's always late. First thing you learn is that you always gotta wait," complained Lou Reed in "I'm Waiting for the Man," a song about buying a $26 score of heroin in a Harlem brownstone in 1967. For people who buy drugs on the street, things haven't improved much since then.

Go online, however, and the consumer experience is in a completely different league. In the comfort of my own living room, with a cup of tea and a package of chocolate cookies under way, I am browsing through reviews of dozens of subtly different varieties of heroin. "AMAZING PRODUCT. Tried a much smaller amount than my usual and it sent me straight to heaven!" says one customer, describing a batch of "Afghanistan high quality heroin" being sold by a vendor called dragoncove for $200 per gram. "Always next day delivery and a really nice guy to chat to. Thanks bro," says a satisfied buyer of "Extra potent #3 Asian heroin," advertised by GentsChoice, which sells for $70 per half gram. Alongside the products are short descriptions by the vendors, many of whom have designed professional-looking logos featuring stylized dragons or old paintings of Chinese opium dens. High-resolution photographs show the products on offer: chalky white powder, or a brownish, crystalline substance like a sugar cube dunked in coffee. Shipping options and lists of terms and conditions lie alongside customer feedback scores. Apart from the goods on sale, the site looks exactly like eBay.

This is Evolution Marketplace, a website where people from around the world anonymously trade illegal goods and services, the most popular by far being drugs. When the Silk Road went offline, for a brief while it looked as if its demise was going to seriously disrupt the online drug trade, so dominant had its role been. At the time of its closure, it was displaying 13,000 drug listings, making it by far the biggest online drug market. The business had been run by the mysterious "Dread Pirate Roberts," which turned out to be the pseudonym of a skinny, young, Texas physics graduate, Ross William Ulbricht. In 2015, Ulbricht, a former Boy Scout, was sentenced to spend the rest of his life in prison for running the site from a computer in San Francisco. But his arrest and conviction have done nothing to slow the online trade in drugs. Indeed, since the Silk Road's closure, the market has grown bigger still, as a succession of imitators has sprung up. Although most of the sites have a limited shelf life—Evolution Marketplace vanished a few weeks after I had checked it out—new ones pop up as quickly as the old ones are taken offline. The Digital Citizens Alliance, a nonprofit group, tracks a dozen such sites. The largest, at the time of this writing, is Agora, whose logo is a masked man carrying an assault rifle. The ten next-biggest have names such as Nucleus, TOM, Middle Earth, and Black Bank. Added together, in early 2015 the top dozen sites were displaying a total of more than 40,000 drug listings—more than double the amount on offer at the time when the Dread Pirate Roberts was still in business.

Buying drugs online sounds like a fantastically dangerous idea for all concerned. Browsing history could be logged, and payments could raise red flags with credit-card firms. Yet these obstacles have been overcome by technological leaps, which have allowed buyers and sellers to cover their tracks. First of all, sites such as Evolution are hidden in the so-called Dark Web, a part of the Internet that isn't indexed by ordinary search engines and can be accessed only using special web browsers. The most popular of these applications, called the TOR browser, uses technology initially developed by the US Naval Research Laboratory to carry out a method of subterfuge known as "onion routing." This bounces web traffic from server to server, creating layer upon layer of encryption like an onion, hence the name. (Hidden websites in the Dark Web have the amusing suffix ".onion," rather than the more usual .com, .net, and so on.) The effect is to make a user's web-browsing history as good as untraceable, which is handy if you are a political dissident, spy, investigative journalist—or drug dealer.

Then there is the problem of how to pay. For this, there is Bitcoin. The world's foremost digital currency system, Bitcoin works without a central bank, instead relying on networks of computers to generate new "coins" by performing complex mathematical operations in a process known as mining. Setting up a Bitcoin account is a bit of a hassle, but not particularly complicated and, like the TOR browser, the currency is perfectly legal to use. Bitcoin's value is ludicrously volatile: its price shot up from less than $15 at the beginning of 2013 to nearly $1,000 in November of that year, before falling back to $300 by the end of 2014. But online shoppers can live with this because, like TOR, Bitcoin provides them with a cloak of anonymity.

The combination of untraceable browsing and anonymous payments has enabled an online criminal market to flourish. As well as drugs, all sorts of other unsavory things are sold on these hidden sites. The Digital Citizens Alliance estimates that illegal narcotics make up about two-thirds of the listings. The remaining one-third is, if anything, still more sinister. Most of the bigger sites draw the line at illegal pornography, as well as contract killings, which are said to be for sale in shadier corners of the Dark Web. But the majority of them have no problem selling weapons, from brass knuckles to handguns and the blueprints for 3D-printable firearms. Stolen credit-card details, counterfeit currency, and fake ID documents also do a roaring trade. Then there are all manner of other weird and not-so-wonderful bits and pieces. Browsing through the "drugs paraphernalia" section of Evolution Marketplace, I find glass pipes for smoking crystal meth ("Made in the USA!!!! Completely lead and additive free unlike the crap you get from the Chinese") and an electrical bag-resealer (which the manufacturer shows being used to seal a stash of marijuana inside an opened bag of Cheetos). Perhaps strangest of all, one vendor is hawking sachets of "synthetic clean urine," aimed at people who need help passing a drug test. For true realism, the vendor, CleanU, also sells an accessory called the ScreenyWeeny, "the world's best fake penis, with Push&Piss technology." The Weeny comes in five colors, from NordicWhite to LatinoBrown. Reviews are generally positive.

How big a chunk of the drugs trade do these sites currently account for? The Global Drug Survey, an annual poll of users, seems to show that buying drugs on the Internet has already become fairly common in some countries. The survey is an opt-in one, which means that the 80,000 or so people from around the world who took part in the latest round were by no means representative of the general population. But it suggests that among those who routinely take drugs, online trading is becoming an important way of getting them. Overall, just over one-tenth said they had bought drugs online. In the United States, the proportion was 14 percent; in the United Kingdom it was the highest, at 22 percent.[2] (In this way the drugs business mimics the legitimate retail trade: Britain does a bigger share of its shopping online than other countries when it comes to regular goods, too.)

Even these figures may somewhat understate the role that the online economy plays, as there is some evidence that a lot of the customers on the Dark Web are themselves dealers, using the sites to buy wholesale. Many vendors offer discounts to shoppers making bulk orders, which are plainly not for personal consumption. On Evolution, a seller called DutchMasters solicits inquiries from people interested in buying more than half a kilogram of cocaine, a quantity that would fetch tens of thousands of dollars if sold by the gram. One academic study of the goods for sale on the original Silk Road estimated that about one-fifth of all its listings were aimed at dealers, and that these "business-to-business" transactions accounted for between 31 percent and 45 percent of the site's trades by value.[3] If that is the case, even drug users who buy their supplies "offline," from a dealer or friend, may well be buying a product that was traded online at an earlier stage in the supply chain.

Measuring the total value of the online drug economy is hard, not least because Bitcoin's price is so volatile. The FBI originally estimated that the Silk Road had done $1.2 billion in business during its two and one-half years online. But it later scaled down this rough calculation: the estimate had been made when Bitcoin's value was near its peak, whereas much of the Silk Road's business was done when the digital currency was less valuable. The FBI did a revised estimate, using the currency's varying value at the time that each different trade was made, and came up with the much lower figure of $200 million. That is a tiny proportion of the global drugs market, which is thought to be worth something like $300 billion. But for two years' trading, it is extraordinary. For comparison, consider that in 1997, two years after its launch and just prior to being floated on the stock exchange, eBay was doing about $100 million in business a year. Nowadays, it annually handles goods worth about $80 billion. If the Silk Road's successors, which are already considerably bigger, are to grow at anything like the same rate that conventional online businesses have, they could account for a large share of the retail narcotics business within a decade or two.

Their future remains somewhat precarious. The fate of the Silk Road shows that sites in the Dark Web are not completely beyond the reach of the long arm of the law. Others, apparently including Evolution, vanish when the people running them decide to pull a fast one. (Evolution's managers are thought to have made off with some $15 million in Bitcoin payments kept in escrow when the site mysteriously vanished in 2015.) And all such sites depend on Bitcoin and TOR, both of which could be pulled from under their feet if the governments of the world decided to ban them.

There is no sign of that for now. Germany's finance ministry has recognized Bitcoin as a currency, meaning its users can be taxed. In the United States, the Winklevoss twins, the nearly men of the dotcom boom who claimed that Mark Zuckerberg had stolen the idea for Face-book from them, have poured money into creating a Bitcoin exchange. Most democratic governments have so far been reluctant to outlaw the TOR browser, on the basis that it has legitimate uses as well as nefar-ious ones. Britain's Parliamentary Office of Science and Technology has argued against a ban, pointing out that TOR was extensively used during the "Arab Spring" of 2011, as well as by Western whistleblow-ers and undercover journalists. Attitudes could change if anonymous online marketplaces come to be seen as a real menace, or if they begin being more widely used to plan or fund terrorism. But those govern-ments that have already tried to ban TOR—including China—have found it impossible. And the speed with which new sites sprang up following the demise of the Silk Road suggests that even if there were a coordinated digital crackdown, it probably wouldn't be long before replacement browsers and digital currencies emerged. Online retailing is here to stay, in drugs as it is in the legitimate economy. The police may not like it. But, as it turns out, their discomfort is nothing com-pared with that of some established drug dealers, for whom the online revolution poses an existential threat.

•   •   •

Hidden markets are different from open ones in a few important ways. Imagine an ordinary, open market in which people are buying and sell-ing a legal product—let's say apples, that trusty standby of economics textbooks. People with apples to sell take them to the market, and peo-ple who want to buy apples go to meet them. The buyers have a look at what's on offer. If an apple seller sets too high a price, the buyers will go elsewhere. If a buyer bids too little, the seller will offer the apples to someone else instead. A price is agreed when both buyer and seller are satisfied that they are getting the best deal they can. This is the basis of the price mechanism that magically matches supply and demand in market economies around the world.

Now imagine the market for an illegal product, such as a banned narcotic. The product's illegality means that deals have to take place in secret. So unless law and order has really broken down, there is no open market where buyers can compare prices and sellers can hawk their wares. Instead, buyers can shop only from dealers whom they know, through some connection or other. In the same way, dealers generally sell only to clients whom they trust to pay up and not get them into trouble with the law.

This means that drug markets don't work anything like as efficiently as they could. A consumer might buy poor-quality cocaine for $200 per gram from a trusted dealer, not knowing that another seller down the road is offering much better stuff for half the price. The buyer might find out about the other dealer eventually, if that buyer is sufficiently well plugged in to drug-taking circles. But it would take time for the news to spread, and without the right set of contacts, the consumer would continue to buy an inferior product at an inflated price. Dealers face the same problem in reverse: there may be potential customers out there who would be prepared to buy their product for a higher price, but they don't have an easy way to identify them. The more they spread the word about their good-value, high-quality drugs, the more they risk arrest: when a product is illegal, there is only so much advertising one can do.[4] The result is called a network economy. Players deal only with people who are part of their network, whether they be family, friends, neighbors, or former cellmates, rather than participating in an open market.

Under these conditions, life is good for the established dealer. A key feature of network markets is that they tend to work strongly in favor of incumbents, who have had time to build up the biggest and strongest networks. Picture the stable, longtime drug dealer, who has been supplying the same city for years. He knows the importers. He has a long list of clients. He may even have contacts in the police whom he pays to turn a blind eye to his business. Now picture the young up-start, someone who spots that the local market is uncompetitive, with watered-down drugs being sold at high prices. It ought to be easy to enter the market and win some business. But entering the drugs mar-ket—a network economy—isn't so easy. Buying wholesale quantities of illegal drugs requires a rare set of high-level contacts. Selling them in smaller quantities requires a second, larger set of potential buyers. Without a network to buy from and sell to, the new dealer won't get far (and that is before even thinking about the possibility that the es-tablished dealer may not take kindly to someone else operating on his patch). The result is that incumbents stay in business, facing only lim-ited competition, even as they charge high prices for poor service. The reason Lou Reed had to spend so much time "waiting for the man" was because there weren't many other people to buy from. "The man" knew this perfectly well, hence his perennial lateness.

The online drugs business turns all of this upside down. When you start shopping online, the first thing you learn is that you *never* have to wait. Poking around the Evolution Marketplace, registered under a pseudonym, I send a few trial messages to vendors, using a messaging system that is built into the site. Within twenty-five minutes, I have my first reply. Everyone gets back to me within a day or two, with po-lite, friendly answers to my queries about dosages, packaging, and so on. Even when I send a deliberately annoying question to a meth-pipe dealer called "vicious86," asking if he does custom engraving of his pipes for gift orders, he sends a nice reply regretting that he can't but wishing me luck in finding someone who will. Unlike most parts of the Internet, where anonymity makes people ruder than in real life, the world of drug dealing seems to be friendlier online than it is on the street.

Indeed, when "the man" goes online, he excels at all forms of cus-tomer service. Unlike street dealers, online sellers spell out their terms and conditions clearly, with most offering some form of compensation if the product fails to arrive. A few even claim that their cocaine is "fair trade" or "conflict free"—a boast that is patently untrue, given that the world's cocaine supply is controlled by a group of murderous cartels, but interesting in that it shows how drug dealers are starting to mimic the tactics used by ordinary retailers. Trust, something that one might think would be hard to establish in an anonymous environment where the players are all crooks, is earned using a "feedback" system modeled on eBay's. Buyers can rate vendors with a positive, negative, or neutral rating, along with a comment. Vendors can see how many successful transactions a buyer has completed. Just as on eBay, participants feel more confident doing business with users who have a string of positive reviews to their name and might avoid doing an expensive trade with someone who doesn't have much of a track record. "We are looking to build a solid customer base because that's the only way we can stay in business and both of us will be happy ☺," says the blurb on the sales page of Snapback, a seller of ecstasy based in Germany. If a shipment is lost, Snapback says it will offer a 30-percent refund or a reshipment at half price to those customers who have completed at least ten trans-actions. Those with thirty transactions under their belts can get a 50-percent refund. Most sellers offer similar terms.

It may seem implausible that crooks can be persuaded to trust each other. But the feedback system seems to have created a sense of honor among thieves. For the strangest example of this, look at the online advertisements for stolen bank details. Whereas some of the people buying and selling drugs put forward a pseudo-moral justification for their business (arguing that it's up to people what they put in their own bodies, that prohibition doesn't work, and so on), there is no ethical defense for draining people's savings. Yet even here, the vendors are anxious to promote their fair-trading standards. One seller, who offers "sniffed" credit-card details (that is, ones stolen from online shopping sites), offers insurance with his sales. A stolen card can be bought for $8. But for $10 he will replace it if it turns out to be dead, provided that the customer has tried to use it within eight hours of buying (stolen credit cards are quickly canceled, once the owner realizes what's up).

His reviews are stellar. "First card was dead and he sent a second one and I shit you not, I bought an iPhone 6 straight from the Apple store! WILL DEFINETLY BUY AGAIN!" says one. Amusingly, buyers and sellers alike take great offense when someone calls into question their honesty. "Called me a scammer after I asked for a replacement. Only 1 worked out of 3," says one indignant customer, outraged at being called a liar when in fact he was simply trying to make an honest living buying stolen credit cards.

Why are drug dealers so serious about customer service on the web, when they are so bad at it offline? The reason is that a Dark Web marketplace such as the Silk Road or Evolution is much more like a conventional market than a network economy. Sellers advertise their products openly, and buyers are free to compare the full range of prices being offered. Buyers and sellers alike can trade with everyone else in the market, rather than just with the people they know. This means that the need for a "network" vanishes—which in turn means that there is no longer much of an incumbent advantage. Sellers are forced to compete more seriously on price, quality, and customer service, rather than being able to stay in business simply because they have built the rare set of contacts required to make it work. What's more, it is relatively easy for new dealers to enter the market, as barriers to entry are extremely low. Buying wholesale quantities of drugs no longer requires connections in the international smuggling business, and selling them no longer means having to hang around on street corners or in nightclubs. Just as sites such as Etsy have made it easy for amateur jewelers to sell their wares, without the hassle and expense of opening a market stall, the Dark Web allows anyone with a laptop and an appetite for risk to set up a drug-dealing enterprise.

Established dealers still retain a small edge over upstarts. New vendors usually have to offer lower prices at first, until they have built a long enough track record to persuade people they aren't going to take their Bitcoins and run. (This is not uncommon: online vendors sometimes pull off "exit scams," in which they bank money for several orders and then vanish, without sending the goods. A long track record reassures customers that the seller has too much to lose to want to carry out such a scam.)[5] Similarly, new customers without a buying history are generally required to pay for things up front, until they have a few successful trades under their belt. Nonetheless, the open nature of the online trading system means that advantages enjoyed by incumbent dealers in the offline drug market are all but eliminated. For the big trafficking networks, the Dark Web represents a serious threat, enabling thousands of new entrants to gobble up customers, in much the same way that Uber has allowed noncommercially licensed drivers to take business away from taxi firms.

So much for the dealers. What does online narco-shopping mean for consumers? The traditional way of getting hold of drugs, through a personal network, provides some basic reassurance to customers that they are taking something that won't fry their brain. But sometimes the assurances can be a bit shaky. Buying powerful mind-altering substances from your friend's brother's girlfriend's roommate, who in turn got them from this guy she met at the local bar, is not much of a guarantee of safety. Online, the feedback mechanism may provide a slightly more reliable endorsement. A couple thousand reviews, 99 percent of them positive, are probably a better indicator of a product's quality than one is likely to get by asking around in the bar. And it does indeed seem that the quality of the drugs sold online is pretty high. A study of synthetic cannabis products in the *Journal of Analytical Toxicology* found that "chemicals obtained from online vendors were of comparable purity to those from traditional research chemical suppliers."[6] Before pouncing on the Silk Road, the FBI made more than one hundred test purchases from the site and found that the substances typically showed "high purity levels" of the drug they claimed to be. Perhaps for this reason, relatively dangerous drugs seem to be especially popular online. A survey of substances for sale on Silk Road 2.0, an illegal site that went up soon after the Silk Road was dismantled (and was itself busted not long after), found that the most widely offered drug for sale was ecstasy. This makes sense: although ecstasy is usually fairly safe, a single pill can kill if a batch is contaminated or particularly strong. Reassurance of quality is therefore extremely important—unlike in the case of marijuana, say, which varies in strength but has never been known to cause an overdose.

Online trading has another advantage regarding safety of a different sort. At a stroke, the move online eliminates the importance of territory. Bloody turf-wars are a signature feature of retail drug markets. In the 1980s, gangsters in Glasgow, Scotland, sold drugs out of ice-cream trucks, leading to the bizarre-sounding "ice-cream wars," in which the ice-cream trucks were targeted for arson attacks and drive-by shootings. Fighting for control of street corners is the subject of countless drug-war dramas, from Scarface to Traffic. But with drugs available online, the corners have become less important, just as the brick-and-mortar outlet has become less important to ordinary retail businesses. "We're past that run and gun shit, man . . . we can run more than corners," says Stringer Bell, a business-minded dealer in The Wire who goes to economics night-classes in between ordering murders. The spread of mobile phones and pagers in the 1990s reduced the need for drug dealers to control territory, as the business moved off the street and indoors, to people's apartments or other rendezvous points that could be set up by phone (some criminologists believe that the fall in violence in New York City in the 1990s was partly due to drug dealers' adoption of mobile phones). The Internet age, in which drugs are ordered online and delivered in the mail, takes this process a step further: dealers no longer even need to leave their homes.

It isn't all good news, however. One consequence of the move online is that prices are likely to be pushed down. Narcotics retailers benefit from the same savings that other web-based enterprises do: just as Amazon doesn't need to pay for expensive storefronts, online drug-dealers don't need to pay employees to stand on street corners or carry out risky deliveries in person. At the same time, the increase in competition brought about by the easier entry to the market will exert even more downward pressure on prices. Cheaper drugs are an unwelcome development for governments that want to curb their use.

It may also be that the simplicity of buying online opens the drug market up to a new range of customers. Until now, getting hold of drugs has been difficult and often unpleasant, requiring a network of dodgy contacts or a nerve-racking trip down a dark alleyway. Buying online makes it easy and lends an almost respectable face to a grubby business. Reading hundreds of reviews of a batch of heroin, written by people who enjoyed it and lived to tell the tale, does a lot to take the scary image away from the drug. (Potential buyers should bear in mind that those customers who overdosed wouldn't have been in a position to leave negative feedback, however.) And buying online is absurdly easy: installing TOR takes minutes, and the browser is as simple to use as any other. Setting up a Bitcoin account is a bit trickier but requires no great technical expertise. If you are capable of buying a book on Amazon, you are probably up to buying crystal meth on the Dark Web. It is easy to imagine a new sort of buyer, lacking contacts and wary of tough-looking strangers, being more willing to buy drugs on the web.

Sites like the Silk Road haven't been around long enough for anyone to draw reliable conclusions about their long-term impact on patterns of drug use, the figures for which tend to be at least a year old. But one can look at a similar trend that has been around for a bit longer: the online sale (on the ordinary web) of prescription painkillers. In 2007, the National Center on Addiction and Substance Abuse at Columbia University in New York estimated that there were 581 websites dedicated to selling prescription drugs. Of these, only two were certified by the US National Association of Boards of Pharmacy; 85 percent were happy to sell drugs without a prescription, and the majority of the rest required only a faxed prescription. In short, even without a browser like TOR or a stash of Bitcoins, it was easy to order drugs online. Drawing a link between the drugs' availability online and their increased usage is tricky. But in one study a pair of academics compared rates of admission for treatment for prescription-drug abuse with the availability of high-speed Internet access in different states.[7] Plotting the number of people seeking help for drugs in a state against the increase in access to broadband, they found that there was a slight correlation. For every 10-percent increase in access to broadband, there was a 1-percent increase in admissions for prescription-drug abuse. In itself, this may not be all that convincing: it could simply show that both Internet access and drug use are more common in heavily urbanized states, for instance. Yet the researchers found that there was no such correlation when it came to admissions for abuse of cocaine or heroin, which at that time were not so readily available online. It may not be long before the impact of sites like the Silk Road starts to show up in drug-use statistics.

· · ·

Maddeningly for the police, online drug dealing is fiendishly tricky to curb. Consider an old-fashioned, offline drug market. Rather than using an open market, like the Silk Road, it works on the basis of a network. And the convenient thing about network economies, from the point of view of the police, is that they are relatively easy to disrupt. Break a link in the chain and a whole chunk of the network can be cut off—rather like when a mouse nibbles through an electrical cable and a whole neighborhood goes dark. Pinpointing exactly where to strike, however, is tricky. A drug-dealing network might have dozens of different members—"nodes," to use the economic term—and the police can't hit all of them at once. So on which member of the gang should they focus their efforts? It might sound straightforward: logic suggests that the most urgent person to nab is the one with the most connections, as taking that person out would break the most chains in the network. But economics shows that this isn't necessarily the best approach.

Consider an example far removed from the modern drugs scene: the marriage market in fifteenth-century Florence. Back then, choosing a partner for your son or daughter was a strategic decision taken with all the care of a cartel kingpin forming his next business alliance. Marrying into an influential family was the best way to enrich and empower

FIGURE 8.1 Family Networks in Florence, 1430s

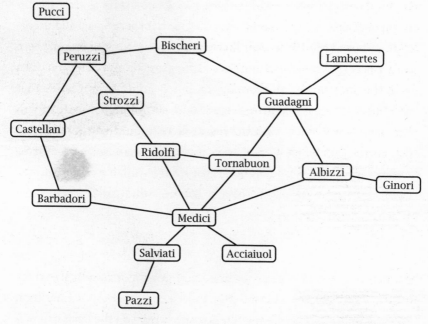

SOURCE: Matthew O. Jackson, *Social and Economic Networks* (Princeton, NJ: Princeton University Press, 2008).

your own kin. But how was a father to determine which family was the most desirable one with which to form a bond? Using data compiled by John Padgett and Christopher Ansell of the University of Chicago, Matthew Jackson of Stanford University produced a network map of how the key Florentine families of the fifteenth century were linked together (see Figure 8.1).[8] Of the sixteen most powerful clans in the city at the time, the unfortunate Pucci family was a bit out in the cold. Signor Pucci could remedy this by setting up a few blind dates for his children with eligible members of the city's other leading families. But which one should he target first?

The most obvious way of determining a family's level of influence is to see how many other powerful clans it is linked to. By this analysis, the Medici are clearly in the lead: they are right at the center of the city's social network, with direct connections to six other powerful families. If none of the young Medici are available, Signor Pucci might want to try the Strozzi or the Guadagni families, which both have links to four other families, more than anyone else. Is one more desirable than the other? Economists have another way of measuring the "centrality" of a node in a network: rather than simply counting the number of connections, they take into account how many connections each of those connections has, and so on. If I have one hundred friends and you have only ten, I might appear better connected than you. But if your ten friends include people who are themselves very well connected— Barack Obama, Angela Merkel, Justin Bieber—you may be more influential than me after all. (Google's page-ranking system works in a similar way: it measures not only how many sites link to a page, but how many sites link to *those* sites, and so on. Being linked to once by the *New York Times* counts for more than being linked to by a dozen unknown blogs.) Applying this to the Florentine families, it seems that Signor Pucci may want to target the Strozzi ahead of the Guadagni, because their connections' connections are more extensive.

But before he packs his daughter off to the nearest trattoria with the most marriageable young Strozzi, Signor Pucci might want to consider one more factor. It's true that the Strozzi score pretty well in their connectedness, and very well in the connectedness of their friends. But sometimes it pays to be in another position: that of the power broker. How often do the other families need to rely on the Strozzi when they want to call in a favor from another family? Look closely at the network and it is clear that the Strozzi are hardly the lynchpins of Florentine society. If the Peruzzi want to get in touch with the Medici, for instance, they can bypass the Strozzi and go through the Castellan instead. Likewise, the Bischeri can use their connections with the Guadagni. If the Strozzi were to disappear, no one would particularly notice. That makes them vulnerable. The Guadagni, meanwhile, are in a stronger position: they are the only way to contact the Lambertes, and they form a useful bridge between the families in the bottom-right and top-left corners of the network. They are useful people to know. Economists clunkily say that people like the Guadagni have a high degree of "betweenness centrality," which they calculate by looking at how frequently a node lies on the shortest path between two other nodes. Signor Pucci might find that a marriage with a Guadagni eventually offered more leverage than throwing in his lot with the disposable Strozzi.

Back to the modern narcotics business. Who is central to a drug-dealing network? Police need to go through the same process as Signor Pucci. The simplest approach—looking at who has the most contacts—would suggest that the street-level dealer is the most important player, as the person with the highest number of connections. He distributes drugs to dozens, perhaps scores, of clients. Arresting him could mean that a hundred or more links are disrupted. It seems like a good place to strike. But there are more valuable targets: if the police apply the Google page-ranking methodology, they will find that the most influential people are those who sit at the top of the chain. They know fewer people—they might deal with only a handful of lieutenants—but through those contacts they are linked to the whole network. Take them out and everybody below them is affected.

Obvious enough, perhaps. But what if the market doesn't look like that? We normally picture a drug-dealing network as a sort of family tree, with a handful of powerful importers at the top, gradually spreading outward to a large army of lowly foot soldiers at the bottom. Yet it may be that narcotics networks look rather different. A study for Britain's Home Office carried out interviews with fifty-one convicted drug dealers.[9] Using this information, the authors pieced together a rough network map of the drugs business in the United Kingdom. What they found was that rather than resembling a pyramid, Britain's drug-trafficking network looked more like an hourglass. At the very top are the big, specialized importers, who bring in large shipments of drugs: 100 kilos or more of heroin or cocaine, 100,000 ecstasy pills, or multiple tons of cannabis. They sell these drugs in smaller quantities to wholesalers, who also specialize in particular substances. The next step is the interesting one: from here, the authors found, the wholesalers sell to a middleman whom they christened the "multi-commodity drug broker." Unlike those above them in the chain, who tend to focus on a single drug, these people deal in the full range of narcotics, from hard drugs to soft, and in fairly large quantities. The researchers found that a typical broker of this sort might put in an order every few weeks for a couple kilograms of heroin, a couple more of cocaine, 30 kilograms of cannabis, 10 kilograms of amphetamine, and 20,000 or so ecstasy pills. He would then sell them in smaller quantities to street-level dealers. The midlevel broker is thus in the very center of the trafficking network, functioning as a clearinghouse for the market. This is the "vital linkage point" in the drug distribution business, the authors wrote.

If Signor Pucci were around today and involved in the drugs business, the "multi-commodity drug broker" is surely the one to whom he would want to marry his daughter. Occupying the very middle of the network, these middlemen are the best-connected people in the business. Furthermore, acting as the link between the wholesalers and the retailers, they have a high degree of "betweenness centrality." The findings of the Home Office report seem to agree with other studies on pricing in the drugs business. The RAND Corporation found that the single-biggest leap in the price of cocaine in the United States occurs during the transfer from middle dealers to retailers, when the price of a kilo shoots up from $19,500 to $78,000.[10] If the police are to focus their energies in one place, it may be that they cause the most disruption not by targeting the small fry on the streets, or even the big fish doing the importation, but instead by aiming squarely at the middle, where the dealers are the best connected and, it seems, making the most money.

The Internet complicates all of this, in a way that may prove fatal to many police efforts to dismantle criminal networks. The listings on sites like the Silk Road suggest that to a large extent, these websites are taking on a role similar to the "multi-commodity drug broker." On these sites, retail buyers, as well as dealers, can find almost any type of drug known to users and buy such drugs in fairly large quantities. This is problematic for the police, because the nature of the online trade means that there is no single central "node": thousands of buyers and sellers are able to interact in an open market, and taking one dealer, or even a dozen, out of business, will not make much of an impact on the supply chain for everyone else. Even if an entire marketplace goes offline, as the Silk Road and Evolution eventually did, new ones pop up to take its place.

Is there anything that can be done? Maybe. Consider a study published in the *American Journal of Sociology*, which again concerns a subject far removed from the drugs world. A team of American academics undertook the unusual exercise of plotting a map of high-school romances.[11] The researchers used a study that had earlier been done at an unnamed high school in the Midwest, in a rural town an hour's drive from the nearest big city, where according to the teenagers interviewed "there is absolutely nothing to do." The study comprised in-home interviews with 832 of the school's roughly 1,000 students, who were asked questions via tape recorder, which they answered by typing responses into a computer. They were each presented with a list of their fellow students at the school and asked to identify those with whom they had had a "special romantic relationship" or a "nonromantic sexual relationship" within the past eighteen months. Of the total, 573 reported that they had been involved in such a relationship with another student at the school.

Armed with these data, the authors drew a kind of sexual map of the school, linking students to each other in a series of daisy chains (see Figure 8.2). There were sixty-three couples in which each individual's only recent partnership had been with the other. Several more students were part of miniature networks containing only three people. The surprise was the discovery of a linked network that included just over half the students in the school. In other words, half the students could be linked to each other via their partners, partners' partners, and so on.

This was an unexpected and potentially important finding. The point of the study was to help epidemiologists better understand how to stop the spread of sexually transmitted diseases (STDs). Such

FIGURE 8.2 Romantic Relationships at "Jefferson High School"

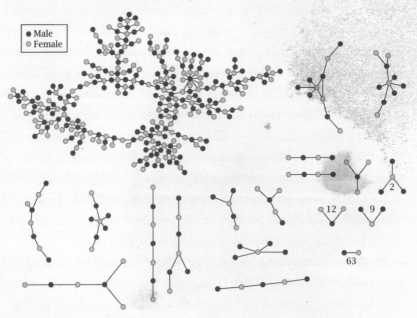

● Male
○ Female

SOURCE: Peter S. Bearman, James Moody, and Katherine Stovel, "Chains of Affection: The Structure of Adolescent Romantic and Sexual Networks," *American Journal of Psychology* 110, 1 (2004): 44–91.

NOTE: Numbers indicate network types that appeared multiple times.

infections are passed from partner to partner, meaning that if one person within a network becomes infected, everyone is at risk. The advice given by schools and parents is that a simple way to limit exposure to infections is to limit the number of sexual partners. Sleeping with only one person must be safer than being promiscuous, the theory goes. It isn't necessarily true. Look at the big network, which contains 288 students. Although the network is very large, many of the people in it have had only one partner (those on the ends of the tree's many small "branches"). In spite of their monogamy, their risk of contracting an infection may be higher than that of someone who has had multiple partners within a smaller network. "Consequently," the authors write, "STD risk is not simply a matter of number of partners."

The study is of limited use to anxious teenagers, who can't draw up such a network map without extensive quizzing of potential partner-nodes, which would probably ruin their chances of linking up. But there is a practical lesson in it for policy makers. Conventional wisdom suggests that if a government wants to stop the spread of illness, it makes sense to aim its safe-sex campaign at those who are the most promiscuous. They are the ones who sleep with the most people, so if they are infected, it will cause the most problems. Persuade them to take the right precautions, and the benefit will be greatest. Just as it makes sense for Signor Pucci to target a family like the Medici, who are connected to many others, safe-sex advertisements should be focused on those individuals who are most likely to sleep around: sex workers, young people, substance abusers, and so on. Correct?

Maybe not, according to the model. The majority of the students are members of a network that is large, but fragile. Most of its members have had only a couple of partners, meaning that in many cases a single person forms the link in a long chain. If any one of these individuals can be persuaded to have safe sex, the chain of infection is broken. As the authors write, "Relatively low levels of behavioral change—even by low-risk actors, who are perhaps the easiest to influence—can easily break a . . . network into small disconnected components, thereby fragmenting the epidemic and radically limiting its scope." Surprisingly, sexual-health education may have more impact if dollars are focused on changing attitudes among those considered *low* risk, rather than targeting the most vulnerable.

What does this mean if translated to the drug world? As we have seen, the conventional model of drug distribution doesn't look much like the high-school sex map: it seems that in many cases there is a single, well-connected node, in the form of the midlevel dealer. But what if the drug market looks more like the sex map than we had thought? Most analysis of the drugs business assumes that once the dealer has sold to the consumer, that's the end of the process. But surveys suggest otherwise. There is pretty good evidence that many people who take drugs—perhaps even the majority—never have contact with a professional dealer at all. Rather, they buy (or are given) drugs by people they know: friends, partners, colleagues, and so on. In Britain, among those adults who took illegal drugs in the past year, 54 percent acquired the drugs in their own home or in the home of someone they knew, according to a government survey.[12] A further 21 percent got them at a party or in a bar or nightclub (from whom the survey does not say—presumably in some cases from friends and in others from dealers). In all, only 11 percent bought their drugs "on the street, in a park, or other outdoor area," the classic territory of the commercial dealer, as depicted in a series such as *The Wire*. A survey of prescription-drug abusers in the United States found that fully 71 percent of users had gotten their drugs from a friend or relative; only 4 percent had bought from a dealer.[13] Drugs are usually sold by professional dealers at some point in their supply chain, but it seems that after that, they are widely passed around through networks of friends.

This could, perhaps, be good news for the authorities as they seek to crack down on the trade amid a boom in online drug-retailing. The move online makes things harder in one way, replacing the old, fragile dealing networks with a vast open market that is resilient to attacks against individual members. But if in fact there is a sort of "after-retail" market, in which drugs are passed around a secondary network of friends and acquaintances, there may be scope for a different sort of intervention. Looking at the map of high-school romances, one can import some of its lessons. The researchers started off with the assumption that targeting the best-connected people would pay the highest dividends. In the school, this meant the people with the most sexual partners; in the drug world, it could mean the dealers. What they found was that it made more sense to target less-well-connected members of the network, because although they were attached to fewer people, they formed links in long chains that were relatively easy to break up. Apply this to the drug world, and it may be that an effective intervention would be to focus on the nonprofessional dealers who informally pass drugs on to friends. These people are the equivalent of the high school students with few partners: they might be relatively easy to influence, and breaking just one link in a friendship "chain"—that is, preventing one person from passing drugs on to others—would mean that a large group of people is severed from the distribution network.

Ways of doing this could include public information campaigns on the risks of passing drugs on to loved ones or of leaving medicine cabinets well stocked and unlocked. A greater effort to publicize the acts of violence in supplier countries that are funded by consumers in the rich world might help to increase the taboo around illegal drugs— particularly cocaine—making them less likely to be offered to family or friends. A harder approach could introduce stiffer penalties for those who buy drugs to share, even if such people are not widely seen as "dealers." As the drug business goes online, where it is easier for ordinary people to buy relatively large quantities, these patterns of informal sharing and dealing among friends may become more common. A campaign of education and deterrence against buying in bulk for friends could offer a new way to break up a different part of the network, now that the upper part has effectively been swallowed up by online marketplaces.

Chapter 9

DIVERSIFYING INTO NEW MARKETS

From Drug Smuggling to People Smuggling

From the Mexican side of the border, the quick scramble from a life of poverty into the glorious, rich surroundings of California doesn't look particularly difficult. Walk through the tumbledown Tijuana suburbs that spill over the hills right up to the frontier, and you come to an old and rusty corrugated-iron fence, topped with ancient barbed wire that in many areas has been pulled away. The metal barrier is as low as eight feet in some places, meaning that even a child standing on an upturned old crate can scale it. Passing objects over the fence is even easier: many residents of Colonia Libertad, an impoverished barrio whose outer edges are squashed right up against the border of the rich world, appear to be in the habit of lobbing their garbage over the fence into the United States.

From the unpaved streets of Colonia Libertad, the crossing might look easy. But from the California side you can see that getting into the United States is a much harder business than it used to be. A few hundred feet beyond the rusty old fence stands another, much newer one. Fourteen feet tall and topped with razor wire, it is illuminated by floodlights and monitored from watchtowers around the clock. Agents from La Migra, as Mexicans call the US immigration authorities, patrol up and down on quad bikes, equipped with night-vision goggles after dark. The fence stretches as far as the eye can see in either direction, following the contours of the hilly scrubland. Camera-equipped drones whirr overhead along its length.

A crackdown on illegal border crossings, which began with a big increase in security spending in the 1990s, has made it far trickier for undocumented migrants to slip into the United States. But young Mexicans with American dreams still try to make the crossing every day—and now they have a powerful new ally. Recent years have seen a growing number of migrants make the difficult and dangerous journey with the help of guides and fixers supplied or licensed by Mexico's drug cartels, which appear to be diversifying into the people-smuggling business. Mexican and American officials have detected the cartels' fingerprints on the increasingly sophisticated attempts to outwit La Migra, as well as more sinister related businesses, such as the trafficking of migrants for exploitation. "We know that these transnational criminal networks do a lot more than drug trafficking—they'll do whatever is profitable. If guns are profitable, they'll traffic guns. If people are profitable, then they will traffic people," Loretta Sanchez, a California member of Congress, told a congressional hearing in 2014.

People smuggling is not the only business into which the cartels are diversifying. As well as the usual criminal rackets—extortion, prostitution, car theft, and so on—the mobs have gone into more unusual areas. If you eat enough guacamole, there is a good chance that at some point you will tuck into an avocado grown or taxed by the Knights Templar cartel, which is said to control much of the agricultural business in the state of Michoacán. Likewise, if you down enough mojitos you may consume a squirt of cartel-grown lime, another industry that in some parts of Mexico is controlled by organized crime. El Salvador was once home to the feared Cártel de los Quesos—the Cheese Cartel—which imported cheap cheese from Honduras. (If you have ever tasted Salvadoran cheese you will immediately understand why this was necessary.) In some areas the cartels are involved in bigger business: Mexican officials have said that the Knights Templar cartel makes more money from taxing the iron-ore industry than it does from drugs. Pemex, the national oil monopoly, loses more than 3 million barrels of fuel a year to bandits who drill into its pipelines, sometimes accidentally blowing themselves up.

The wide range of businesses in which the cartels are now involved means that some analysts say it no longer makes sense even to refer to the cartels as mere drug traffickers. Some institutions, including the FBI, now call them "transnational crime organizations," or TCOs. (Online, it seems, the term has yet to catch on: a Google search for "Mexican TCOs" prompts the question: "Did you mean: Mexican *TACOs*?") Whatever you call them, one thing is clear: drug cartels are spreading their tentacles into new industries.

• • •

Their branching out mimics the behavior of legitimate companies. Firms looking to grow, and especially those with surplus cash to invest (always a problem for criminal organizations, for whom banking is tricky), strike out into new markets where they believe their existing expertise could give them a head start. The diversification of Mexico's cartels comes a few decades after corporate America's last great wave of diversification. In 1950, fewer than one-third of companies in the Fortune 500 operated in more than one industry. By 1974, nearly two-thirds did. Diversification mania reached its peak in 1977, when Coca-Cola attempted to enter the wine industry, with the acquisition of Taylor Wines. Perhaps unsurprisingly, no one much liked the idea of Château Coke, and the idea flopped. Since then, the trend has been in the opposite direction, with companies returning to focus on a few things that they do really well. But the wave of diversification is instructive, because the ideas that motivated it help to explain what is driving the current trend in the criminal world.

Take Coca-Cola wine (a good match with Salvadoran cheese, perhaps). It may have been a failure, but it is a good example of what management gurus call "concentric diversification," when a company makes use of its expertise in one area to launch a product line aimed at new customers. Coca-Cola knew nothing about wine. But it has a genius for marketing and branding, and it runs one of the most sophisticated distribution networks on earth. Its bet was that it could apply its marketing know-how and distribution muscle to the wine industry. Drug cartels getting into people smuggling are making a similar bet. They have no immediate expertise in the migration business; and the "clients" in that industry—Mexican peasants who want to move to the United States—represent a new market, different in every way from the rich Americans who buy the cartels' main product. But the business of smuggling things over the border in secret, bribing or intimidating public servants along the way, is a skill that can be applied across various industries. If you can smuggle drugs, why not people?

One man who knows a lot about crossing the border, both legally and illegally, is Víctor Clark Alfaro, an academic based in Tijuana who teaches anthropology classes at San Diego State University. Like many people in the border region, he lives an international existence, crossing into the United States twice a week to give his lectures. I go to meet him in his Tijuana home, which doubles as the Binational Center for Human Rights, a small NGO that he runs. After climbing the outdoor stairs of his apartment block, I come to a heavy-looking front door, which Clark carefully unchains, apologizing for the delay as he does so. Five months earlier, the state government had removed the bodyguards they had earlier assigned to him for the dirt-digging investigative work he does. In the past, he has blown the whistle on state officials selling police IDs to the local cartel. That sort of thing can earn a man enemies.

Inside, in an office lined with books and papers, Clark, whose research interests focus on Tijuana's ample underbelly, tells me about market conditions in the people-smuggling business. He regularly chats with the local "coyotes," as people-smugglers are known; some of them have even participated in his lectures in San Diego, appearing via Skype to talk to American students about the smuggling game. Broadly, he says, there are two types of service. The basic option is to sneak over the frontier with a guide on foot, hoping to avoid the US Border Patrol's sentries. For those with deeper pockets, or without the stamina to wade through rivers or cross deserts and mountains, there is a luxury option: crossing "in the line," meaning walking up to the immigration desk with fake documents. Coyotes buy a secondhand visa for $100 or so, and make the client up to look like the person in the photo. A guide surreptitiously directs the migrant to whichever line is moving fastest—a sign that the person on duty is giving the documents only a cursory check. No detail is overlooked: the coyotes even put souvenirs in their clients' bags to make them look like day-trippers.

Lately, however, the industry has been turned upside down, Clark says. "The attacks of 9/11 caused the United States to see the border as a subject of national security. The border is now extremely well patrolled—practically closed." The crackdown has made it harder for the coyotes to provide their usual services. As a result, they have jacked up their prices: foot crossings, which used to cost $2,000, now cost $5,000 in Tijuana. Crossing in the line, which used to cost $5,000, can now cost as much as $13,000. The local coyotes are "in crisis," he says.

The following day I walk over the border myself, at the checkpoint in San Ysidro. Although my British passport is in order, my conversation with Clark has left me feeling oddly nervous about walking into the United States. I wonder how many of the people in the line around me are using false documents or carrying bags full of hastily bought souvenirs in an attempt to pass themselves off as tourists. Once through customs, I meet up with Mike Jimenez, a supervisory agent with the Border Patrol in the San Diego region. To give an idea of the sort of reception that illegal migrants face, he takes me on a tour of the Tijuana border from the American side. It is a frightening gauntlet to run. Seismic sensors check for footsteps (though they are also sometimes tripped by deer). Ground-penetrating radar scans for tunnels; remote-controlled robots trundle around the sewer system, into which migrants have sometimes burrowed. The heavier policing of the land around the border means that more people are going by sea, a passage that costs between $5,000 and $9,000. On foggy days, up to twenty-five people at a time are ferried up the coast in rickety speedboats, sometimes landing as far north as Santa Barbara, nearly two hundred miles from the Mexican border.

At the same time, the penalties have been stiffened for people involved in the smuggling business. Sometimes in the past there would be no consequences for US citizens caught driving illegal migrants away from the border area. Now, they are prosecuted the first time. A biometric database, shared with the FBI, tells the Border Patrol if the person has previous convictions. And people are now arrested even for ferrying small groups of people; previously, guides were more likely to be let off if their group numbered fewer than seven. "It's harder to get people to do the job [of people smuggling] if the penalties are stiffer," Jimenez says.

It is still possible to cross, of course, but the extra level of security has ramped up smugglers' costs. Guides who face a higher risk of being jailed demand higher salaries. To prevent the guides from being captured, some organizations have increased the size of their vehicle fleet, so that a car of migrants can follow a car driven by the guide, meaning that if the migrants are stopped, the guide can get away. At the border fence, some guides have cut through the sturdy wire mesh using portable battery-powered saws. Jimenez says that many coyotes have invested in night-vision goggles of their own. Some may even be using drones. Unmanned aircraft overloaded with drugs have occasionally been known to crash near the border; the same technology could presumably be used to monitor the positions of border guards, helping migrants to cross undetected.

As well as driving up smugglers' costs, technology has given more bargaining power to their clients, who are able to determine which coyotes are the most trustworthy by using feedback on social media. Just as sites such as the Silk Road have raised competition in the drugs business, social networks have allowed would-be migrants to swap price and customer-service information about border crossings. "Does anyone know a coyote who can help me cross the border to the United States?" asks one person on the Spanish-language section of the Yahoo! website. "Juan Carlos" replies, offering help and promising that he has GPS, experience in the desert, and "speaks 90 percent English." These changes mean that migrants can drive a harder bargain than they did in the days when hiring a coyote meant having to loiter near one of the international bridges as night fell.

Just how bad for business have the extra enforcement measures been? A research paper by a group of statisticians at the US Department of Homeland Security tried to answer this question.[1] Using information from interviews carried out with captured migrants, the authors were able to amass thousands of pieces of data on the prices paid to coyotes. Elderly people, children, and women (particularly pregnant women) have to pay extra, the authors found, presumably because these clients are more time-consuming to guide over the border. They also discovered that people from parts of central Mexico that have traditionally sent a lot of migrants to the United States generally pay a bit less, perhaps because their familiarity with the market means they are able to negotiate a better price. They found that smugglers offer group discounts—but impose penalties on really large parties, which are harder to shepherd across undetected. And there is greater demand for coyotes' services ahead of the American harvest season, and during construction booms, both of which rely on cheap Mexican labor.

The researchers plotted prices over time, taking data from the Border Patrol's interviews and from surveys carried out by other agencies in both the United States and Mexico. All of them showed that the price of crossing the border had risen steadily, and steeply, from a range of about $700–$1,400 in 1993, to $1,500–$2,400 by 2007 (all of those prices are in 2007 dollars). The average price has therefore

FIGURE 9.1 Migrants vs. La Migra

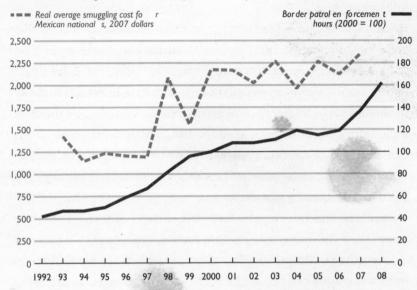

SOURCE: Bryan Roberts et al., "An Analysis of Migrant Smuggling Costs Along the Southwest Border," US Department of Homeland Security, Office of Immigration Statistics working paper, November 2010.

nearly doubled in real terms. Alongside this, the researchers plotted a line showing the number of staff-hours spent policing the border. The two lines match almost perfectly. (See Figure 9.1.) The report seems to confirm what Víctor Clark's smuggler sources claim: the extra enforcement on the American side has driven up the cost of crossing the border illegally.

After reading all this, and having seen the fearsome border obstacle course with my own eyes, I began to wonder what the cartels saw in this difficult market. Thanks to all the extra hours spent watching the line, crossing the border has become much more difficult. The Border Patrol now numbers some 21,000 officers, making it about the same size as Canada's active-duty army. Local coyotes are going out of business, and those who remain are charging far higher prices, which presumably dampens demand. Is there really any money to be made in people smuggling?

In San Diego, I go to see David Scott Fitzgerald, the co-chair of the Center for Comparative Immigration Studies at the University of California–San Diego. Since 2005, his department has carried out a fascinating annual survey of people in Jalisco, a state in central Mexico that sends a lot of migrants to America. His surveys suggest that the people-smuggling business is alive and well, and growing increasingly sophisticated. Some outfits now offer a door-to-door service, collecting migrants in groups from villages in Mexico's interior and handling all aspects of the journey to a city in the United States. A package from central Mexico to Los Angeles costs between $2,500 and $3,000—cheaper than the more basic packages offered by Tijuana's local coyotes, according to the prices quoted by Víctor Clark. To travel in more comfort, migrants can pay an extra $1,000 to rent forged documents, giving them a better chance if stopped by immigration officers. Customer satisfaction is high: Fitzgerald says that 95 percent of those who try to cross the border succeed, though not always on the first attempt. Between one-third and one-half of attempts are turned back, according to his survey. That is why most smugglers offer the migrant as many tries as it takes to get across, all included in the fee.

All the extra security at the border has had the effect of giving a competitive advantage to the more professional smugglers, Fitzgerald says. "A result of US enforcement is that coyote networks are more extensive, and those networks more criminalized." The relationship between coyotes and cartels is complex: rather than handling the migrants themselves, the cartels usually farm the job out to people smugglers, who pay the cartel for *derecho de piso*—literally "floor rights," or a license to use the cartels' turf and contacts around the border. In some cases, it seems that the cartels have allowed their valuable drug-trafficking infrastructure to be used to smuggle migrants. In 2014, a tunnel being used for people smuggling was discovered in

Colonia Libertad in Tijuana. Mexican police raided two buildings: one a safe house for guarding the migrants (who often come from Central America, and therefore have to keep a low profile in Mexico, where they do not have permission to be), and another just a few yards from the border, containing the hidden entrance to a tunnel that emerged in California.

As the people-smuggling business gets tougher, the cartels, or at least cartel-aided coyotes, seem to be gaining market share over the more basic, one-person operations. That may not be desirable. But it may be tolerable if the overall size of the market is shrinking. Making the border harder to cross must make people less willing to cross it, one would think.

Yes and no. A tougher border probably does put some people off. But it has persuaded others that taking out the services of a coyote is essential. Getting past the ground sensors and night-vision cameras in San Diego, or trekking through the Arizona desert alone, is beyond the capability of most would-be migrants ("suicide" is how Víctor Clark succinctly describes the idea). So seeking professional help has become more appealing. Survey evidence seems to back this up. In the early 1970s, only 40–50 percent of illegal migrants engaged the services of a coyote. In 1990, the figure was 80 percent. By 1999, it had grown to 90 percent. A survey in 2006 (this one only questioned first-time cross-ers) found that 95 percent used a coyote.[2] Increased enforcement has helped to turn a cheap service that most migrants ignored into a very high-earning one that nearly all of them decide to purchase.

Could it still be that fewer people are making the trip overall, and that the cartels are simply getting a bigger share of a shrinking market? If you look at recent years, that looks like a plausible theory. No one knows quite how many people cross the American border illegally, but some of the best estimates come from the Pew Hispanic Center. It cal-culates that since 2000, the annual flow of immigrants from Mexico has fallen from about 770,000 a year to fewer than 150,000, a steep drop that neatly coincides with the ramping up of border patrols.[3] But the story before then is different. Between 1991 and 2000, during which time border-patrolling hours increased by about 150 percent, there was no fall in migration at all. In fact, quite the reverse: annual migration doubled during this period. This makes it hard to believe that border security is a major factor in determining the number of people who make the crossing. In other words, it seems that although the crackdown at the frontier has an impact on the cost of crossing, it doesn't seem to put people off trying to get to America.

Maybe that shouldn't be so surprising. Mexican laborers moving to the United States stand to quadruple their real wages, even once the higher cost of living is taken into account. And the cost of crossing is often subsidized by family members already working in the United States. To get an idea of what makes people decide to make the dangerous crossing, I go to one of Tijuana's several "migrant houses," stopping-off shelters for people who are making the journey north. The Instituto Madre Assunta, which is run by a network of Catholic missionaries, allows female migrants to stay for up to two weeks, during which time they are given three meals a day, clean clothes, and access to medical and legal help. In a small computer room off a sunny courtyard, women talk to their children on Skype. Mary Galván, the center's director, is depressed about the US approach to immigration. "We had great hopes for Obama. We expected there would be a big reform to help migrants," she says. But it was "*todo lo contrario*"—exactly the opposite. During Obama's first presidential term, from 2009–2013, an average of nearly 400,000 illegal aliens was deported each year—double the number at the turn of the century, and nearly ten times more than in the early 1990s. These days, most of the women in the migrant shelter are people who have just been deported. Most of them are planning immediately to return.

The women I speak to all have different reasons for wanting to go to the United States. Some are economic. Ángela, a dark-skinned woman in her thirties from the southern state of Oaxaca, has just been deported after spending nearly four years in San Bernardino, California, where she worked in a recycling plant. There she was earning what was then the minimum wage of $8 per hour; Mexico's minimum wage averages under $5 per *day*. All the women I speak to mention the jobs they held in the United States: one in a hotel and a gas station, another as a seamstress in a swimsuit factory and a nanny. Others mention family. Rosa, a forty-five-year-old, left her home in Guadalajara at age twenty-one, fleeing a violent husband. Like Ángela, she has been living in San Bernardino, with a new husband and three daughters. Being deported means she has "lost everything," she says. But she is hopeful that she can fool the border agents with the ID and birth certificate of a friend, who, with a quick change of hairstyle, she more or less resembles. Another woman, Trinidad, who seems to be slightly disturbed, is aiming to go back north to find her nine-year-old son, a US citizen who, she says, was taken from her by the government. She is planning to go back with the help of a coyote, as she has once before. "There are animals and snakes. It takes maybe one or two days. You suffer. Some die. There is cold, there is heat, there is no water." But the "great pain" of being without her son means she has no choice, she says.

Making the border harder to cross has made migrants like these women almost certain to pay for the help of a coyote, when previously they might not have. It has increased the price that they (or their American relatives) will hand over to the people smugglers. It has increased the chances that those people smugglers will be linked to serious organized-crime networks. All this, and yet it seems to have done very little to dissuade them from making the journey. Hearing the women's stories, of the chance to earn in an hour what in Mexico it would take a day to make, or of the hope of being reunited with a lost child, makes it seem fanciful to think that the need to pay an extra thousand dollars or so would make them turn back. The vast increase in spending on border security has inadvertently transformed the people-smuggling business from an optional, cheap, amateur affair into a near-compulsory, very expensive, and cartel-dominated one. It is a gift to organized crime.

·　　·　　·

Cartels' "concentric diversification" into people smuggling seems to have been more successful than Coca-Cola's foray into winemaking. But they haven't stopped there. Instead, they are experimenting with other new markets, via a type of diversification that management gurus call "horizontal."

For a good example of this from the legitimate business world, look at a company that is about as different from a drug cartel as one could get: Disney. The Walt Disney Company started off making cartoons. Those cartoons established a following among children and their families, so Disney set about diversifying into all manner of other businesses, from theme parks to vacation cruises to television broadcasting, which it now sells to the same customers. "I suppose my formula might be: dream, diversify and never miss an angle," Walt Disney once said. He followed his own advice: the Mickey Mouse silhouette can now be found on toys, clothes, books, stationery, and a multitude of other products. Disney has diversified not through its key skills—after all, running a theme park or a cruise ship has little in common with making a cartoon—but through its audience. The people who go to Disney's theme parks or buy its branded clothes are the same people who enjoy watching its cartoons and movies. This strategy—launching completely different products, aimed at existing customers—is horizontal diversification in action.

How does this work for drug cartels? First, examine their market: drug takers, mostly in the rich world. What substances do they consume? Estimates of exactly how much money the Mexican cartels make from different drugs vary widely, but everyone agrees that cocaine and marijuana make up the lion's share of their drug income. Depending on whose estimate you trust, the proportion of total drug income accounted for by cocaine and marijuana alone is probably somewhere between 74 percent (based on a midpoint estimate by the RAND Corporation) and 90 percent (according to a slightly dubious calculation by the US Office of National Drug Control).[4]

Focusing so much on just two product lines is a dangerous strategy, especially in the notorious faddy market for drugs. Drugs go in and out of fashion with every generation; teenagers don't take much LSD nowadays, any more than they wear flared pants. Focusing on cocaine and cannabis has looked especially risky in recent years. Cocaine, the biggest money spinner for Mexican cartels according to most estimates, has been going out of fashion in the United States. No one is quite sure why—especially given that it has become more popular in Europe at the same time—but coke consumption in America fell by one-half in the years 2006–2010. The cannabis market looks healthier, with consumption going up by nearly one-third during the same period. But there are different threats to the cartels there, in the form of powerful new American competitors that are operating in the states that have legalized the marijuana business, and that now threaten to take over the market (see Chapter 10).

In the face of such stormy conditions, Mexico's cartels have diversified into other drugs. One is crystal meth. Meth can be made anywhere, but keeping a clandestine laboratory running is easier and cheaper in a relatively lawless country like Mexico than it is in the United States. In recent years the Mexican authorities have uncovered some setups that make Walter White's lab in *Breaking Bad* look like a kitchen operation. One raid in 2012 saw them blow open a warehouse just south of Guadalajara to uncover a professional-looking laboratory containing fifteen tons of the drug, along with seven tons of the precursor chemicals used to make it. Discoveries like that used to be unusual. But lately they have become far more common: whereas in 2008 the police in Mexico discovered twenty-one meth labs, the following year they found 191.

The US border authorities have intercepted a growing amount of Mexican meth bound for America, too. In 2001, they discovered 1.3 tons of the drug; by 2010, the annual figure had risen to 4.5 tons.

The Mexican cartels' move into meth has been helped enormously by American law-enforcement agencies. Until recently, making meth in the United States was fairly easy. The main ingredient, pseudo-ephedrine, could be found in common cold medicines, so brewing up a batch meant simply making a trip to the drugstore and following an online recipe. Although the process is potentially explosive—addicts have been known to blow their hands off—it is not especially difficult. But homemade meth became much tougher to create following the Combat Methamphetamine Epidemic Act of 2005, which restricted the sale of medicines containing pseudoephedrine and other similar chemicals. Now, anyone buying more than a small quantity faces arrest—whatever their motive. One of the first such arrests to be reported was of a man stocking up on allergy medicines for his son, who was going off to church camp.

The law worked, but it had two unintended consequences. One was that American meth manufacturers recruited armies of their friends and family, along with unemployed people looking to make a fast buck, to buy small quantities of cold medicine from different pharmacies and then sell it to the manufacturer at a profit. Thousands of these "smurfs," as the straw-purchasers were known, were thus introduced to the drugs business. Sometimes paid in product, as well as cash, many of them developed meth addictions of their own.

These "smurfing" operations are expensive to run, however, and so it wasn't long before many American meth makers went out of business. But then came the second unintended consequence. The business moved south of the border, to Mexico—and the Mexicans turned out to be much better at it. Mexican cartels, which have in the past bribed local police to overlook entire fields full of marijuana plants, had little trouble setting up crystal meth factories of a scale unheard of in the

United States. And just as Walter White found, when you make the drug on a larger scale, using more sophisticated equipment, you come up with a much better product. Since the Mexican labs came onstream, the average purity of meth in America has doubled. Not only that: the efficiency of the labs means that Mexican meth is far cheaper than the amateurish stuff cooked up in American kitchens. The average price of the drug in the United States has fallen by more than two-thirds following Mexicans' ramping up of supply. And the manufacturers seem to be taking their cues from *Breaking Bad:* blue crystals, Walter White's signature product, reportedly command a higher price than the regular off-white variety (unlike White, manufacturers apparently fake the blue effect by using food coloring).

Encouraged by their success in meth, the cartels have started to diversify into another, potentially even more profitable drug: heroin. From the point of view of the Mexicans, heroin is an especially appealing market to get into. Unlike cocaine, which they have to import from South America, or meth, which is made from chemicals usually brought in from the Far East, heroin can be made at home. Poppies are cultivated in the mountains of the Sierra Madre by farmers known as *gomeros,* or "gummers," for the way that they harvest the gluey sap from the poppies. The process is simple: a razor blade is drawn across the side of the flower's bulging seed pod, causing a milky sap to ooze out. Left in the sun, the sap hardens into gum, which the *gomeros* scrape off. This is raw opium. The opium gum is boiled with water and lime in order to extract morphine, which is then turned into heroin with the help of a few readily available chemicals: sodium carbonate, hydrochloric acid, and a bit of charcoal. By now barely 5 percent of its original weight, the finished product is ready for shipment. Keeping the business vertically integrated, from production to distribution, allows the cartel to reap greater rewards. "The profit margins are higher on heroin—there's no payback to Colombia," says Kevin Merrill, the assistant special agent in charge of the DEA's division in Denver, Colorado.

Mexican cartels have historically been reluctant to enter the heroin market for two reasons. The first concerns the demand side. Americans fell in love with heroin in the 1960s and 1970s, when the Velvet Underground released a song dedicated to the drug and the Rolling Stones sang jauntily about relaxing "with a needle and a spoon." But the relationship soon soured. Public-information campaigns educated teenagers about heroin's addictiveness and the risk of overdose, and a few of the famous people who had made the drug seem so glamorous eventually died of it. Heroin's reputation quickly went from rather exciting to straightforwardly terrifying. By the 1980s, its status as a vice only of the inner-city poor was cemented. By the early 1990s, it had lost even that title, as it was overtaken by crack cocaine. Once so promising, the heroin market withered.

The second reason is that the Mexicans have always faced a barrier on the supply side. Opium poppies are easy to grow, but the hills of the Sierra Madre are patrolled on foot and from the air by the Mexican armed forces, and they destroy any sign of the *gomeros'* poppy cultivation. Colombian planters, who enjoy harder-to-access terrain and weaker enforcement, have long been able to produce the poppies more cheaply than their Mexican rivals. With ebbing demand and difficulty organizing supply, the Mexicans saw little reason to get into heroin.

But then two things happened that changed all of this. To understand what turned the American heroin market around, meet Cynthia Scudo. A young-looking grandmother with a slim figure and a neat, dark haircut, she draws up in a Subaru SUV, smartly dressed in black and carrying a Louis Vuitton handbag. Scudo's family, which lives in a well-to-do suburb of Denver, has been touched by heroin addiction. That may seem surprising: heroin has the reputation of a drug of the inner-city poor, not of the comfortable, suburban middle classes. But stranger still, the addict in the family was not Scudo's son, or grandson. It was Scudo herself. We meet at CeDAR, the Center for Dependency, Addiction, and Rehabilitation, the Denver clinic where she recently put an end to nine years of heroin addiction. Sitting down at a table on the clinic's pleasant grounds, she recalls with a shudder how, on admission to the detox program, she vomited every fifteen minutes for the first six days. Even before that she had been left skeletal by the drug, finding herself buying children's-size pants. In rehab, her weight dropped to eighty-nine pounds.

Scudo's case shows how well the cartels have managed to overcome the first obstacle—heroin's image problem. Heroin has a frightening reputation, and rightly so: the margin between an effective dose and an overdose is narrower than that of any other mainstream narcotic. A paper in *Addiction*, an academic journal, estimated the quantity of various drugs needed to get an average person high versus the amount required to kill them.[5] In the case of alcohol, it found that the ratio was about ten to one—in other words, if a couple of shots of vodka are enough to make you tipsy, twenty shots might kill you, if you can keep them down. Cocaine, it found, was slightly safer, with a ratio of fifteen to one. LSD has a ratio of 1,000 to one, whereas marijuana is safest of all: it is impossible to die of overdose, as far as anyone can tell. Even with the edibles, there is no evidence that one can die of overdose— you simply have a stronger and longer-lasting effect than you may have wanted. For heroin, the ratio between an effective dose and a deadly one is just six to one. Given that batches vary dramatically in their purity, each shot is a game of Russian roulette. Dealers may not care much about this if their market is people who feel they have nothing much to live for. But for the product to really sell, the drug's appeal has to be broadened, which means softening its image.

Fortunately for the cartels, they had an unwitting accomplice: America's doctors, who in recent years have done more to improve the reputation of opiates than any drug dealer could have hoped. Scudo's ordeal began when she sustained a hip injury. Her doctor was happy to help—too happy, as it turned out. She was prescribed a daily dose of six pills of OxyContin, a powerful opioid painkiller. "I suppose doctors want patients to be satisfied so that they come back," she says. And she did come back, again and again. "I was hooked. I was finishing my thirty-day script in ten days." The doctor kept the pills coming. But then one day he left, and his replacement, horrified, cut down Scudo's dose. Desperate, she began crushing, snorting, and smoking the pills, to enhance their effect. It wasn't enough. Extra OxyContins were available on the black market. But at $80 each, they were too expensive for Scudo to be able to buy enough to keep away the sickness of withdrawal. Then, through a shady friend of her daughter, she was introduced to a drug that would have exactly the same effect, for a fraction of the cost. That drug was heroin. Whereas a single day's supply of black-market OxyContin cost $480, an entire week's supply of heroin cost only about $350, part of which she was able to afford by selling her small supply of OxyContins. As if from nowhere, Scudo had become a heroin addict.

Her story may sound fantastical, but hundreds of thousands of Americans have ended up in this vulnerable position, thanks to a surge in prescriptions of opioid painkillers during the 1990s and 2000s. The quantity of powerful opioid drugs being dished out by doctors is breathtaking: in some states, concentrated in the South, the number of prescriptions made each year is now greater than the population. The drugs help to save some patients from excruciating pain. But the rampant overprescription means that they are widely abused: about 11 million Americans a year take them illegally, more than the number who use cocaine, ecstasy, methamphetamine, and LSD combined.

Prescribed by kindly doctors, in packaging with the reassuring logo of a well-known pharmaceutical company, they put a respectable face on hard drugs. Art Schut, the head of Arapahoe House, another Denver rehab clinic, tells me that many of the heroin addicts he sees now are well-off young people of college age who get into heroin via OxyContin or similar pills. "Most of them are middle or upper-middle class, and the pathway is prescription drugs. Prescription drugs are pure, they're medicine, we think they're good for us. It's a pretty easy step," he says. Nationwide, two-thirds of America's heroin addicts started off by abusing prescription painkillers.

Recently there has been something of a crackdown. OxyContin's manufacturer, Purdue, has come up with a chewy version of the pill, which cannot be so easily ground up for snorting or injection. Doctors must now check patients' records to see if they have been prescribed painkillers elsewhere; clinics that break the rules are shut down. But in the short term, this has left millions of painkiller addicts in the same position that Cynthia Scudo was in, without access to their normal supply, and desperate for a substitute.

For the cartels, this represents an extraordinary opportunity to tap a new market. For one thing, the heroin brand has been decontaminated by prescription drugs. Better still, the people taking those gateway drugs are a group that drug dealers have historically found hard to reach: older, richer women. Already, the cartels have started successfully turning these people into customers. A fascinating study led by Theodore Cicero of Washington University in St. Louis, Missouri, compares today's heroin users with those of past generations, finding that the typical addict today is from a completely different demographic than the one who took the drug a generation ago.[6] Whereas in the 1960s, more than 80 percent of heroin addicts were men, the gender balance now is nearly 50-50, with women in the slight majority. Users' ethnic background has changed, too. In 1970, fewer than half of heroin users were white. Now, 90 percent are. And their average age has gone up. In the 1960s, the average age of first-time use was harrowingly low, at just sixteen. Now the average first-timer is twenty-four, positively ancient by the standards of the drugs business, which is mainly a young person's game.

The demand side of the heroin market has been transformed. What changed things on the supply side? The answer lies south of the border, in a decision taken in 2006 by the new president of Mexico, Felipe Calderón. He had squeezed into the presidency that year by the slimmest of margins, beating his nearest rival by less than 1 percent. Opposition parties were unfairly but noisily crying fraud; a protest at his inauguration meant that the new president had to scuttle out of the congressional offices by the back door. It was a humiliating start to his presidency, and in a show of strength, Calderón made a bold promise: he was going to crush the country's murderous drug cartels once and for all. In the following years, as sky-high levels of violence erupted in Mexico's ports and border cities, Calderón called in the firepower of the army, sending thousands of soldiers to patrol the streets where cartels were terrorizing the locals. Cities such as Juárez bristled with troops, with mixed results (see Chapter 2). But one consequence of this strategy was that the armed forces were taken off their ordinary duties—including patrolling the Sierra Madre. Suddenly, the poppy plantations were left unwatched.

The *gomeros* wasted no time. "It's like any other business. Where there's demand, they'll look to provide that product," says Kevin Merrill of the DEA. From 2006, poppy production surged, reaching a high of nearly 20,000 hectares, or almost 50,000 acres (at the start of the decade, total cultivation had been barely 2,000 hectares, or just under 5,000 acres, according to the United Nations). Mexico is now the world's third-biggest poppy grower, after Afghanistan and Myanmar. And most of it seems to be heading north. The amount of heroin seized at the US border with Mexico octupled, from about 250 kilograms in 2005 to more than 2,000 kilograms in 2013. For the United States, the DEA figures that Mexican cartels now supply virtually all the heroin in the West, and about half of that in the East (the rest is mostly from Colombia and Afghanistan).

The vertical integration of the heroin business has been maintained, with the cartels selling the drug through cells of mainly Mexican and Honduran dealers. Members of the cells are recalled to Mexico every four to six months, outfoxing the DEA's attempts to infiltrate the groups. Dealers work the streets between 6:00 a.m. and 5:00 p.m. before counting up the proceeds and reporting back to base in Mexico, where the "command and control" still takes place, Merrill says. When setting up shop in a new neighborhood, it is common for them to give away free samples. Although Mexican heroin is of lower purity than other types, it suits the new, middle-class market well. Some users say that "brown" Mexican heroin is easier to smoke or snort than the "black tar" variety more prevalent in Asia. The possibility of smoking the drug has made it easier to market to new, wary users, who are put off by needles and the "junkie" image that goes with them. "I somehow thought that if I didn't inject it, I wasn't a heroin addict," Scudo says sheepishly. She would often buy her drugs, packaged in little balloons that the dealer kept in his mouth, ready to swallow, at the intersection of Sixth Avenue and Sheridan Boulevard in Denver. Passing that intersection still brings a shiver of temptation, she says. "After rehab, I was driving home and my hands started shaking on the steering wheel."

She resisted the temptation to pull over. But many do not. Some 680,000 Americans used heroin in 2013, nearly double the number that had used it only six years earlier. For the cartels, this represents an extraordinarily successful diversification of their business. A drug that many believed was dying out has been rehabilitated, now sold to an unsuspecting and lucrative new market. As cocaine goes out of fashion and cannabis is taken over by the legal market, the cartels can be expected to push even harder at their deadly Plan B.

Chapter 10

COMING FULL CIRCLE

How Legalization Threatens the Drug Lords

There is no sign on the door of the large gray warehouse that I have driven out to on the edge of Denver, Colorado. But I check my phone's map and this seems to be the place: an unmarked lot in a nondescript business park in one of the city's less glamorous neighborhoods. No one much is around, though I imagine someone watching me through the CCTV cameras that are trained on the warehouse's entrance as I walk up the ramp to the door. I buzz the unlabeled entry phone, and after a short wait the door is opened by a cheerful young man with a broad grin and a mop of blond hair, wearing Bermuda shorts and flip-flops. In a reception area inside, he carefully makes a copy of my driver's license, as more CCTV cameras look on. Opening another door, we are met with warm air and the faint hum of high-wattage lights and air conditioners. Most noticeable of all is an overpowering smell of marijuana.

This is the cannabis-growing facility of Denver Relief, which runs Denver's oldest legal marijuana dispensary. The firm was started in 2009 by Ean Seeb, a young Coloradan who became a devotee of medical marijuana after a skiing accident left him with an injury that only cannabis seemed to soothe. As if fate were giving him a hint, he later lopped off the tip of one of his fingers in another painful accident, which further persuaded him of the power of pot. Starting off with savings of just $4,000 and a stash of half a pound of marijuana, Denver Relief began as a delivery service, ferrying cannabis to the city's registered medical-marijuana patients, who have been allowed to use the drug with a doctor's permission since 2000. On January 1, 2014, Denver Relief broadened its market to include recreational users, after Colorado became the first place in the world to legalize the sale of marijuana for nonmedical purposes.

Nick Hice, the company's chief horticulturalist, shows me around the nursery. Wearing a white lab-technician's coat, he pushes open the double doors of the first growing room, where about a hundred mature plants—the "moms," as he calls them—are lined up against the walls, with 350 or so smaller plants sitting on tables in the center. Tiny cuttings are planted in pots of rockwool, where they are allowed to develop for two weeks before being moved to the tables. There they sit in soil, gobbling up imported European plant food and basking under the glare of a bank of halide lights. There are probes to test the pH level of the soil, and quantum meters to measure the amount of photons being given off by the lights. Temperature and humidity are minutely controlled. Everything is uploaded to a computer system, so that if there is a problem with a particular crop, the company can check back over one-hour periods for months, to see what happened.

Hice, whose parents run a more conventional sort of plant nursery in Ohio, modestly says that cultivating cannabis is "just like growing tomatoes." But he takes obvious pride in the immaculate facility. "There are a lot of books out there that are geared towards the amateur grower. But now we're finding out what really works: the amount of light, the temperature and humidity, the levels of nitrogen and phosphates," he enthuses. After a few weeks, the "girls" are carefully transferred to a second growing room, and then a third. Overall, it takes 140 days for the plants to be ready for harvesting, with plump buds that ooze a sticky sap that covers the leaves near the tops of the plants. The buds are plucked and set aside to be dried and sold, and the lower leaves are mashed up and filtered into a concentrated solution, which can be added to edible products or smoked.

For the cartels that have until now had total control over the cannabis market, Denver Relief's drug farm and the dozens more like it that have popped up in Colorado represent serious competition. For many years, the illegality of America's favorite drug meant criminal organizations held the exclusive rights to the market. And what a market: despite its illegality, about four out of ten Americans admit to having tried marijuana. Across the country, cannabis is thought to be worth roughly $40 billion a year—about the same as the recorded music industry. Until recently, every cent of that went to criminal organizations. But in 2014, Colorado, and then Washington state, became the first places in the United States, and the world, to allow law-abiding, tax-paying folk such as Seeb and Hice to enter the market. Later that year, Alaska and Oregon voted to follow suit. Many other states have vowed to do the same. In these few places, licensed businesses can now grow, process, and sell marijuana to anyone over the age of twenty-one, including those from other states or other countries. By the end of the first year of trading, Colorado's dispensaries alone had reached about $700 million in cannabis sales[1]—money that the cartels saw as rightfully theirs.

. . .

Colorado's legal businesses enjoy several important advantages over those that inhabit the black-market economy. Take the cultivation side of the industry first. Cannabis cultivation, like any other form of agriculture, benefits enormously from economies of scale. One big warehouse can grow crops more efficiently than lots of small ones. In the illegal economy, the danger of being discovered puts a natural ceiling on the scale of operations. In Mexico, some drug producers have managed to get away with hiding enormous cultivations, but usually only in remote, outdoor locations, where growing is nothing like as sophisticated as what goes on in Denver Relief's facility. Some Colorado growing rooms are larger than 100,000 square feet—about the size of a big supermarket. Each plant can produce about 75 grams of usable marijuana, with a retail value of a little over $1,000. This means that even a fairly modest grow-site, housing 1,000 plants, would have hundreds of thousands of dollars of cannabis under cultivation at any time. This is presumably why Denver Relief doesn't advertise its name on the side of its warehouse. But operating a large facility is far riskier for illegal operations, which don't have the option of taking out insurance— and, of course, they can hardly call the police if they are burgled.

Illegal cannabis plantations are also kept small by another constraint: electricity. Growing cannabis indoors—the best way to achieve a potent, valuable crop—requires the plants to be kept under bright, energy-intensive lights for many hours each day. That means a suspiciously large electricity bill. Online forums for cannabis enthusiasts buzz with messages from people wondering how much power they can use before their electricity provider reports them to the police. "Guides for growers used to say that as a rule of thumb a big TV uses about 1,000 watts. So if someone was growing in a five-bedroomed house, they could use maybe 5,000 watts without it looking too suspicious," says Hice. That is a puny amount: Denver Relief's facility uses about 150,000 watts of light, plus around another 100,000 watts in air-conditioning and other gadgetry. The bill comes to $800 per day.

For illicit growers, all the lights create another problem: heat. The police have caught on to this, and many departments now use infrared cameras to scan neighborhoods for suspiciously hot homes. Seen through the heat-sensitive camera of a police helicopter, a cannabis-growing house glows a giveaway bright-white in an otherwise dark street. The cops aren't the only ones who hunt for cannabis farms in this way: criminals in Birmingham, England, have been caught using drones equipped with infrared cameras to spot hidden grow-sites, to rob or extort the owners. "They are fair game," a drone-using extortionist told the local *Halesowen News*. "It is not like I'm using my drone to see if people have nice televisions. I am just after drugs to steal and sell. If you break the law then you enter me and my drone's world."[2]

The obstacles to growing cannabis illegally on any serious scale mean that unlicensed growers are at a big disadvantage when it comes to competing with the warehouses of Colorado in terms of quantity. But what of quality? Not much of a connoisseur of these things, I seek help from an expert. Genifer Murray meets me in the reception area of Cannlabs, a company she founded that in the words of its glossy investors' brochure, is "leading cannabis innovation." Murray, who wears a necklace from which dangles a diamante marijuana-leaf pendant, got a degree in microbiology and developed a fascination for the scientific side of weed. She started her business in 2010, in a tiny 150-square-foot laboratory. In 2014, following Colorado's recreational pot boom, Cannlabs moved to a high-tech, 2,000-square-foot lab, where increased its staff to more than thirty. Inside, many Coloradan strains are put through their paces.

Murray has seen the marijuana-growing business change. "Four years ago, it was very unsophisticated: people were just putting together soil, water, and light. Previously it was some guy who had been growing illegally in his basement. Nowadays, you have to have a horticulturalist. You need to treat [the grow-site] more as a pharmaceutical facility," she says. For $80, Cannlabs will test a single batch of marijuana, calculating the concentration of nine different cannabinoids, the elements that affect everything from the user's state of mind to his or her appetite. A gleaming silver gadget—"the Bentley of instrumentation," Murray proudly calls it—checks samples for pesticides. Other contaminants that may be flagged include heavy metals, as well as traces of butane and propane gas, which some manufacturers use in the production of concentrates and fail to eliminate before sale.

The upshot of this sophisticated testing is that consumers of legal marijuana know exactly what they are smoking, and what effect it is likely to have on them. Marijuana dispensaries in Denver have "menus" that list the various strains for sale. The options are accompanied by little descriptions that, with their flowery language, remind me of the blurbs you read on wine labels. "Pungent, peppery lemon with a kick of ammonia . . . a powerful, soaring, euphoric 'up' high," reads the description of a strain called Trainwreck on sale at The Clinic, one of Denver's biggest chains. "Licorice with citrus and minty undertones . . . very clear and cerebral" is how it describes Durban Poison, another strain being offered. Alongside the description is information about the concentration of different cannabinoids, showing that Durban Poison, for instance, is quite a bit stronger than Trainwreck. Some manufacturers even provide a time chart showing how long it will take the drug to kick in, and how long the effect will last—handy for consumers who need to drive the following morning.

Criminal dealers aren't totally inept when it comes to this sort of thing: illegal online marketplaces such as the Silk Road usually advertise their products with the same jazzy names and descriptions that legal dispensaries use. But the laboratory-backed information about potency and contaminants gives legal vendors an advantage over street dealers, particularly with new customers who may be nervous about smoking an unknown strain.

When it comes to those new customers, the legal market has devised various new ways to get people interested in lighting up. In downtown Denver, I meet Peter Johnson, the head of Colorado Green Tours, which is pioneering the intriguing new field of "marijuana tourism." In sunglasses, leather jacket, and slicked-back hair, Johnson meets me in the lobby of the Warwick Hotel, which, in spite of banning the consumption of marijuana on its premises, has become a favorite destination for pot tourists, owing to the fact that each room has a secluded balcony, ideal for a crafty smoke. Although cannabis has more or less come out into the open in Colorado, Johnson still suggests that we take a table in the corner of the restaurant, so that we can talk with more privacy.

Johnson describes himself as a "serial entrepreneur" who dabbled in technology during the dotcom boom. Now that reefer fever has come to Colorado, he has decided to make a go of the marijuana business. He says he has more than thirty different projects under way, including Cannabeds.com, which aims to be a pot-centric rival to Airbnb, the online lodging service, and an as-yet-unnamed taxi service, which he bills as a cannabis-friendly version of Uber, the taxi-calling smartphone app. He has a cannabis-themed hotel in the works, too, along with umpteen other projects. Is there really demand for all this stuff? "Absolutely!" Johnson exclaims. "It reminds me of the dotcom era in the 1990s. That was moving fast. But *this?*"—he looks around conspiratorially, as if hoping no one else will steal his idea—"This is moving faster." Comparisons to the dotcom bubble don't seem to me to be totally reassuring. And there is indeed a bubbly feeling to Colorado's marijuana market: by the end of 2014, the state had licensed 833 recreational marijuana dispensaries, to serve an estimated half a million monthly consumers.[3] Even if each of those customers stocks up every month, it would mean that each dispensary would see an average of only about twenty customers a day, which doesn't seem like enough to sustain a retail business. A spell of consolidation surely looms.

Customers from out of state are picking up some of the slack. According to Priceline.com, a hotel-booking service, among American students Denver was the third-most-searched-for spring break destination in the world in 2014. During the first nine months of recreational marijuana being on sale, 44 percent of sales in the Denver metropolitan area were to people from outside Colorado. In touristy mountain communities, such as Summit County, San Miguel, and Clear Creek, the figure was 90 percent. Johnson says that guests on his tours are mostly American, but he has had clients from all over the world: Europeans, especially, but also people from Australia, Japan, and Canada, as well as a lot of Brazilians. In contrast to the spring-break market, most of his customers are somewhere between thirty-five and sixty-five years old. Many haven't smoked in a while and are "looking for a little bit of hand-holding," he says. Some are people whose partners are in Denver on business, so they find themselves at loose ends during the day. Another niche is people with a few hours to kill at Denver's airport, one of the busiest in America. Those stuck with time on their hands can call 1-855-WEED-TOUR, and Johnson will send a limousine to pick them up and drive them around while they smoke in the back. All of these services, aimed at casual or first-time users, low on confidence and lacking contacts in the state, are ones that the illegal market cannot easily provide.

As I wander around Denver, seeing businesspeople go in and out of hotels and the convention center, I try to imagine their husbands and wives nervously lighting up a joint in the back of a Colorado Green Tours limo. It seems a bit improbable at first. But then legal firms are finding all sorts of ways of packaging cannabis in formats that appeal to different sorts of consumers. Walk into a marijuana dispensary and in addition to the shelves displaying glass jars of cannabis buds, and the cabinets of prerolled joints for novices, you will often see a refrigerator stocked with brightly colored drinks bottles, and shelves piled high with plastic packs of chocolates. Cannabis enthusiasts have long experimented with different ways of ingesting the drug, from hash brownies to the Indian *bhang lassi*, a yogurty, ganja-infused drink. Now, legalization has allowed players with real expertise to enter the market. So far, Colorado has licensed more than 250 "infused product manufacturers," or companies that take cannabis and turn it into tempting products that are impossible to find in the illegal market.

The biggest in Colorado is a company called Dixie Elixirs, which makes a range of cannabis drinks, chocolates, and pills. The inside of the Dixie factory looks rather like the crystal-meth laboratory in *Breaking Bad*. But it owes as much to Willy Wonka as it does to Walter White. While some of the white-coated technicians are working with concentrated narcotics, others are stirring vats of molten chocolate or plucking aluminum bottles off an assembly line. Chuck Smith, the company's chief financial officer, walks me around the factory, pausing to admire something called an Apeks Supercritical CO_2 Extraction Machine, a $100,000 spaghetti of dials, wires, and metal cylinders that extracts the active ingredients from cannabis plants. Different parts of the factory put together cannabis-infused drinks, in flavors such as Watermelon Cream and Sparkling Pomegranate, and even such products as massage oils.

Like the rest of the industry, the marijuana edibles market has become far more sophisticated since the recreational market was legalized. "Every year sees a quantum leap in technology. Five years ago we were in a small kitchen doing everything by hand," says Smith. In 2014, the company moved into a 30,000-square-foot factory, where visitors can peer into the glass-walled mixing rooms. The rapid development of new methods of consuming cannabis—from drinks to chocolate bars to Dixie's "dew drops," a highly concentrated liquid form of the drug that can be absorbed under the tongue—shows the nimbleness of entrepreneurs in the legitimate business world in coming up with new ways to reach new customers. Just as lager was invented to persuade more women to drink beer and "light" cigarettes were developed to target health-conscious smokers, edible or quaffable cannabis products may well open up a new market of potential potheads who don't like the idea of smoking a joint.

Dixie has made the most of the booming market, with revenues growing fivefold within the first six months of recreational weed being legalized. But as the firm's profile has risen, it has had to counter accusations that its products are more dangerous than its customers realize. Although marijuana is an unusually safe drug—it seems to be as good as impossible to overdose, with no fatalities ever recorded—taking too much of it can be a nasty experience, causing attacks of paranoia that can last for hours. Edibles firms have been singled out for criticism because it is far easier to overindulge with edible products than through smoking. Whereas the effects of a joint come on quickly, a chocolate bar or drink can take forty-five minutes to get the user high. A common mistake among first-timers is to have a nibble, feel no effect, and wolf down the rest—locking them into a prolonged, frightening experience from which they have no way out.

Maureen Dowd, a *New York Times* columnist, made this mistake on a reporting trip to Denver when she tucked into a chocolate bar that she later learned should have been shared among sixteen people. As she later wrote in the *Times*: "For an hour, I felt nothing. But then I felt a scary shudder go through my body and brain. I barely made it from the desk to the bed, where I lay curled up in a hallucinatory state for the next eight hours. . . . I was panting and paranoid, sure that when the room-service waiter knocked and I didn't answer, he'd call the police and have me arrested for being unable to handle my candy. . . . As my paranoia deepened, I became convinced that I had died and no one was telling me."[4]

A handful of people have come off much worse. Levi Thamba Pongi, a nineteen-year-old exchange student from Congo who was studying in Wyoming, leaped to his death from the balcony of the Denver Holiday Inn after eating a marijuana cookie that was supposed to be divided among six people. According to his friends, an hour after eating the cookie, he began speaking in French, throwing things around the hotel room, and trying to talk to a lamp. He then bolted from the room and threw himself off a balcony before they could stop him. Another man, Richard Kirk, was accused of shooting dead his wife after eating a marijuana cookie. Kirk pleaded guilty by reason of insanity.

Since those tragedies, Colorado has tightened up its rules on edibles, demanding clearer labeling and child-safe bottle tops. People in the edibles business point out that other products, notably alcohol, are far more dangerous and yet more loosely regulated. But pot companies have also realized that it is in their own interest to tread cautiously. "The thing that's going to kill the industry is if [companies] do it wrong, and give the industry a bad name," says Chuck Smith. Dixie's original range of drinks, which come in cute little bottles smaller

than a can of Coke, say in small letters on the side that they contain
up to 7.5 servings. That strikes me as a very high dose for a bottle that
contains barely seven gulps. Many customers seem to agree; Dixie has
responded to demand with a new range of lower-dose drinks called
Dixie One, which contain only 5 milligrams of tetrahydrocannabinol,
or THC, the chemical in cannabis that gets you high, rather than the
75 milligrams that its strongest drinks contain.

I leave Dixie's strange chocolate-drug factory feeling a bit more skeptical about the supposed harmlessness of cannabis. If a single chocolate
bar or a few gulps of pomegranate drink can make you go temporarily
crazy, it seems that the drug has evolved into something stronger than
is commonly thought. Still, it is encouraging that market forces seem
to be pulling firms such as Dixie in the direction of making milder
ranges of their product, rather than pushing them toward developing
ever-stronger versions. One thing is clear, though: however terrifying a
cannabis cookie is to Maureen Dowd or to other potential consumers,
it is a far scarier prospect for the cartels that currently deal marijuana
in America. No organized crime group, so far as I know, is in the business of smuggling chocolate hash brownies. Legal cannabis firms, by
contrast, are popularizing a new way of consuming drugs that could in
time bring in millions of new customers who don't like the idea of puffing on a bong but might be persuaded to try a THC-loaded drink. How
will the cartels fare against these new, legal competitors, who outdo
them in quantity, quality, and innovation?

. . .

The vast American cannabis market remains the cartels' to lose. Americans burn their way through more than 3,000 tons of marijuana a
year (some estimates put the figure two or three times higher). Some
is homegrown, and a little is imported from countries such as Canada and Jamaica. But for many years, the lion's share of that pot has
come from Mexico. In 2011, the US National Drug Intelligence Center, a now-defunct agency of the Department of Justice, estimated with

"high confidence" that Mexican cartels controlled "most" of the distribution of marijuana in more than 1,000 cities across the United States.
The previous year, a more detailed study by the RAND Corporation
estimated that the Mexicans supplied somewhere between 40 percent
and 67 percent of all the pot consumed in the country.[5]

Amid all the excitement in Denver, it is easy to forget that, as of
2015, only four of America's fifty states—Colorado, Washington, Oregon, and Alaska—have fully legalized cannabis. They are all smallish
ones, too: their combined population is only about 17 million, equivalent to 5 percent of the national population. Cartels might struggle
to compete with the legal cannabis industry in those four states, but
for the time being the remaining 95 percent of Americans have to buy
their weed on the black market (unless they can persuade a doctor to
give them a license to smoke medical marijuana, which is allowed in a
further twenty-one states, as well as the District of Columbia).[6] However, to the irritation of drug cartels and American police officers alike,
legal marijuana has a habit of finding its way into neighboring states. In
places where the drug is still outlawed, consumers now have a choice
between buying cannabis that is imported from Mexico or that which
is smuggled in from American states where it is legal. How much illicit
interstate trade goes on?

To find out, I go to see the man with the task of trying to contain
Colorado's marijuana: Tom Gorman, head of the Rocky Mountain
High-Intensity Drug Trafficking Area program, a federal counternarcotics initiative. In states where cannabis has been legalized,
federal-government outposts play a confused role, notionally continuing to fight a battle against marijuana even though a local cease
fire has been declared. Lying on the edge of town and decorated with
presidential portraits, star-spangled banners, and eagle statuettes, the
Rocky Mountain office has the feel of the last remaining garrison in a
rebellious province. But none of that seems to bother Gorman, an un-
stoppable one-man war on drugs. In black leather cowboy boots and a
bristling sandy moustache, he looks a bit like Chuck Norris's tougher

(if a little shorter) younger brother. On the wall of his office, mounted on a wooden plaque, is a dagger with which he was stabbed in the leg while raiding a house in California in the 1970s. (He washed the blood off his trousers, got his wife to sew up the hole, and continued to wear the same trousers on the beat, he says.) I briefly wonder if the solution to Latin America's cartel wars would simply be to send Gorman over there for a few days to teach the *bandidos* a lesson. Yet it turns out that even he is struggling to keep a lid on Colorado's new marijuana industry.

"The legal market has become the black market for the rest of the United States," he says. All you need is an ID proving you are over twenty-one years old to walk into a Colorado dispensary and buy up to a quarter of an ounce of marijuana. There is then little to stop you from driving over the border to states where cannabis is illegal. Police on the highways can do their best to intercept such traffic. But the borders are only state lines, not international frontiers: cops are not allowed simply to set up a checkpoint and carry out searches. To stop a vehicle, the police need there to have been a traffic violation and must then develop probable cause before being able to carry out a search. "I'd guess we're seizing 10 percent or less," says Gorman. Coloradan pot isn't only leaking out along the highways. It is also being sent through the mail. In 2010, the year after medical marijuana dispensaries mushroomed in Colorado, the US Postal Service intercepted fifty-seven pounds of marijuana being sent out of Colorado. By 2013, that figure had increased to 497 pounds, bound for thirty-three different states. And those are just the shipments that are spotted; no one knows how many make it through undetected.

It is hardly surprising that legal weed is seeping out. "Colorado marijuana is premium stuff. It doesn't have pesticides. Buy a pound of it here and you could double your money in Missouri or Iowa," says Gorman. Of course, the interstate trade in illicit goods is neither new, nor limited to drugs. Chatting to one cannabis retailer in Denver, I was told that just as Coloradan marijuana dispensaries do a roaring trade near the border with Wyoming (where the drug is banned), retailers in Wyoming make good money selling fireworks to residents of Colorado, who are not allowed to buy them in their home state. A quick look on-line confirms this: just as there are marijuana dispensaries listed not far from the Colorado state line, the Wyoming border is home to a wonder-world of fireworks, including Pyro City, "just two miles north of the Colorado/Wyoming border."

Illegal dealers are doing their best to cling on by serving niches that the legal market cannot reach. In Colorado, for instance, dispensaries have to close for the day at 7:00 p.m. So the evening shift still belongs to the black market. Nor are recreational-pot dispensaries allowed to offer home delivery, something that illegal dealers have long specialized in because it is less risky than hanging around on street corners. In any case, many existing drug-users will stick with their current supplier, if only out of habit, Gorman thinks. "There's a mystique about drug dealers that's totally wrong. They're very regular people. I might call you for marijuana because you're a buddy of mine. If you're a dealer, and I'm already buying dope from you, what changes?"

The thing that might change is the wholesale end of the market. It may be that Gorman is right, and that some chronic users will keep getting cannabis from their current dealer, out of habit, loyalty, or a preference for home delivery late in the evening. But the big question for the drug cartels is where dealers like that get their own supply. In other words, will America's black market in cannabis remain one in which Mexican weed can compete? Or will it turn into a "gray market," in which illegal dealers buy weed through legal channels and make their money by selling it illegally—in states where it isn't allowed, at times when it is banned, or to people under age twenty-one? The latter model is how the black markets in alcohol and tobacco have turned out, for instance. Visit any college campus on a Saturday night, and it is obvious that there is a thriving market in illicit alcohol. But underage drinkers don't buy illegally brewed beer that has been smuggled in from Mexico.

Instead, they buy booze that was made legally, and sold in an ordinary shop, but acquired illegally via a "dealer," who in practice is probably an older brother or friend. Likewise, most illegal cigarettes are ones that were produced legitimately for one market, and diverted illegally to another market where cigarettes are subject to higher taxes. (By one estimate, more than half the cigarettes smoked in New York are smuggled in from other states for this reason.)[7]

The only way that the cartels will be able to compete in this gray market is if they can beat the legal growers on price. How do they measure up? Back in the offices of Denver Relief, Ean Seeb, the boss, says that the firm's nursery can produce a gram of smokable marijuana for about $2. That puts the company roughly in line with other established players in Colorado: most of Denver's big producers aim to produce a pound of cannabis for $1,000, or about $2.20 per gram. After tax, it retails for about $11 to $15 per gram in medical dispensaries, and more like $16 to $20 in recreational outlets, where taxes are higher.

On that basis, illegal Mexican pot looks pretty competitive. According to the White House annual drugs report, the average price of illegal cannabis in the United States is about $15 per gram, or a little cheaper if bought in large quantities. Cannabis dispensaries in Denver say that illegal suppliers have been cutting their prices since the legal market was born, in order to retain clients. One retailer estimates that illegal marijuana is 20–30 percent cheaper than the store-bought variety. But that does not take the strength of the pot into account. According to the White House, the THC content of illegal cannabis averages only about 7 percent. That is pretty puny compared with the stuff on sale in Colorado's legal marijuana emporiums, where plenty of strains advertise THC content of more than 20 percent. In other words, you would have to smoke almost three times as much Mexican marijuana to get the same effect that you would from a single dose of the Colorado variety. If they want to stay competitive, then cartels will have to offer their inferior product for less than one-third of the price of the legal stuff.

Their ability to do that varies from state to state. A basic law of drug smuggling is that the further the product has to travel, the more expensive it becomes. Every step of the contraband's perilous journey involves someone taking a risk, for which they expect to be compensated. So just as heroin becomes gradually more expensive as it makes its way from Afghanistan to Europe, cannabis becomes pricier the further it has traveled from the Mexican border. *Narcotic News*, an online source of all kinds of drug-related information, keeps a database of drug prices from around the United States, supplied by law-enforcement officers. The cheapest illegal weed is found in the border region: in El Paso, Texas, the wholesale price of a kilogram can be as little as $200. By the time it reaches New York City, the same drug costs upward of $1,000. Pity the person who wants to get high in Hawaii, where a kilo of marijuana costs $6,000, wholesale.

To calculate the cost of smuggling, researchers at the Mexican Institute for Competitiveness (IMCO), a think tank based in Mexico City, drew up a chart plotting the price of the drug in forty-eight cities, comparing it with those cities' distance by road from the Mexican border. On average, they found, marijuana's wholesale price rises by $500 for every 1,000 kilometers (620 miles) that it has to travel within the United States. It seems reasonable to assume that American traffickers in Colorado or Washington would face similar costs if they wanted to smuggle their own products to other states. So the team at IMCO did the calculations, assuming that the wholesale price of legal marijuana was $2,000 per kilo (the same as what most Colorado growers say it costs to make their own batches). They then constructed a map of America, plotting how much it would cost to smuggle Coloradan and Washingtonian cannabis to other states, assuming smuggling expenses of $500 for every 620 miles. Adjusting for purity, smuggled cannabis from Colorado or Washington came out cheaper than Mexican weed in forty-seven of the forty-eight mainland states. Only in Texas, right on Mexico's doorstep, is the cartels' product a better value.[8]

The potential loss of most of the US cannabis market would represent a serious blow to Mexico's criminal gangs. IMCO reckons that the cartels earn about $2 billion a year from selling marijuana in the United States. That makes the pot business almost as valuable to them as the cocaine trade, from which they are thought to make about $2.4 billion. According to IMCO's calculations, the spread of legal cannabis from Colorado and Washington to other states could mean that Mexico's cartels lose nearly three-quarters of their current business, cutting their cannabis revenues to $600 million. And those calculations were done before other states started to legalize. For every new place in the United States that starts growing legal cannabis on a large scale, the illegal market will shrink, and the smuggled cannabis that feeds it will increasingly come from American states, not from Mexico.

Already, there is evidence of the problems that the cartels are facing. From Denver, I call an old contact in Mexico City, Antonio Mazzitelli, a wily Italian who runs the UN Office on Drugs and Crime in the region. I ask him how the Mexican cannabis industry is doing, in the face of America's change of heart on prohibition. "The impact has been dramatic," he says. A few weeks earlier, Mexican police had raided a warehouse in Tijuana and found 30 tons of marijuana, a big stash by any standard. "Why stock such a huge quantity? Because you don't have a buyer on the other side. These days there is simply better quality [cannabis] produced in the United States or Canada," he says. The use of drug-trafficking tunnels for smuggling illegal migrants, mentioned in the previous chapter, may be another sign that the cartels are struggling. Migrants bring in less money than drugs, and they have a habit of sneezing at the wrong moment, giving away the location of the tunnel. "This is not how you do it. You build up such an infrastructure for drugs, and keep it very low profile," says Mazzitelli, sounding almost annoyed at the cartels' idiocy for misusing such a valuable resource. "The very moment you use that same infrastructure for moving hundreds of migrants, you do it because you don't any longer have a market for your most valuable item. Otherwise, you don't risk it." Such desperate measures suggest that, for cartels that export a lot of cannabis, these are desperate times.

•   •   •

What next for the legal marijuana industry? With every new state that liberalizes its laws, the market attracts the interest of bigger investors. The cannabis industry has already moved out of the closet (which is quite literally where much of America's weed used to be grown) and taken on most of the attributes of any other big business: lobby groups, public-relations companies, trade shows—including an annual bash in Las Vegas that attracts more than 2,000 entrepreneurs—and a lively trade press, with news sources such as the *Marijuana Business Daily*. The *Denver Post* even has a marijuana editor, Ricardo Baca, who has appointed a cannabis critic and a cannabis-recipe writer and, most recently, advertised for a cannabis-focused sex columnist.

The growth of the business means that an increasing amount of money is being put behind efforts to legalize it. In the past, campaigns to liberalize the cannabis laws were led mostly by students and hippies (as well as a few libertarians, including the editors of the *Economist*), who ran amateurish campaigns that were easily squashed by the better-funded opposition. Nowadays, the money is changing sides. Take the 2014 ballot initiatives. In Alaska, the "yes" campaign won over a skeptical public partly thanks to $850,000 that was pumped into the campaign by the Marijuana Policy Project and the Drug Policy Alliance, a pressure group that is partly funded by George Soros, a wealthy financier who has long campaigned for legalization on moral grounds. The "no" campaign, by contrast, raised only $108,000. In Oregon, the race was even more one-sided: the "no" campaign raised $168,000, mostly from the state Sheriffs' Association, whereas the "yes" side raised $7.5 million. The Florida campaign, the highest-spending of the lot, was closer. Sheldon Adelson, a billionaire who made his money running casinos, helped the "no" side to raise $4.7 million. But the "yes" campaign raised $6.1 million. Much of it came from John Morgan, a wealthy Orlando lawyer. Businesses from as far away as California, Colorado, and Nevada chipped in, too.

In the end, the Florida initiative narrowly failed. With its population of 20 million, the state would have been by far the biggest cannabis market to date. "You know, [business] was not the angle we talked about because we were focused on the compassion issue, but the lost opportunity is huge," Morgan said after the results came in. "It's gigantic. All you have to do is look at Colorado: real estate is up, 30,000 jobs added, retail is up, state tax [revenues] up." The business is getting so big that many mainstream investors have interests in cannabis, perhaps unwittingly. Warren Buffett, the "Sage of Omaha" whose shrewd investments have made him one of the world's richest men, has a stake in the marijuana industry via Cubic Designs, a company that provides mezzanine floor-space for warehouses. Cubic Designs dropped flyers off at 1,000 marijuana dispensaries, urging them to "double your growing space," with a picture of metal flooring loaded with cannabis plants. The Sage himself made no comment.

As more states jump on the legalization bandwagon, it seems ever stranger that the federal authorities are ignoring the issue. Sam Kamin, a law professor at the University of Denver who helped to draft the Colorado law, thinks that federal legalization will come perhaps a decade after Colorado's experiment began, in 2024. Legalization in California, Illinois, and New York would make federal reform irresistible, he believes. If that did happen, the people currently involved in the legal cannabis business would rejoice. The federal illegality of the drug is the main constraint on marijuana companies: it hampers everything from their banking to their ability to operate in more than one state. Repealing the ban would allow them to grow much more easily; Smith says he wants Dixie Elixirs to become "the PepsiCo of the cannabis industry."

But there is another possibility: that federal legalization would mean that much bigger companies, so far wary of entering the marijuana business, would decide to dip their sizable toes in the water. One of the striking things about the legal marijuana industry so far is that no seriously large firm has joined the gold rush. Colorado has the most-developed recreational marijuana market in the world, but it doesn't have a single big chain: as of 2014, no marijuana dispensary had more than ten branches. Most of the state's cannabis start-ups are run by people who are weed enthusiasts first and entrepreneurs second. It is hard to imagine them surviving a serious onslaught from a big, well-funded household name. The way the industry is set up means that large companies would have big advantages: better able to navigate complex regulations; better placed to exploit the economies of scale inherent in agriculture; and better able to reassure nervous new customers, with a trusted, nationally known brand. How would Dixie's drinks fare against a THC-infused beer made by Budweiser? Would people still buy Dixie's edibles if they could buy Ben and Jerry's cannabis ice cream? And would small chains of marijuana dispensaries survive if people could buy a pack of twenty cannabis Lucky Strikes at the 7-Eleven?

Household names still have a little way to go before getting into cannabis. As long as it remains illegal in most of the United States—not to mention every other country in the world, apart from Uruguay— the marijuana industry will be risky in both legal and public-relations terms. Even someone like Richard Branson, an outspoken advocate of legalization, has been unwilling to risk the Virgin brand for the sake of one experimental new sideline. (I asked his office for an interview; and though he is never usually one to turn down free publicity, Branson declined to comment.) Investors are champing at the bit: a research note by the tobacco-research team of RBS Capital Markets, an investment bank, argued that "it is only a matter of time until investors start asking questions about how [marijuana legalization] will fit into the bigger picture . . . we believe full federal legalization of marijuana in the US would likely lead tobacco companies to reconsider this space."[9]

Publicly, the Big Tobacco companies have denied any interest in marijuana. Privately, however, they have been pursuing the idea of cannabis cigarettes for decades. A trio of academics went digging in the archives of the big cigarette firms and made some extraordinary discoveries.[10] Hiding among 80 million pages of previously secret internal documents was proof that Big Tobacco has put serious thought into how to become Big Pot. The researchers found that since at least the 1970s, tobacco companies have taken a keen interest in marijuana—both as a rival to tobacco, and as a potential line of new products. The earliest interest was found in a memo by Alfred Burger, a professor at the University of Virginia who supervised a fellowship in chemistry sponsored by Philip Morris, one of the world's great tobacco giants. The year was 1969, when polls showed that 12 percent of Americans in their twenties had tried cannabis, and 10 percent of those who hadn't said they would like to. Burger wrote to the head of chemical research at Philip Morris's laboratories: "I can predict that marihuana smoking will have grown to immense proportions within a decade and will probably be legalized. The company that will bring out the first marihuana smoking devices, be it a cigarette or some other form, will capture the market and be in a better position than its competitors to satisfy the legal public demand for such products. I want to suggest, therefore, that you institute immediately a research program on all phases of marihuana."

Later that year, Philip Morris contacted the Department of Justice to request a sample of cannabis on which it could carry out tests. Billed as an offer of help to the government in understanding the drug, the request was granted by the Department of Justice, which promised to supply the company with "good quality" pot. In a memo soon afterward, the president of Philip Morris USA, Ross Millhiser, wrote:

"While I am opposed to its use, I recognize that it may be legalized in the near future and put on some sort of restricted sale, if only to eliminate the criminal element. Thus, with these great auspices, we should be in a position to examine: 1. A potential competition, 2. A possible product, 3. At this time, cooperate with the government."

There was interest on the other side of the Atlantic, too. In 1970, Sir Harry Greenfield was president of the International Narcotics Control Board, the body charged with monitoring and implementing the UN conventions on drugs. But he was also a consultant to British American Tobacco (BAT). In that year he wrote to BAT's management concerning "the possibility of drawing upon the immense amount of research done by the tobacco industry into the smoking of tobacco and utilizing it for research on Cannabis." He explained that he had already talked it over with one Sir Charles Ellis, an eminent physicist who at the time was working as the principal technical adviser to BAT. Sir Charles was "rather taken with the idea," he said. Later that year, Sir Charles put together a memo for BAT in which he argued, "Smoking [a marijuana] cigarette is a natural expansion of current smoking habits which, if a more tolerant attitude were ever taken to cannabis, would be a change in habit comparable to moving over to cigars." As for BAT's own marijuana program, he suggested, "The starting point must be to learn how to produce in quantity cigarettes loaded uniformly with a known amount of either ground cannabis or dried and cut cannabis rag." He proposed experiments to test the effect of cannabis on mice.

Over the years, the tobacco companies continued to keep an eye on the marijuana scene. In 1972, an R. J. Reynolds planning document stamped "Secret" estimated that there was a 15-percent chance that cannabis would be legalized by 1980. A 1976 report for Brown & Williamson (another big cigarette firm, now extinct) predicted that pot would be decriminalized and perhaps legal by 1990, which would have "important implications for the tobacco industry in terms of an alternative product line." All the while, they denied it; *Time* magazine even apologized for running a story suggesting that tobacco firms were eyeing the cannabis business, after the companies protested.

Some of the ideas kicked around by Big Tobacco in the 1970s are still relevant today. One internal report for Brown & Williamson imagined a scenario in which marijuana was just starting to be legalized in the United States—much as it is at the moment. To begin with, it imagined, "While marijuana products seem to be a logical new industry for tobacco companies, severe stockholder dissention prohibits several from immediately entering the market." It then imagines that, following the US lead, foreign governments legalize marijuana. After this, "South America and Indonesia are the primary suppliers to the world for this commodity due to low production costs, adequate quality, and hence, cheaper prices."

This may well come to pass. Latin American governments are among the most dissatisfied with the regime of prohibition, which has handed a multibillion-dollar market to the region's powerful drug cartels. Uruguay has already taken the plunge and legalized cannabis. Former presidents of Brazil and Mexico have endorsed the same policy. More recently, the sitting presidents of Colombia and Guatemala have called for legalization. It is hard to imagine Mexico fighting a war against cannabis in Tijuana when the same drug is freely available over the border in San Diego. If legalization in Latin America follows, the analysts at Brown & Williamson nearly forty years ago may be proved correct. Just as NAFTA has led to the sprouting up of factories in Mexico assembling televisions and refrigerators to be exported to the United States, cannabis warehouses would surely move south of the border, to take advantage of low rents and wages. Vicente Fox, a former Coca-Cola executive who served as Mexico's president from 2000 to 2006, has said that he himself would be interested in turning his *rancho* in Guanajuato into a cannabis farm. "Once it is legitimate and legal, sure, I could do it, I'm a farmer," he told a local newspaper in 2013. The industry "would take millions of dollars away from criminals . . . the money would go to businesspeople, and not to 'Shorty' Guzmán [of the Sinaloa cartel]," he said.

If Mexico does start producing cannabis for the American market, the warehouses of Denver may go the same way as the car factories of Detroit: bust, having been undercut by cheaper competition from abroad. And so legalization may turn the cannabis industry full circle: from illegal production in Mexico, to legal production in the United States, and eventually back to Mexico. The only difference will be that the Mexican cannabis farmers will be working for Philip Morris and the like, rather than for the drug cartels.

Conclusion

WHY ECONOMISTS MAKE THE BEST POLICE OFFICERS

One of the most startling successes in the history of the war on drugs took place recently in an office in Austin, Texas. Officials in the state's Department of Public Safety executed an operation that, at a stroke, seized more than $1.6 billion in drugs from organized crime. The operation was notable for its stealthiness. It was carried out without a single shot being fired, or a single person being hurt. In fact, no officers even had to get up from their desks, let alone draw their weapons. The billion-dollar bust was made when officials decided that instead of calculating the value of the drugs they seized at the border using *wholesale* prices, they would instead calculate them using much higher *retail* prices. With a single tweak to a spreadsheet, the value of drugs intercepted in the state shot up from $161 million to $1.8 billion. Conveniently, the tenfold upward revision came just a week before the department was due to hand in a performance review.[1]

Whether it is Mexican generals fanning the value of a marijuana bonfire or Texas border agents nudging up the worth of their drug seizures, the people in charge of the war on drugs often seem to demonstrate a selective understanding of economics. It may not be all that surprising that police officers make unreliable economists. But what would happen if economists were given a chance to be police?

239

The idea isn't as strange as it sounds. In an office block set in parkland in south Wales, a group of statisticians is compiling data on some highly unusual subjects. The analysts, who work for the Office for National Statistics, Britain's official number-cruncher, devote most of their time to recording everyday things such as inflation and unemployment. But since 2014, as well as measuring the size of the regular economy they have been ordered to measure the economic activity carried out by criminals. So far they have restricted their inquiries to the markets for drugs and sex, using the same accounting model that they apply to legitimate businesses. Their early findings suggest that the illegal-drugs market in Britain contributes about $7.4 billion a year to gross domestic product, making it roughly as big as the advertising industry. The prostitution business is even larger, generating about $8.9 billion per year. Put together, sex and drugs are worth more to Britain than agriculture.

There is something strange about reading through the statisticians' methodology, which drily explains how they have subtracted the cost of electricity from cannabis-growers' profits and the cost of "rubber goods" from those of prostitutes. The calculations have been done in detail and with great care: cost assumptions regarding marijuana cultivation are based on agricultural data from the Department for Environment, Food and Rural Affairs, and prostitutes' expenses are calculated to include $170 per month on clothes and 70 cents per client on condoms. If it were not printed on official stationery, it might look like satire. But the sober analysis of crime as business is being used ever more widely, as governments realize that there is something to be learned from looking at organized crime as a profit-making enterprise. Every country in the European Union now includes the sex and drugs businesses in its national accounts. Britain is considering enlarging its own program to include illegal gambling, pirated music and software, and "fencing," or the handling of stolen goods. What will the world learn as crime comes to be analyzed not simply as a war or a moral crusade, but as a business?

In this book I have done my best to examine cartels' operations using the sort of approach that might be used to investigate any other industry. The similarities between mobsters and ordinary managers are striking, from the headaches caused by human resources to the threat posed to brick-and-mortar businesses from online retailers. But what is also noticeable is the frequency with which policies aimed at stifling the drug trade seem to be misdirected. Regulatory approaches that in the ordinary business world would be discarded for their ineffectiveness have been allowed to endure for years in the world of counternarcotics. Running through this book is evidence that official efforts to tackle the drugs industry have been hampered by four big mistakes.

MISTAKE ONE: THE OBSESSION WITH SUPPLY

Whereas the relentless focus of the war on drugs is on the supply side of the business—the traffickers—there is an overwhelming case instead for prioritizing the demand side, the consumers. In the first chapter of this book we saw how disrupting the supply of coca leaves in the Andes, by dumping weed killer from light aircraft, has done remarkably little to alter the price of cocaine, in spite of decades of investment and a considerable amount of violence. One reason is that the cartels have used their buying power to force farmers to absorb any cost increases, just as Walmart squeezes its own suppliers. More significant, the cost of coca leaf, the drug's raw material, is simply too low to have much impact on the final price of cocaine. The bundle of leaves required to make a kilo of powder costs only a few hundred dollars. So even doubling the cost of growing coca adds less than 1 percent to the price of the finished product, which sells for the equivalent of more than $100,000 per kilo. If the supply side is to be attacked, it should be at the end of the chain, in the rich world, where the product is valuable enough for its confiscation to do some economic damage to those who sell it.

There is another reason that focusing on the supply side is misguided, even if it can be made to work. When the price of a product goes up, the amount consumed generally falls. But the size of the fall in consumption varies. Demand for some goods is "elastic," meaning that it drops dramatically following even a small increase in price. Demand for other products is "inelastic," meaning that consumers will keep buying more or less the same amount as before, even in the face of big price rises. Measuring elasticity in drug markets is tricky, because the data on both price and consumption are so hard to verify. But most of the evidence suggests that demand for drugs is inelastic. One survey of the evidence in the United States[2] quoted studies suggesting that the elasticity of demand for marijuana was about −0.33, meaning that a 10-percent rise in price would lead to only a 3.3-percent drop in demand. Other studies that measured the likelihood of drugs showing up in the urine tests of arrestees found an even weaker relationship: −0.17 for cocaine and −0.09 for heroin, meaning that for every 10-percent increase in the price of cocaine, the number of people testing positive fell by only 1.7 percent, and that in the case of heroin, the effect was less than 1 percent.

The idea that demand for drugs is inelastic fits with intuition, especially in the case of addictive substances. Users such as Cynthia Scudo, the heroin-addicted grandmother in Denver, are unlikely to stop taking their drugs just because the price has gone up a bit. We came across the same idea when examining how drug cartels have diversified into people smuggling. Even though tougher patrolling of the United States border has raised the cost of crossing illegally, the increase in price hasn't made much of an impact on people's demand for safe passage. The demand for coyotes seems to be as inelastic as that for drugs. Again, this is unsurprising: crossing the border to be reunited with one's children, or even to get a much-better-paying job, is a decision that is unlikely to be swayed much by a small increase in price.

The inelasticity of demand for illegal goods and services has two worrying implications for a policy that focuses on supply. First, it means that even big successes in forcing up the cost of drugs (or coyote crossings, for that matter) translate to only small victories in what counts, namely, the number of people buying the drugs (or crossing the border illegally). Governments are thus condemned to invest large amounts of resources in return for only meager gains. Second, large increases in price coupled with only small decreases in demand mean that with every enforcement "success," the value of the market increases. Imagine a small town in which competing dealers between them sell one kilo of marijuana per week, for $10 per gram, making $10,000 in total. Better policing in the town then raises the dealers' costs, forcing them to up their prices by 10 percent, to $11 per gram. If we believe the elasticity calculation quoted above, this will cause demand to drop by 3.3 percent. So the dealers will now sell 967 grams of marijuana per week, for $11 per gram: a total of $10,637. The successful crackdown has resulted in slightly lower consumption, but at significantly higher prices, making the criminal economy bigger overall than it was before.

What would happen if governments instead focused on the demand side of the equation? Imagine that our small town begins a policy that succeeds in discouraging people from taking drugs: a public-health campaign; better leisure facilities for teenagers; rehab for addicts; take your pick. Demand drops. At this point, the dealers are likely to react by cutting their prices as they fight among themselves for the smaller pool of customers.[3] So both consumption and prices fall, meaning that the criminal market is reduced on two fronts. Again, the same logic could be applied to other illegal markets. Rather than cracking down on coyotes, who run the supply side of the illegal migration business, it might make more sense to drain the demand for illegal border crossings. This could be done by friendly measures (such as issuing more visas, so people can cross legally) or by hostile ones (such as making the United States a harder place to live without documentation). Either way, reducing the number of people wanting to cross illegally would lower not only the number of clandestine crossings but also the prices that the coyotes were able to charge.

Whether the subject is drugs, migration, or another illegal business, the point is the same: whereas attacking supply can only reduce consumption by driving up prices—and therefore criminal revenues—attacking demand can reduce both.

MISTAKE TWO: SAVING MONEY EARLY ON AND PAYING FOR IT LATER

Even though the number of inmates is rising, the state of New Hampshire is spending less on its prisons. One was closed in 2009, causing inmates to be crammed into the state's remaining institutions. Trimming another $15 million off the budget in 2014 meant cutting educational courses and rehabilitation programs for prisoners. All of this is a shame, politicians admit, but resources are scarce: there simply isn't enough money to run the system at as high a standard as everyone might like.

The claims of scarce cash must seem odd, though, to anyone visiting the small New Hampshire town of Keene. Keene is not a violent place. Between 1999 and 2012, it saw only three homicides. Yet its police department has spent nearly $286,000 on an armored personnel carrier known as a BearCat. Asked why a town like Keene needed a vehicle better suited to trundling around Baghdad, the police chief explained that it would be used to patrol Keene's "Pumpkin Festival and other dangerous situations."[4]

The case of Keene shows that when it comes to fighting crime, money is no object—as long as it is spent on enforcement, rather than prevention. Governments argue, to cheers from voters, that public security is priceless, and so acquisitions like the BearCat go ahead without much complaint. The Department of Homeland Security disbursed $35 billion to state and local police forces in 2002–2011, allowing them to buy toys like this. Money spent on prevention, by contrast, is audited with great care. If funds are scarce, prisoners, drug addicts, and other potential offenders are often among the first to feel the pinch. It is understandable that society isn't in a hurry to lavish money on these characters. But it has turned out to be an expensive principle to uphold.

Making cuts to rehab and education programs in jails might save a few thousand dollars. But if it means even a handful of prisoners failing to learn to read, or to kick their drug addiction, and as a result reoffending rather than finding work on their release, the cost is immense. One classic study[5] attempted to calculate how much cocaine consumption would be prevented by each of a range of different government interventions. It estimated that for every $1 million spent on controlling supply in "source countries" in Latin America, there would be a reduction of about 10 kilograms in the total amount of cocaine consumed in the United States. If $1 million were spent trying to intercept cocaine further down the supply chain, on its way to America, that would save more like 20 kilograms. Prevention programs in schools were a bit more effective, saving about 25 kilograms per $1 million. All of these interventions were vastly outdone, however, by treatment programs for drug addicts. For every $1 million spent on treatment, the consumption of more than 100 kilograms of cocaine is averted. In other words, treatment is up to ten times more cost effective than enforcement (perhaps partly because it addresses demand rather than supply, as outlined in the previous section). The boring but unsurprising truth is that it costs less money to get someone off drugs and into a job than it does to chase that person down in a BearCat.

In several separate instances in this book, we have seen cases where huge gains could be made by diverting resources toward early, cheap prevention, and away from expensive cure. In the Caribbean, prisons serve as recruitment centers for cartels because governments are unwilling to spend enough money to make them safe (or even provide inmates with lunch). In Mexico, cartels win support from locals by carrying out acts of "corporate social responsibility" that succeed because the government has failed to provide basic public services. Andean governments could spend tiny amounts to get farmers growing tomatoes instead of coca, but instead they invest much greater quantities in destroying their coca crops by force. Rather than shell out for job-creation programs for young men, Central American countries prefer the more expensive option of hunting them down when they eventually find work with criminal gangs. Instead of spending a small amount on rehabilitation for prescription painkiller addicts, the United States allows them to slip into addiction to heroin—which it then spends a colossal amount attempting to suppress.

It is easy to call for more spending as a solution to the world's every social problem. The difference in the drug world is that more than enough money is already being spent—it is just focused on the wrong area. It is time for governments' generosity toward the police and miserliness toward development to be reversed.

MISTAKE THREE: ACTING NATIONALLY AGAINST A GLOBAL BUSINESS

While drug traffickers have embraced globalization, running truly borderless businesses that span multiple countries and even continents, most attempts to thwart them have stuck to rigidly demarcated national boundaries. This approach has led to many examples of apparent success in one country that in fact comes at the expense of a failure of equal size somewhere else. Frequently in this book we have seen examples of "squeezing the balloon," or, in the Latin American terminology, the "cockroach effect," in which the drugs business is driven out of one place only to pop up in another. In the 1990s, coca cultivation was pushed out of Peru—"a remarkable achievement," in the words of the UN chief drug-control officer at the time[6]—only to crop up in Colombia. Within a decade, Colombia had forced it back out—"a remarkable achievement," the United Nations noted again[7]—straight back into Peru, where it had originated. In spite of these two remarkable achievements, remarkably little was actually achieved.

The same cat-and-mouse game is played on the trafficking side of the business. The shutting down of the Caribbean smuggling route in the 1980s caused the cocaine kings to shift their attention to Mexico. A more recent crackdown there has persuaded the cartels to begin offshoring more of their work to the weak states of Central America. Now, there are early signs that increased vigilance in Central America is nudging the business to move on yet again—back to its old haunts in the Caribbean. The cartels are no less nimble when it comes to switching retail markets. Cocaine use fell admirably in the United States in the early 2000s—but it rose by a very similar amount in Europe during the same period. In the war on drugs, it seems, national successes are common, whereas global ones are rare. "The only thing you can do is push it elsewhere, and make it someone else's problem," a senior official in one northern Mexican state told me gloomily, as we drove around a cartel-controlled neighborhood in his armored SUV.

It is hardly surprising that national governments don't think much about problems that exist beyond their own borders. Colombia's crackdown on coca cultivation has been perfectly successful from Colombia's point of view, even if it hasn't done much damage to the international market. The trouble is that whereas cartels are multinational businesses, there exists no real multinational regulator to keep on top of them. The closest thing is the UN Office on Drugs and Crime. But it seems to be so committed to defending the strategy of suppressing supply that it isn't a very honest assessor of the policy's shortcomings. Its drug monitors have continued to trumpet isolated national successes, spending little time dwelling on the distinctly less impressive aggregate results. If a multinational company tried the same trick, highlighting strong results in one market while glossing over the disappointing bottom line, its shareholders would not allow the firm to get away with it for very long.

The reason it goes on is that the most influential UN shareholders—the wealthy member states that pay the lion's share of its upkeep—are reasonably satisfied with the way the war is currently being fought. Rich countries, which consume most of the world's drugs, are happy for the fighting to occur far away from their own populations. As noted earlier, disruptions to drug-supply networks are most effective when they are made at the end of the supply chain, when the product is most valuable and its confiscation is most damaging to the dealers. Yet the number of helicopter gunships deployed over London or Washington, DC, is conspicuously low. As Hugo Almada, the academic from the University of Juárez, pointed out so bitterly, the United States (along with its wealthy allies) wages the war on drugs much more pragmatically on its own soil than it does on foreign turf. Four out of ten Americans admit to having taken illegal drugs, a figure that suggests that society has decided to tolerate a certain amount of dealing so long as it comes without violence. By contrast, other countries that fail to tackle drug traffickers with sufficient force are singled out for punishment. "Those that do not [cooperate] face the consequences: public shaming, economic sanctions, or back-channel punitive uses of American influence with international funding agencies like the World Bank and IMF [International Monetary Fund]," writes Moisés Naím, an expert on organized crime and himself a former executive director of the World Bank.[8]

Latin American presidents no longer bother to hide their exasperation with this state of affairs. "If [Americans] want to take all the drugs they want, as far as I'm concerned let them take them. I don't agree with it but it's their decision, as consumers and as a society. What I do not accept is that they continue passing their money to the hands of killers," Felipe Calderón told me, livid at having spent his six years as president of Mexico fighting a war against a product that his neighbors insisted he wipe out, even as they imported it by the ton.

The structure of the global market has made this political deadlock inevitable. Historically, most countries have fallen into one of three categories: those where drugs are produced (such as Colombia), those where they are trafficked (such as Mexico), or those where they are consumed (such as Europe and the United States). This has allowed governments, and their voters, to see only one side of the drugs industry. Consumer countries, which simply want to stop the drugs reaching their shores, have argued for attacks on the trade to be as severe as possible and to be made at the earliest point in the supply chain, even though it isn't very effective. For their part, producer and transit countries don't see why they should invest their own money and lives in suppressing a business whose ill effects are felt mostly outside their own borders.

But this is changing, as two global trends begin to force all countries to see the drug trade in the round. One is that the interests of producer and consumer countries are aligning, because the very categories of "producer" and "consumer" are blurring. Drugs are predominantly a middle-class vice, and as developing countries get richer, their emerging middle classes are starting to take more of them—just as they are buying more cars, taking more foreign vacations, and acquiring other middle-class habits. The most visible example of this is in Brazil, which is now the world's second-biggest market for powder cocaine, and the biggest bar none for crack. At the same time, consumer countries are seeing more domestic production of drugs. One strand of this trend is in marijuana, which now tends to be grown locally, especially in America. Another is in synthetic drugs, which can be made in kitchen laboratories anywhere. As consumer countries have started producing more drugs of their own, they have realized that attacking supply networks is ineffective. Faced with a booming local marijuana market, America has forgone Colombian-style crop eradication programs in favor of legalization. New Zealand came to a similar conclusion with "legal highs," which it is haltingly trying to regulate in a similar way.

The second big trend affecting the global politics of drugs is a shifting balance of power. The poor countries that have historically been home to producers and traffickers are getting richer and gaining more clout. In 2000, the UN drugs office received 96 percent of its funding from the "major donors group," a collection of twenty mainly wealthy countries. By 2014, the major donors contributed only 60 percent of the office's budget. One-third of its funding now comes from "emerging" donor countries. The biggest of these in recent years have been Colombia and Brazil, both of whose governments have expressed frustration with the current, enforcement-led approach to drug control. Other emerging powers take a different view: Russia, which makes occasional large donations to the UN drugs office (and managed to get a Russian diplomat, Yuri Fedotov, installed as the agency's boss in 2010), runs a highly punitive antidrugs policy at home. China sometimes celebrates the annual International Day Against Drug Use and Illicit Trafficking by executing smugglers. The emerging powers contain plenty of hawks as well as doves, and the former may yet prevail. But the international drug-control regime is in play as never before.

MISTAKE FOUR: CONFUSING PROHIBITION WITH CONTROL

In 1998, the United Nations held an event with the slogan: "A drug-free world: we can do it." In many ways it was an admirable aim. Of the roughly 250 million people who take drugs every year, most have a good time, but a large minority suffer horribly. About 180,000 die of overdose; unknown millions more are harmed or do harm to others. No one who has seen the everyday devastation wrought by addiction can support legalizing drugs, Tom Gorman, the drug-warrior cop of Denver, told me. "There are people who can use drugs responsibly and there are the people who are victimized because of it," he said. "My bias is on their behalf."

So is mine. But everything that this book has described about the drugs trade—from its roots in South America to its traffickers in the Caribbean, and from its consumers in Colorado to its retailers in cyberspace—points to the conclusion that if you really want to get drugs under control, to put the cartels out of business and protect the public, prohibition is not an effective way to do it. Since the optimistically titled UN conference, there has been no sign of the promised "drug-free world." Despite governments spending well in excess of $1 trillion enforcing prohibition, the net result since 1998 is that total consumption of marijuana and cocaine has increased by half, and consumption of opiates has almost trebled. This is not what success looks like.

Legalizing drugs is a cause that for many years was promoted mainly by people who enjoyed smoking pot, who pointed out that it was less dangerous than plenty of other substances that were already legal. This was perfectly true, but it failed to persuade the public; most people understandably took the view that the world had enough dangerous distractions already, without adding marijuana (and perhaps other, more harmful drugs) to the mix. In recent years, however, the argument has been inverted. The case now most often made for legalizing drugs is not that drugs are safe—it is that they are dangerous, and that bringing them within the law is a more effective way to control them than leaving them to the mafia.

What might a legally regulated drug market look like? In Colorado we see the first one in action. Drugs are tested for safety and strength, clearly labeled, packed in child-safe containers, and sold in limited quantities to those over twenty-one. The state gains a new stream of income from taxation and licensing—worth $76 million to Colorado in its first year in operation—and saves money by making many fewer arrests. The number of people charged with marijuana possession each year in Colorado has fallen from about thirty thousand before legalization to about two thousand now (the people still being charged include those found with excessive or unlicensed quantities, or those who are underage). Sales worth more than $700 million per year have been taken away from organized crime and handed to legitimate businesspeople. It is too early to be sure about the impact on consumption, partly because so much of the demand is from out-of-state visitors. But legalization doesn't seem to have opened any floodgates. Nearly half the US states have legalized marijuana in some form—most of them for broadly defined "medical" purposes—and the amount consumed has not changed much since the mid-1990s.

These tentatively positive results have encouraged others. Three more states joined the legal recreational-weed club within a year of when Colorado's experiment began. Uruguay became the first whole country to legalize the drug in 2014. And in 2015, Jamaica announced that it would legalize *ganja* for medical and religious purposes, while decriminalizing it for everyone else. The fact that the revolution began in the United States has for once prevented its federal government from criticizing countries that take a lenient line. "Jamaican law is of course Jamaica's own business and Jamaica's sovereign decision," said William Brownfield, the US assistant secretary of state for counternarcotics, who faces the awkward task of defending prohibition abroad while it is ignored at home.

Compared with the policy disasters outlined elsewhere in this book, marijuana legalization so far looks something like a success. But what of harder drugs? The only place that has attempted to legalize other recreational narcotics so far is New Zealand. Starved of conventional hard drugs, the country became a world leader in cooking up synthetic ones. Attempts to ban those "legal highs," in New Zealand as elsewhere, have become an endless exercise in balloon squeezing and cockroach herding, with one ban being immediately followed by the invention of a nearly identical substitute. In the case of legal highs, not only has prohibition been ineffective: in some cases it has been positively dangerous. Drugs such as MDMA, or ecstasy, that pose a relatively low risk if consumed in small doses, have been replaced by nastier alternatives. Many of the people who die nowadays from "ecstasy" have in fact unwittingly taken PMA, a close but far more dangerous cousin. In banning MDMA, governments have shooed away a small and relatively harmless cockroach, only for it to be replaced by dozens of deadly ones. Authorizing a limited number of lower-risk, officially tested chemical highs, as New Zealand's system could if it ever properly gets going, would surely be safer than the current approach of trying to ban everything and in practice banning nothing.

When it comes to the most dangerous drugs of all, legalization seems to be even more effective. The case for bringing drugs under legal control, and out of the hands of the mob, is motivated by the fact that they are harmful, not that they are safe. Consider heroin. Although they don't much like to talk about it, a handful of European countries, including Switzerland, the Netherlands, and the United Kingdom, have already legalized it in a very limited way. None of their programs involves selling the drug to just anyone, along Colorado lines. Rather, specialized doctors have been given permission to prescribe heroin, free of charge, to addicts. The idea is that through managed, rationed use, addicts are gradually able to wean themselves off the drug. In Switzerland, whose program is the most well-established, doctors targeted 3,000 hardcore addicts, who made up 10–15 percent of the country's users but accounted for up to 60 percent of consumption in the country. By providing them with free heroin, which they took under supervised conditions, the government reduced the number of robberies they committed by 90 percent.

But that was just the beginning. By removing these heavy users from the market, the program took away the industry's most valuable customers, making the heroin market far less viable in terms of demand. At the same time, it struck an unusually deadly blow against supply. The heavy users' habits were so prodigious that most of them also dealt the drug, in order to pay for their own drug use. Taking them out of the game therefore simultaneously removed most of the country's dealers, making it much harder for casual users to get a fix. By taking on as a patient anyone who was a serious customer, the program caused the market to collapse. In Zurich, the number of new addicts registered in 1990 was 850. In 2005, it was 150.[9] Legalizing heroin—through a strictly limited, doctor-run program—has made the drug far harder to access than banning it ever did.

•   •   •

A few months after coining the phrase "war on drugs," Richard Nixon was in the Oval Office discussing a government-designed antidrugs brochure with his chief of staff, H. R. Haldeman. Nixon was furious.

"They put in as a quote from the president on the front of the pamphlet, with a picture, and a good strong picture and the rest, that said that the problem of drugs is our number one and must be dealt with 'in a variety of ways,'" Nixon fumed. "When I saw 'variety of ways' I god damned near puked. And I thought, for pity's sake, we need . . . 'all-out war,' or 'all fronts,' or, uh, 'despicable.'"

Haldeman agreed. "Handle it 'in a variety of ways' really says we don't know how to handle it," he told the president. "Which may be the truth. But it sure as hell isn't the thing to say."[10]

This has been the approach of most governments ever since: unsure how to handle the world's growing addiction to drugs, they have resolutely stuck to the unsuccessful policies already in place. With every passing year, the result becomes plainer to see: the "all-out war" approach has failed to cut the number of consumers, while it has driven up the price of a few cheap agricultural commodities to create a hideously violent, $300-billion global industry.

The time has surely come to try out more "varieties of ways" of tackling the drugs industry. Until there is a radical change in strategy, business conditions for the mafia will remain promising. Half a century after Nixon's war was declared, sadly, there has never been a better time to run a drug cartel.

Acknowledgments

Narconomics started life as an article in the *Economist*'s issue of July 28, 2012. Robert Guest, the business editor at the time, asked me to come up with a business column about Mexico, and I wrote what would become a sort of pilot chapter of this book (if you're not sick of the subject already, you can read it at www.economist.com/node /21559598). Robert was one of many people at the *Economist* who was incredibly helpful. Michael Reid, the Americas editor during my stint in Mexico, is a Latin America encyclopedia. John Micklethwait, now at Bloomberg News, was the editor brave enough to hire me in the first place and to send me to Mexico, despite my knowing nothing about the place. Celina Dunlop kindly helped me track down the photographs used in this book, and Adam Meara expertly put together the maps and charts. Andrew Palmer put me in touch with his agent, Andrew Stuart—another person without whom the book would never have gotten under way. John Mahaney and his colleagues at PublicAffairs were imaginative enough to take a chance on a first-time author with a weird idea. More generally, I am grateful to the hundreds of people who helped me, sometimes at a certain amount of risk to themselves, in the course of my researching this book: in Britain, the United States, Mexico, Guatemala, El Salvador, Honduras, Bolivia, the Dominican Republic, Portugal, and New Zealand, among other places. Lastly, and mostly, thanks to my wonderful family.

Notes

INTRODUCTION: CARTEL INCORPORATED

1. Executive Secretariat of the National Public Security System, "Reports of Incidence of Crime by Year," 2010 (in Spanish), at http://secretariadoejecutivo.gob .mx/incidencia-delictiva/incidencia-delictiva-fuero-comun.php.

2. These estimates—which are necessarily rough—are from the UN Office on Drugs and Crime (hereafter UNODC). See, for instance, "Time for Policy Change Against Crime, Not in Favor of Drugs," 2009, at https://www.unodc.org/unodc/en /about-unodc/speeches/2009-03-11.html.

3. Beau Kilmer et al., "Reducing Drug Trafficking Revenues and Violence in Mexico," RAND Corporation occasional paper, 2010, see p. 19 at http://www .rand.org/content/dam/rand/pubs/occasional_papers/2010/RAND_OP325 .appendixes.pdf.

4. Moisés Naím, *Illicit: How Smugglers, Traffickers, and Copycats Are Hijacking the Global Economy* (New York: Doubleday, 2005), p. 68.

CHAPTER 1 COCAINE'S SUPPLY CHAIN: THE COCKROACH EFFECT AND THE 30,000 PERCENT MARKUP

1. "Plurinational State of Bolivia, Monitoring of Coca Cultivation 2014," UNODC, August 2015 (in Spanish), at https://www.unodc.org/documents /bolivia/Informe_Monitoreo_Coca_2014/Bolivia_Informe_Monitoreo_Coca _2014.pdf.

2. "World Drug Report 2006," UNODC, 2007, at https://www.unodc.org /unodc/en/data-and-analysis/WDR-2006.html.

3. See p. 75 at http://www.whitehouse.gov/sites/default/files/ondcp/policy-and -research/2013_data_supplement_final2.pdf.

4. Tom van Riper, "The Wal-Mart Squeeze," *Forbes*, April 24, 2007, at http://www .forbes.com/2007/04/23/walmart-suppliers-margins-lead-cx_tvr_0423walmart .html.

5. Charles Fishman, "The Wal-Mart You Don't Know," *Fast Company,* December 2003, at http://www.fastcompany.com/47593/wal-mart-you-dont-know.

6. Jorge Gallego and Daniel Rico, "Manual Eradication, Aerial Spray and Coca Prices in Colombia," unpublished paper, 2012, available online at http://www.mamacoca.org/docs_de_base/Fumigas/Daniel_Rico_GallegoJorge_Manual_Eradication_Aerial_Sparying_and_Coca_Prices__2012.pdf.

7. Oeindrila Dube, Omar Garcia-Ponce, and Kevin Thom, "From Maize to Haze: Agricultural Shocks and the Growth of the Mexican Drug Sector," Center for Global Development, 2014, at http://www.cgdev.org/sites/default/files/maize-haze-agricultural-shocks-growth-mexican-drug-sector_0.pdf.

8. "Colombia Coca Cultivation Survey 2005," UNODC, June 2006, see p. 7 at http://www.unodc.org/pdf/andean/Colombia_coca_survey_2005_eng.pdf.

9. "Recommended Methods for the Identification and Analysis of Cocaine in Seized Materials," UNODC, 2012, at http://www.unodc.org/documents/scientific/Cocaine_Manual_Rev_1.pdf.

10. Beau Kilmer and Peter Reuter, as quoted in *Foreign Policy,* October 2009, at http://foreignpolicy.com/2009/10/16/prime-numbers-doped.

CHAPTER 2 COMPETITION VS. COLLUSION: WHY MERGER IS SOMETIMES BETTER THAN MURDER

1. The apocryphal tale is dramatically recounted in "Fifty Thousand Red Roses," a *narcocorrido,* or narco-ballad, by Lupillo Rivera.

2. "Ciudad Juarez Man Sentenced for Eight Years for Bribery/Drug Smuggling," US Immigration and Customs Enforcement news release, September 15, 2008, at http://www.ice.gov/news/releases/ciudad-juarez-man-sentenced-8-years-briberydrug-smuggling.

3. Stephen S. Dudley, "Drug Trafficking Organizations in Central America: Transportistas, Mexican Cartels and Maras," Wilson Center, 2010, at http://www.wilsoncenter.org/sites/default/files/Chapter%202-%20Drug%20Trafficking%20Organizations%20in%20Central%20America%20Transportistas,%20Mexican%20Cartels%20and%20Maras.pdf.

4. US Securities and Exchange Commission, see p. 15 at http://www.sec.gov/Archives/edgar/data/1467858/000146785812000014/gm201110k.htm#s8EF7834BE4E777188CAF1031CB30C168.

5. Gianluca Fiorentini and Sam Peltzman, eds., *The Economics of Organised Crime* (Cambridge: Cambridge University Press, 1997).

6. Christina Villacorte, "Tattoo Removal in Prison Gives Inmates a Second Chance," *Huffington Post,* September 4, 2013, at http://www.huffingtonpost.com/2013/09/04/tattoo-removal-prison_n_3864222.html.

CHAPTER 3 THE PEOPLE PROBLEMS OF A DRUG CARTEL: WHEN JAMES BOND MEETS MR. BEAN

1. "The Illicit Drug Trade in the United Kingdom," Matrix Knowledge Group/Home Office, 2007, at http://webarchive.nationalarchives.gov.uk/20110220105210/rds.homeoffice.gov.uk/rds/pdfs07/rdsolr2007.pdf.

2. Joe Palazzolo and Rogerio Jelmayer, "Brazil Files Bribery Charges in Embraer Aircraft Sale to Dominican Republic," *Wall Street Journal*, September 23, 2014, at http://www.wsj.com/articles/brazil-files-bribery-charges-in-embraer-aircraft-sale-to-dominican-republic-1411502236.

3. David Skarbek, *The Social Order of the Underworld: How Prison Gangs Govern the American Prison System* (Oxford: Oxford University Press, 2014).

4. David Grann, "The Brand," *New Yorker*, February 2004, at http://www.newyorker.com/magazine/2004/02/16/the-brand.

5. "The Illicit Drug Trade in the United Kingdom," Home Office, 2007.

6. Melvin Soudijn and Peter Reuter, "Managing Potential Conflict in Illegal Markets: An Exploratory Study of Cocaine Smuggling in the Netherlands," 2013, at http://www.trimbos.org/~/media/Programmas/Internationalisering/Further%20insights%20into%20aspects%20of%20the%20EU%20illicit%20drugs%20market.ashx.

7. Charles Bowden, *Murder City: Ciudad Juárez and the Global Economy's New Killing Fields* (New York: Nation Books, 2010).

8. One exception is Roy Y. J. Chua of Harvard Business School, whose experiments tentatively suggest that people who work in settings where there is some level of "cultural conflict" are less likely to perform well in tests of creativity.

9. Moisés Naím, *Illicit: How Smugglers, Traffickers, and Copycats Are Hijacking the Global Economy* (New York: Doubleday, 2005), p. 73.

10. Cited by Common Sense for Drug Policy, at http://www.csdp.org/research/nixonpot.txt.

11. International Centre for Prison Studies, http://www.prisonstudies.org.

12. Ruth Maclean, "We're Not a Gang, We're a Union, Say the Drug Killers of Ciudad Juárez," London *Times*, March 27, 2010, available on the author's website at https://macleanandrickardstraus.wordpress.com/2010/03/27/were-not-a-gang-were-a-union-say-the-drug-killers-of-ciudad-juarez.

CHAPTER 4 PR AND THE MAD MEN OF SINALOA: WHY CARTELS CARE ABOUT CORPORATE SOCIAL RESPONSIBILITY

1. *Reforma*'s regular opinion poll, April 1, 2014, p. 8 (in Spanish), as cited at http://www.funcionpublica.gob.mx/sintesis/ComSoc_historico/2014/abril/01/t5.pdf.

2. You can listen to the bouncy ballad at https://www.youtube.com/watch?t
=39&v=pfGtRJjkS-g.

3. "El Chapo Accuses Governor of Chihuahua of Helping Juárez Cartel," *Proceso,*
September 15, 2010 (in Spanish), at http://www.proceso.com.mx/?p=101344.

4. Al Ries and Laura Ries, *The Fall of Advertising and the Rise of PR* (New York:
HarperCollins, 2012).

5. A 2008 estimate cited in Nick Davies, *Flat Earth News* (London: Chatto and
Windus, 2008).

6. "What Do You Want from Us?" *El Diario de Juárez*, September 19, 2010, at
http://diario.mx/Local/2010-09-19_cfaade06/_que-quieren-de-nosotros/?/.

7. Alison Smith, "Fortune 500 Companies Spend More Than $500bn on Corpo-
rate Responsibility," *Financial Times*, October 12, 2012, at http://www.ft.com/cms
/s/0/95239a6e-4fe0-11e4-a0a4-00144feab7de.html#axzz3lqtuDTmC.

8. As quoted in *La Jornada*, September 20, 2005 (in Spanish), at http://www
.jornada.unam.mx/2005/09/20/index.php?section=politica&article=022n1pol.

9. Herschel I. Grossman, "Rival Kleptocrats: The Mafia Versus the State," in Gianluca Fiorentini and Sam Peltzman, *The Economics of Organised Crime* (Cambridge
University Press, 1997).

10. Leopoldo Franchetti, *Political and Administrative Conditions in Sicily* (1876).

11. Diego Gambetta and Peter Reuter, "Conspiracy Among the Many: The Mafia
in Legitimate Industries," in Fiorentini and Peltzman, *The Economics of Organised
Crime*.

12. FBI, "Investigative Programs: Organized Crime," at http://www.fbi.gov
/about-us/investigate/organizedcrime/cases/carting-industry.

13. Tom Wainwright, "Señores, Start Your Engines," *Economist*, November
24, 2012, at http://www.economist.com/news/special-report/21566782-cheaper
-china-and-credit-and-oil-about-start-flowing-mexico-becoming.

CHAPTER 5 OFFSHORING: THE PERKS OF DOING
BUSINESS ON THE MOSQUITO COAST

1. Alan Blinder, "Offshoring: The Next Industrial Revolution?" *Foreign Affairs*
(March 2006), at https://www.foreignaffairs.com/articles/2006-03-01/offshoring
-next-industrial-revolution.

2. Clair Brown et al., "The 2010 National Organizations Survey: Examining the
Relationships Between Job Quality and the Domestic and International Sourcing
of Business Functions by United States Organizations," Institute for Research
on Labor and Employment, December 2013, at http://www.irle.berkeley.edu
/workingpapers/156-13.pdf.

3. "Latin America: Tax Revenues Continue to Rise, but Are Low and Varied
Among Countries," OECD, January 20, 2014, at http://www.oecd.org/ctp/latin

-america-tax-revenues-continue-to-rise-but-are-low-and-varied-among-countries
-according-to-new-oecd-eclac-ciat-report.htm.

4. In the end, the divorce strategy proves unsuccessful: shortly after my meeting with Colom, his ex-wife's candidacy is ruled illegal after all. The couple has not remarried.

5. See http://kevinunderhill.typepad.com/Documents/Opinions/US_v_One _Lucite_Ball.pdf, and also http://www.collectspace.com/news/usvmoonrock.pdf.

6. Tom Wainwright, "Dicing with Death," *Economist*, April 12, 2014, at http://media.economist.com/sites/default/files/media/2014InfoG/databank /IR2a.pdf.

7. "Country Report: Honduras," US Department of State, 2014, at http://www .state.gov/j/inl/rls/nrcrpt/2014/vol1/222904.htm.

8. "Cocaine from South America to the United States," UNODC, at https://www .unodc.org/documents/toc/Reports/TOCTASouthAmerica/English/TOCTA _CACaribb_cocaine_SAmerica_US.pdf.

9. This point is well made by Peter Reuter in "The Limits of Supply-Side Drug Control," *Milken Institute Review* (First Quarter 2001), at http://faculty.publicpolicy .umd.edu/sites/default/files/reuter/files/milken.pdf.

10. Miguel L. Castillo Girón, "Land Ownership Transfers in the Petén, Guatemala," Western Hemisphere Security Analysis Center, Florida International University, February 1, 2011, at http://digitalcommons.fiu.edu/cgi/viewcontent .cgi?article=1019&context=whemsac.

11. Natalia Naish and Jeremy Scott, *Coke: The Biography* (London: Robson Press, 2013), p. 18.

12. El Salvador is something of an exception: the WEF's data suggest that it is a little easier for cartels to do business there than in Nicaragua, and yet its murder rate is far higher. One explanation may be that the country's bloodthirsty street gangs drive up the level of violence; the data in this table are from before the signing of the truce outlined in Chapter 2. Honduras's murder rate, meanwhile, was particularly high in 2012, partly as a hangover from the country's coup in 2009.

CHAPTER 6 THE PROMISE AND PERILS OF FRANCHISING: HOW THE MOB HAS BORROWED FROM MCDONALD'S

1. "Ricardo" is a pseudonym. The other details are unchanged.

2. "Incidence of Crime 2014," National System of Public Security, 2015 (in Spanish), http://secretariadoejecutivo.gob.mx/docs/pdfs/estadisticas%20del%20 fuero%20comun/Cieisp2014_012015.pdf.

3. Chris Kanich et al., "Spamalytics: An Empirical Analysis of Spam Marketing Conversion," *CCS'08*, 2008, http://cseweb.ucsd.edu/~savage/papers /CCS08Conversion.pdf.

4. Roger Blair and Francine Lafontaine, *The Economics of Franchising* (Cambridge: Cambridge University Press, 2005).

5. Antonio O. Mazzitelli, "Mexican Cartels' Influence in Latin America," Florida International University, Applied Research Center, September 2011, at http://www.seguridadydefensa.com/descargas/Mazzitelli-Antonio-Mexican-Cartel-Influence-in-Central-America-Sept.pdf.

6. Peter Drucker, *The Daily Drucker* (New York: HarperCollins, 2004).

7. See Rodrigo Canales's excellent TED talk on Mexican cartels, at http://www.ted.com/talks/rodrigo_canales_the_deadly_genius_of_drug_cartels/transcript?language=en.

8. In 2004, there were 539 murders; in 2014, there were 1,514. See http://secretariadoejecutivo.gob.mx/incidencia-delictiva/incidencia-delictiva-fuero-comun.php.

9. Charles G. Miller, "Hot Litigation Topics in Franchising," unpublished paper, at http://www.bzbm.com/wp-content/uploads/2012/07/HOT-LITIGATION-TOPICS-IN-FRANCHISING.pdf.

10. Témoris Grecko and David Espino, "War for the 'Red Gold' Tears Guerrero Apart," *El Universal*, February 3, 2015 (in Spanish), at http://www.eluniversal.com.mx/nacion-mexico/2015/impreso/guerra-porel-8216oro-rojo-8217flagela-a-guerrero-222823.html, and Julio Ramírez, "Government of the Republic Identifies Nine Cartels; They Control Forty-three Gangs," *Excelsior*, September 16, 2014 (in Spanish), at http://www.excelsior.com.mx/nacional/2014/09/16/981925#imagen-2.

CHAPTER 7   INNOVATING AHEAD OF THE LAW: RESEARCH AND DEVELOPMENT IN THE "LEGAL HIGHS" INDUSTRY

1. "Drugs Use Map of the World," *Guardian*, July 2, 2012, at http://www.theguardian.com/news/datablog/interactive/2012/jul/02/drug-use-map-world.

2. Tom Wainwright, "Legal Highs: A New Prescription," *Economist*, August 8, 2013, at http://www.economist.com/news/leaders/21583270-new-zealands-plan-regulate-designer-drugs-better-trying-ban-them-and-failing-new.

3. See, for instance, C. Wilkins et al., "Legal Party Pill Use in New Zealand," Centre for Social and Health Outcomes Research and Evaluation, Massey University, Auckland, at http://www.whariki.ac.nz/massey/fms/Colleges/College%20of%20Humanities%20and%20Social%20Sciences/Shore/reports/Legal%20party%20pills%20in%20New%20Zealand%20report3.pdf.

4. "World Drug Report 2013," UNODC, June 26, 2013, at http://www.unodc.org/lpo-brazil/en/frontpage/2013/06/26-world-drug-report-notes-stability-in-use-of-traditional-drugs-and-points-to-alarming-rise-in-new-psychoactive-substances.html.

5. "Controlled Drugs: Licences, Fees and Returns," Home Office, July 24, 2015, at https://www.gov.uk/government/publications/controlled-drugs-list.

6. The transcript of the ridiculous exchange is immortalized in Hansard, the official record of the Houses of Parliament, under Parliamentary Business, Publications and Records, July 23, 1996, at http://www.parliament.the-stationery-office.co.uk /pa/cm199596/cmhansrd/vo960723/text/60723w10.htm.

7. As quoted in "Is Irish Ban on Legal Highs Driving Market Underground?" *Guardian*, June 30, 2015, at http://www.theguardian.com/society/2015/jun/30 /risks-of-legal-highs-drive-bereaved-mother-to-campaign-for-uk-ban.

8. "Psychoactive Substance Regulations—Regulatory Impact Assessment," Treasury of New Zealand, August 5, 2014, at http://www.treasury.govt.nz /publications/informationreleases/ris/pdfs/ris-moh-psr-jul14.pdf.

9. "Pharmaceutical Industry," Programmes, World Health Organization, at http://www.who.int/trade/glossary/story073/en.

10. Joseph A. DiMasi, "Innovation in the Pharmaceutical Industry: New Estimates of R&D Costs," Tufts Center for the Study of Drug Development, November 18, 2014, at http://csdd.tufts.edu/files/uploads/Tufts_CSDD_briefing_on_RD _cost_study_-_Nov_18,_2014.pdf.

11. "The Price of Failure," *Economist*, November 27, 2014, at http://www .economist.com/news/business/21635005-startling-new-cost-estimate-new -medicines-met-scepticism-price-failure.

12. Lena Groeger, "Big Pharma's Big Fines," *ProPublica*, February 24, 2014, at http://projects.propublica.org/graphics/bigpharma.

13. "Regulatory Impact Statement: Amendment to the Psychoactive Substances Act 2013," Treasury of New Zealand, May 2014, at http://www.treasury.govt.nz /publications/informationreleases/ris/pdfs/ris-moh-apsa-may14.pdf.

14. Amanda Gillies, "Matt Bowden's Legal High Company in Liquidation," *3 News*, May 16, 2015, at http://www.3news.co.nz/nznews/matt-bowdens-legal-high -company-in-liquidation-2015051617#axzz3eYIB5tSf.

CHAPTER 8 ORDERING A LINE ONLINE: HOW INTERNET SHOPPING HAS IMPROVED DRUG DEALERS' CUSTOMER SERVICE

1. See http://www.pizzahut.com/assets/pizzanet.

2. Global Drug Survey, 2014, at http://www.globaldrugsurvey.com/facts-figures /the-global-drug-survey-2014-findings.

3. Judith Aldridge and David Décary-Hétu, "Not an 'eBay for Drugs': The Cryptomarket 'Silk Road' as a Paradigm Shifting Criminal Innovation," Social Science Research Network, May 13, 2014, at http://papers.ssrn.com/sol3/Papers .cfm?abstract_id=2436643.

4. For an extreme version of this problem, consider the Honduran colonel trying to sell a piece of moon rock in Chapter 5. Finding a buyer was so difficult that he was forced to drop his asking price from $1 million to $10,000 and a refrigerated truck. There may well have been a buyer somewhere in the world who was willing to pay more—but how could he have identified that person?

5. Sometimes the people carrying out successful "exit scams" even own up to it. A vendor called DataProV left the following message on his Evolution trading page in early 2015, shortly after pulling off an exit scam worth £34,900 ($52,000): "Huge apologies, Most of you it won't effect. Some of you, it will. . . . Some for over £10,000! Peace out guys."

6. B. C. Ginsburg et al., "Purity of Synthetic Cannabinoids Sold Online for Recreational Use," *Journal of Analytical Toxicology* 36 (1) (January 2012).

7. Anupam B. Jena and Dana P. Goldman, "Growing Internet Use May Help Explain the Rise in Prescription Drug Abuse in the United States," *Health Affairs*, May 12, 2011, at http://content.healthaffairs.org/content/30/6/1192.full .pdf+html.

8. Matthew O. Jackson, *Social and Economic Networks* (Princeton, NJ: Princeton University Press, 2008).

9. Geoffrey Pearson and Dick Hobbs, "Middle Market Drug Distribution," Home Office Research Study 227, November 2001, at http://eprints.lse.ac.uk/13878/1 /Middle_market_drug_distribution.pdf.

10. Beau Kilmer and Peter Reuter, "Prime Numbers: Doped," *Foreign Policy*, October 16, 2009, at http://foreignpolicy.com/2009/10/16/prime-numbers-doped.

11. Peter S. Bearman, James Moody, and Katherine Stovel, "Chains of Affection: The Structure of Adolescent Romantic and Sexual Networks," *American Journal of Sociology* 110 (1) (July 2004), at http://www.soc.duke.edu/~jmoody77/chains.pdf.

12. "Findings from the 2013/14 Crime Survey," Home Office, 2014, at https://www.gov.uk/government/publications/drug-misuse-findings-from-the -2013-to-2014-csew/drug-misuse-findings-from-the-201314-crime-survey-for -england-and-wales.

13. "Popping Pills: Prescription Drug Abuse in America," National Institute on Drug Abuse, 2011, at http://www.drugabuse.gov/related-topics/trends-statistics /infographics/popping-pills-prescription-drug-abuse-in-america.

CHAPTER 9 DIVERSIFYING INTO NEW MARKETS: FROM DRUG SMUGGLING TO PEOPLE SMUGGLING

1. Bryan Roberts et al., "An Analysis of Migrant Smuggling Costs Along the Southwest Border," Department of Homeland Security, working paper, November 2010, at http://www.dhs.gov/xlibrary/assets/statistics/publications/ois-smuggling -wp.pdf.

2. Ibid.

3. Jeffrey S. Passel, D'Vera Cohn, and Ana Gonzalez-Barrera, "Net Migration from Mexico Falls to Zero—and Perhaps Less," Pew Hispanic Center, April 23, 2012, at http://www.pewhispanic.org/2012/04/23/net-migration-from-mexico-falls-to-zero-and-perhaps-less.

4. Both are cited in Beau Kilmer et al., "Reducing Drug Trafficking Revenues and Violence in Mexico," RAND Corporation, occasional paper, 2010, at http://www.rand.org/content/dam/rand/pubs/occasional_papers/2010/RAND_OP325.pdf.

5. Robert S. Gable, "Comparison of Acute Lethal Toxicity of Commonly Used Psychoactive Substances," *Addiction* 99 (6) (2004).

6. T. J. Cicero, "The Changing Face of Heroin Use in the United States," *JAMA Psychiatry* 71 (7) (2014), at http://www.ncbi.nlm.nih.gov/pubmed/24871348.

CHAPTER 10 COMING FULL CIRCLE: HOW LEGALIZATION THREATENS THE DRUG LORDS

1. Ricardo Baca, "Chart: Colorado Marijuana Sales Hit $700 Million in 2014," *Cannabist*, February 12, 2015, at http://www.thecannabist.co/2015/02/12/colorado-marijuana-sales-2014–700-million/27565.

2. Adam Smith, "Tech-Savvy Criminals Now Using Heat-Seeking Drones to Target Cannabis Farms," *Halesowen News*, April 17, 2014, at http://www.halesowennews.co.uk/news/11155386.print.

3. First annual report of the Colorado Marijuana Enforcement Division, 2015, at https://www.colorado.gov/pacific/sites/default/files/2014%20MED%20Annual%20Report_1.pdf.

4. Maureen Dowd, "Don't Harsh Our Mellow, Dude," *New York Times*, June 3, 2014, at http://www.nytimes.com/2014/06/04/opinion/dowd-dont-harsh-our-mellow-dude.html?_r=0.

5. Beau Kilmer et al., "Reducing Drug Trafficking Revenues and Violence in Mexico," RAND Corporation occasional paper, 2010, see p. 19 at http://www.rand.org/content/dam/rand/pubs/occasional_papers/2010/RAND_OP325.appendixes.pdf.

6. "Mapping Marijuana," *Economist*, January 20, 2015, at http://www.economist.com/blogs/graphicdetail/2015/01/daily-chart-11.

7. Chris Dolmetsch, "New York Expands Fight on Smuggled Cigarettes with UPS Suit," *Bloomberg*, February 18, 2015, at http://www.bloomberg.com/news/articles/2015-02-18/new-york-expands-fight-on-smuggled-cigarettes-with-ups-lawsuit.

8. "Possible Impact of the Legalization of Marijuana in the United States," IMCO, October 2012 (in Spanish), at http://imco.org.mx/seguridad/posible_impacto_de_la_legalizacion_de_la_marihuana_en_estados_unidos.

9. Sam Ro, "Wall Street Analyst Argues Big Tobacco Will Soon Have to Answer Big Questions About Pot," *Business Insider*, December 10, 2014, at http://uk.businessinsider.com/rbc-analyst-on-marijuana-2014-12.

10. Rachel Ann Barry, Heikki Hiilamo, and Stanton Glantz, "Waiting for the Opportune Moment: The Tobacco Industry and Marijuana Legalization," *Milbank Quarterly* 92(2) (2014), at http://www.milbank.org/uploads/documents/featured -articles/pdf/Milbank_Quarterly_Vol-92_No-2_2014_The_Tobacco_Industry _and_Marijuana_Legalization.pdf.

CONCLUSION: WHY ECONOMISTS MAKE THE BEST POLICE OFFICERS

1. Kiah Collier and Jeremy Schwartz, "DPS Boosts Drug Seizure Values as It Seeks More Border Money," *Austin American-Statesman,* February 26, 2015, at http://www.mystatesman.com/news/news/state-regional-govt-politics/dps -boosts-drug-seizure-values-as-it-seeks-more-bo/nkKbc.

2. Peter Reuter, *Understanding the Demand for Illegal Drugs* (Washington, DC: National Academies Press), at http://www.nap.edu/catalog/12976/understanding -the-demand-for-illegal-drugs.

3. The extent to which they cut their prices, if at all, depends on the elasticity of supply. For further discussion of this, see this 2002 paper on the elasticity of the demand and supply of drugs, published by the Department of Justice: William Rhodes et al., "Illicit Drugs: Price Elasticity of Demand and Supply," at https://www .ncjrs.gov/pdffiles1/nij/grants/191856.pdf.

4. Keene's dangerous Pumpkin Festival was reported in "Cops or Soldiers?" in the *Economist* on May 22, 2014, by my fearless colleague Jon Fasman, at http://www .economist.com/news/united-states/21599349-americas-police-have-become-too -militarised-cops-or-soldiers.

5. "The Benefits and Costs of Drug Use Prevention," RAND Corporation, re- search brief, 1999, at http://www.rand.org/pubs/research_briefs/RB6007/index1 .html.

6. Quoted by Thalif Deen, "UN Body Praises Peru, Bolivia for Slashing Output," Inter Press Service, March 7, 2000, at http://www.ipsnews.net/2000/03/drugs-un -body-praises-peru-bolivia-for-slashing-output.

7. UN press release, "UNODC Reports Steep Decline in Cocaine Production in Colombia," June 19, 2009, at http://www.unodc.org/unodc/en/press/releases /2009/june/unodc-reports-steep-decline-in-cocaine-production-in-colombia .html.

8. Moisés Naím, *Illicit: How Smugglers, Traffickers, and Copycats Are Hijacking the Global Economy* (New York: Doubleday, 2005), p. 80.

9. "War on Drugs: Report of the Global Commission on Drug Policy," June 2011, at http://www.globalcommissionondrugs.org/wp-content/themes/gcdp_v1/pdf /Global_Commission_Report_English.pdf.

10. Richard Nixon and H. R. Haldeman in a private conversation in the Oval Office, March 21, 1972, at http://www.csdp.org/research/nixonpot.txt.

Index

Courtesy of the author

Tom Wainwright is the Britain editor of the *Economist*. Until 2013, he was the magazine's Mexico City correspondent, covering Mexico, Central America, and the Caribbean, as well as parts of South America and the border region of the United States. Before working in journalism he read philosophy, politics, and economics at Oxford University. Wainwright was born in 1982 in London, England, where he lives today.